Against the Current

AGAINST

Selections from

Edited, with an Introduction
and Notes, by George Ivask

TRANSLATED FROM THE RUSSIAN BY
GEORGE REAVEY

THE CURRENT

the novels, essays, notes, and letters of
Konstantin Leontiev

Weybright and Talley   New York

Contents

PHILOSOPHY

LITERARY CRITICISM

The Other Russian:
Konstantin Leontiev

ALEXANDER BLOK, one of the greatest Russian poets of the twentieth century, has said: "It is worth living if only to make absolute demands on life." He had in mind the demand for *real being*—what Tolstoy and Dostoyevsky called the *living life*—a life that excluded not only evil and injustice, but also routine and inertia. Some Russian critics have defined such an approach to life as a maximalist one.

The great Russian poet Alexander Pushkin was able to accept life as it is. All the discontents he had experienced provoked in him either embitterment or a "lucid sadness." He did not claim or hope for anything better or more absolute.

A new age in the life of the Russian educated class, the intelligentsia who appeared on the social scene after the death of Pushkin, began with a metaphysical poet, Mikhail Lermontov; the great master of grotesque "realism," Nikolai Gogol; and the Russian philosophers of the 1840's. The intelligentsia were soon to become split into two opposing factions—the Slavophiles and the Westernizers, both of whom were influenced by Hegelian philosophy. The brilliant dandies and swashbucklers—the country gentle-men and professional officers—with moderate romantic dreams or revolutionary aspirations now gave way to more "serious" and less balanced people who had studied the German philosophers or the French Socialists and who discussed the destinies of Russia and the whole of mankind. A few of the latter—the greatest of whom after Gogol were perhaps Tolstoy and Dostoyevsky—were involved in religion, while the majority of them were interested above all in social problems. Later, in the 1860's, they became radicals, so-cialists, and even fanatic revolutionaries. All of them made great demands on life. But since the Russian government hindered any political or even social activity, the intelligentsia was often lost in unrealistic utopian dreams. By reading N. Chernyshevsky's tenden-tious novel *What to Do?*, which recommended that intellectuals join socialist working communities, many generations of Russian radicals learned how to live. The peaceful anarchists, the Christian fundamentalist Tolstoy, and the Russian messianist Dostoyevsky, also had their utopian dreams. Russian literature after Pushkin be-came didactic (H. MacLean) or prophetic (N. Berdyaev). Some-times sermons and prophesies infringed upon the artistic unity of the works of fiction. Nevertheless, the great Russian novels of the nineteenth century could not have been written without these various "absolute demands" being made. A few writers were in-spired by ethical or religious beliefs in moral regeneration; the majority of them, however, believed in a total political, social, and economic revolution as an initial step preceding the regeneration of mankind as a whole.

Konstantin Leontiev, who also belonged to this great age, had his own vision of the real life or of the "living life." But his philosophy was essentially different from all the other ideas so dear to his contemporaries. His main reality was Beauty and nothing else. Truth, Good, and sometimes God too, were only aspects of Beauty which, in his opinion, could not be expressed and realized in classical harmony. Leontiev conceived of Beauty as a romantic disharmony composed of picturesque contrasts and marked by an exuberant variety in an elastic unity of opposites which he some-times called "form." Such a formal unity excludes chaos, but does not necessarily establish order: It is an organic principle shaping and animating the growth of various forces in nature, history, and art. Great vitality produces great variety in the luxuriant realms of mighty and tragic civilizations. But while vitality is subordinated to natural laws, variety is always unpredictable, free and beautiful.

How did Leontiev arrive at these main theses of his philosophy? His aestheticism had preceded both his naturalism and his bio-logical interpretation of history.

II

As I have already explained in my introduction to his novel *The Egyptian Dove*, Leontiev was a sort of tragic Narcissus who was never satisfied with himself because he could never consider his own ego worthy of love. According to Berdyaev, he was also an androgynous type of man, physically a normal male who was pos-sessed of certain feminine features and moods. From his numerous reminiscences and from his partly autobiographical novels we know that he was often in love, but never passionately so, not only in his youth but also in his later years. He rather liked to admire girls, sometimes boys, picturesque houses, colorful dresses, and, in particular, the world of Oriental bazaars and Balkan festivals. He had served for a decade as a Russian diplomatic agent in the Balkans, and there he felt himself even more at home than in snow-bound Russia. Since his early youth Leontiev had regarded life as an amazing spectacle performed especially for his own delectation. In his dreams, this Narcissus wished to play a more active role on the historical stage, the role of an arrogant and attractive adventurer, the role of Alcibiades, the witty interlocutor of Socrates.

Leontiev's narcissistic aestheticism developed very early, rather unconsciously at first. Perhaps it was first formulated during a long conversation with a young radical writer, Piotrovsky, in front of the

St. Petersburg palace of Prince Belozersky-Beloselsky. Commenting on this conversation, his biographer, A. Alexandrov, stated that, in the early 1860's, Leontiev "imagined that, if the majority of people would acquire good taste and aesthetic ideas, and would listen to his sermons, life would have a new and unprecedented variety of good and evil, plenty of contrasts, an abundance of poetry beginning with idylls (such as the one described in Gogol's *Old-World Land-Owners*) and ending finally with tragic popular uprisings." But later on Leontiev lost these optimistic beliefs in the possibility of the triumph of Beauty and even tried to renounce his own "rapacious aesthetics."

Leontiev's naturalist and even materialist philosophy had been formed in Moscow, where he studied medicine for four years and developed a particular interest in phrenology. At that time he began to believe in certain "iron" laws of nature which determined the life of all creatures, including human beings. In his long essay *Byzantinism and Slavdom*, written in 1873 in Constantinople, he attempted to interpret world history in terms of biology. His scientific or pseudo-scientific methodology is reminiscent of that of the Slavophile N. Danilevsky. Leontiev was indeed influenced to some extent by the latter's book *Russia and Europe*. But, unlike Danilevsky, Leontiev was not an anti-Western thinker: he extended his condemnation only to the modern trends in European civilization.

According to Leontiev, all nations are subject to a natural law, and their history passes through three stages of development. The first stage of this "rule of three" is primitive society. He found the source of civilization in backward Turkey and in the Greek and Slavic provinces of the Ottoman Empire. He admired the natural or the semi-natural man who lived there and who was not Rousseau's meek savage but rather Byron's picturesque beast, no lamb but a wolf, a bold warrior or a robber (although a pious one) who believed in Allah or was able to find penance in a Greek-Orthodox monastery. For Leontiev, the "rapacious and God-fearing aesthete," such a civilization in its first, primitive stage was beautiful.

He also admired the second stage, the period of "exuberant

growth and complexity," the luxurious summer of classical Greece, late Republican and early Imperial Rome, Byzantium up to 1000 A.D., Medieval Europe, Renaissance Italy, England and France in the sixteenth and seventeenth centuries, and Russia in the reign of Catherine the Great. The unifying force of the second stage lay in the authoritative rule of a dictator, a monarch, a patriarch, or a pope. Such rulers somehow limited the excessive variety of life; they suppressed uprisings and eradicated heresies; but they failed to eliminate all the causes of discontent and discord. They liked to fight and grew stronger in the struggles with rebels and heretics. At this stage all opponents of authority were welcome, Leontiev affirmed, because there would be no movement, no dynamics in the austere but flexible framework of an empire or a church without any opposition. Indeed, he admired the great historical tragedies as they were enacted by kings and soldiers, rebels and robbers, saints and martyrs, and heretics. Thus the beauty of history consisted in the presence of variety within a unifying system. Leontiev particularly liked the Middle Ages. In that age of exuberant growth and complexity, Caesars, Popes, and Patriarchs were often dethroned, blinded, or killed. There were many revolts and heresies of which he approved but, despite them, the empires, the Eastern and the Western, as well as the Papacy and the Patriarchates, remained strong and stable, and this delighted him too.

In Leontiev's view the nineteenth century represented the third stage of civilization, the age of "secondary simplification," of capitalism, democracy, socialism, and industrialization. Since this was also an age characterized by dissolution and disintegration, Leontiev argued that any development in this direction must be checked in order to prevent the final destruction of society. The modern state, he affirmed, is weak and flaccid; man has become soft and corrupt in the Western democracies, and the poetic mankind of the past is now dying out. Leontiev despised all the representative types of this new age, to him so devoid of Beauty—the self-satisfied bourgeoisie in their dark suits and derby hats, the rebellious proletarians in their dirty blouses—and all of its tenets too, particularly the concept of equality. Equality, Leontiev maintained, was only for decomposing corpses and fleshless skeletons; great men make their appearance in response to inequality, in opposition to elemental forces or to an authoritative hierarchical order.

III

Leontiev constantly complained of his isolation, but actually he would not have been so isolated if he had only known those contemporary thinkers who held views more or less similar to his own. He was, in fact, an original and outstanding representative of the great nineteenth-century counterrevolution which defended

> *beauty against ugliness,*
> *quality against quantity,*
> *the talented minority against the mediocre majority,*
> *a colorful personality against the colorless masses,*
> *nature against technique,*
> *truth against advertising and propaganda,*
> *freedom against plutocracy, bureaucracy and revolutions,*
> *art against the press.*

Goethe, Schopenhauer, de Tocqueville, Flaubert, and Kierkegaard were among those who, each in his own way, were taking part in this counterrevolution. Leontiev was sometimes very close to thinkers like Carlyle and J. S. Mill, as well as J. de Maistre, Gobineau, Nietzsche, and Ruskin. All these thinkers were antagonistic to the political and industrial revolutions of the eighteenth and nineteenth centuries, those revolutions that had produced the collective mediocrity of the bourgeoisie and the proletariat, both alike hostile to the concepts of personality and authority—concepts variously called the *Pope* by de Maistre, the *Hero* by Carlyle, the *Eccentric* by Mill, the *Aryan* by Gobineau, the *Superman* by Nietzsche, the *Artisan* by Ruskin, and the *Beautiful Man* by Leontiev.

Leontiev had never read Nietzsche, Gobineau, or Ruskin. He was more impressed by Mill than by Carlyle. At first sight it would seem that Mill, the English liberal and utilitarian, had nothing in common with a Russian "reactionary" and a devout Greek-Orthodox. Nevertheless Leontiev regarded Mill very much as his ally, as he did Herzen, the emigré leader of the Russian revolutionaries in London who, after the failure of the Revolution of 1848, had been deeply disillusioned by the conformity of the German and French radicals. Leontiev rejected mediocrity, the tyrannical mediocrity of modern democracy, as emphatically as Mill and Herzen had done.

The problem as a whole was, of course, more complex: there were many strong personalities and great pioneers among both the bourgeoisie and the proletariat.

I also believe that we do not have to take very seriously Leontiev's biological laws as he applied them to the development of various civilizations. He was an amateur historian who had never studied historical sources, and his interpretation of history was actually based on a small number of reference books. He knew the natural sciences much better, but he was no more than an average student of medicine. Finally, his biology of history may be as sharply criticized as some other attempts in the same direction. Besides Danilevsky and Leontiev, such German historians as Karl Friedrich Vollgraf, Heinrich Rueckert, and Peter Ernst Lasaul, as well as Oswald Spengler and to some extent Arnold Toynbee, have applied natural-science methods to history, but they came to very different conclusions.

None of these philosophizing historians seems to have realized that the methods of natural science cannot necessarily be applied to history. According to W. Windelband and H. Rickert, natural scientists establish natural laws while historians have it as their function to analyze unique and nonrecurring facts. Human beings are also animals but, since they are more unpredictable than other mammals, they tend to digress from natural laws, which are perhaps merely working hypotheses and can be disputed as much as certain mathematical axioms. Nevertheless Leontiev may be praised, if not for his methodology, then for his sharp and witty criticism of our civilization, which is marked by shocking conformity and tragic dehumanization.

Leontiev was the most pessimistic of all the historian-naturalists. Like his contemporary Donoso Cortez, the Spanish diplomat and thinker, whose books he had never read, Leontiev prophesied that there would be a bloody revolution in the coming century—not in the West as Karl Marx had expected, but in economically backward Russia. "Who knows," Leontiev wrote in one of his articles, "perhaps, like the Jews who never expected a Teacher of the *New Faith* to issue from their womb, we shall also unexpectedly give birth to an Anti-Christ in the next hundred years. . . ." According to him, a tyrannical socialist society would govern the former Russian Empire, and the new dictators would have more power than all the dynasties of the Ruriks and the Romanovs. In Dostoyevsky's *The Possessed* we also find a grotesque philosopher of a modern totalitarian state in the person of Shigalev. The author himself, however, believed that *Shigalevism* could never succeed in his Holy Russia, but Leontiev had no such illusion, and he sharply attacked and ridiculed Dostoyevsky's "rosy-colored Christianity." Unfortunately, Leontiev proved a better prophet than the creator of *The Brothers Karamazov*.

Leontiev once recommended that Russia be "frozen." He approved of the most rigorous reaction, a reaction excluding any progress, in order to postpone the revolution which he considered to be inevitable in about twenty years' time.

It is well known that Leontiev also made another proposal, namely, to "warm up" Russia as an autocratic socialist monarchy. But this project of his was shelved by such high dignitaries of the Russian bureaucracy as K. Pobedonostsev and T. Filippov.

Yet Leontiev did not seriously believe that a Tsar, either a reactionary or a socialist, could prevent the fatal progress of both the liberal and the revolutionary forces that were leading Russia to destruction and, eventually, to a communist society populated by dull, colorless Philistines living in their comfortable anthills.

It is interesting to note that Leontiev hated the extreme radical revolutionaries less than he did the moderate liberals. On one occasion, Leontiev stated that he preferred the cruel Robespierre to Gambetta, the moderate ideologist and politician of the Third French Republic.

In Leontiev's writings we find some other predictions. He stated that Germany would be strong enough to make one or two but not more than three wars: that Russia would find herself threatened by a fierce and powerful China; and that modern technology would lead to universal destruction after horrible apocalyptic conflicts.

Leontiev often directed his attacks against modern nationalism. Nationalism, he believed, did not produce a new, original culture, but merely accelerated the process of *secondary simplification,* turning the newly unified Italians and Germans, and the emancipated Greeks, Rumanians, and South Slavs into the same self-satisfied, mediocre bourgeoisie already existing in France and the Scandinavian countries.

United Italy, wrote Leontiev, is less original than the divided Italy which had inspired Goethe, Byron, Musset, and Gogol. Once upon a time the English, Germans, French, and Russians had crossed the Alps and entered a fairyland but, after 1861, the new Apennine kingdom more and more resembled any other European country. Gone were the picturesque processions in Rome and the carnivals in Venice, and the "corrupt and pious, despotic and idle, yet enchanting kingdom of Naples had disappeared forever."

Leontiev admired Bismarck, the iron chancellor, but he disapproved of his anti-Catholic policy and of the concessions he made to the liberal bourgeoisie and the Social Democrats. The new German Empire, like the new kingdom of Italy, was now more homogeneous than it had been before 1870, and the Germans, despite their arrogant national pretensions, were becoming average Europeans.

He also despised the illusions of the Russian Slavophiles and the local emancipators of the Balkans: the native leaders there only pretended to be nationalists. Actually they were dooming their countries to a process of denationalization in the melting pot of a colorless modern European civilization, in which all citizens would finally become as equal as skeletons. Therefore, according to Leontiev, the very principle of equality was likewise hostile and fatal to both Life and Beauty.

Leontiev expressed his detestation of liberal-bourgeois nationalism and its program of leveling all individuals in the following grandiloquent rhetorical question:

> Is it not awful and pitiful to think that Moses climbed Sinai, that the Hellenes built their graceful Acropolis, that the Romans fought the Punic Wars, that the handsome man of genius Alexander in a feathered helmet crossed the Granicus and fought at Arbela, that Christ's disciples propagated the faith, the martyrs suffered, the poets sang, the artists painted, and the knights shone in tournaments, just so the *French, German, or Russian bourgeois in their ugly and comic attire* might enjoy themselves both individually and collectively on the ruins of all that great past?

If hate is indeed expressed here, there is also love for our ancient Judeo-Hellenic-Latin civilization which Leontiev tried to preserve in the name of Beauty and of *living life*.

IV

The maximalism of this "other Russian" is expressed in this first commandment of his philosophy: *Be beautiful* (meaning also full of life) or perish either in totalitarian wars or in the communist slavery that he had predicted. Leontiev's second commandment was a religious one: *Save your soul.*

Leontiev used to maintain that people cannot be saved in the company of others. He hated the illusory Holy Russia proclaimed by "rosy-colored Christian" Dostoyevsky no less than he did the atheist, whether bourgeois or revolutionary. He regarded himself as a "transcendental egotist," who did not care about the salvation of his neighbors. Once he referred proudly to his servant girl Varia who, in his opinion, was wiser than all the Russian

Messianists including Dostoyevsky himself: "God help me to save my own soul; others I cannot save."

What was Leontiev's religion? As a boy Leontiev never experienced any deep piety. His early vision of the coming of the Bridegroom at midnight, a vision described in his novel *Podlipki*, was just one of the moods he cherished. In the Balkans, he regarded the Greek-Orthodox Church as the cultural and political force linking the Greeks and the Slavs with their common Byzantine spiritual heritage, which he valued as the last stronghold against the modern European ideas of liberal and technological progress. All that was to change after the miraculous cure from cholera or dysentery which he experienced in Salonika when he was praying before an icon of the Holy Virgin. At that hour he made a solemn promise to Her to take monastic vows, and later he became a devoted believer although he postponed his consecration to the last year of his life. He often emphasized that God was not the God of Love, but the God of Fear, and that His Kingdom would never be realized here on earth as the "rosy-colored Christians" Tolstoy and particularly Dostoyevsky believed. In his view the whole world would be eliminated before the Last Judgment. Until that apocalyptic *moment*, our life would remain a battlefield of light and darkness, hatred and love, a sort of exciting tragic opera in which ferocious and sad motives would alternate with tender and touching ones, and there would be *nothing else*. . . . Furthermore, he added: "Blessed are the peacemakers, for discord is inevitable; there will be no truth here." And it seems that he sometimes enjoyed this "opera" fully.

How was it possible then to save one's soul? While listening to the alluring music of good and evil? Only by obeying the Church, Leontiev claimed; and he followed the advice of his spiritual father and confessor in the Optina monastery, the elder Ambrosius, who was not inspired by Leontiev's terrifying God but by a loving God. Father Ambrosius never demanded much from his spiritual children, provided that their hearts were open to repentance and to divine revelation. Perhaps this wise elder also knew that his proud and tormented disciple would finally find his own way to the Lord.

Indeed, Leontiev finally realized that his two commandments, "be beautiful" and "save your soul" were incompatible. He understood that God commands us to make a final choice between Him and Satan. A Christian believer cannot enjoy both good and evil as aspects of beauty. At the end of his life he tried to solve this tragic antinomy of a rapacious aestheticism and ascetic soteriology. In a letter written to his younger friend V. Rozanov on August 13, 1891, he admitted: "What is to be done? Out of (our) transcendental egotism, fear of the judgment beyond the grave, and for the salvation of our souls, we are obliged to assist Christianity even if we have to renounce our beloved aesthetics. We still must resist such modern progress as is harmful to both Christianity and aesthetics."

Nevertheless, this declaration, made three months before his death, was not a final one. In other letters addressed to the same correspondent he continued to discuss various problems from the aesthetic point of view only. During his last agony he shouted: "We'll fight, fight. . . ." We shall never know what he had in mind. Was he going to fight for earthly beauty or for the Kingdom of Heaven, against the hated liberal progress or against his own aesthetic temptations?

Many outstanding Russian theologians, including V. Soloviev, the Metropolitan Antonius (Khrapovitsky) and, more recently, the Reverend G. Florovsky, have doubted whether Leontiev was a Christian at all. Florovsky regarded him as a decadent Romanticist who, instead of genuine beliefs, had only his moods and dreams.

For a long time Leontiev remained the idol of various obscure reactionaries who tended to simplify the complexity of his controversial philosophy. The arguments of his admirers showed more insight. Berdyaev, as many others (S. Frank and V. Zenkovsky, for example) had done, rejected Leontiev's concept of history, determined as it was by the very hypothetical laws of nature he had himself invented. Nevertheless, Berdyaev shared his hatred of the bourgeois Philistines of the West and valued highly Leontiev's boldness and integrity, the independence of his thought, and even his controversial aestheticism. Vasily Rozanov, with whom Leontiev corresponded during the last year of his life, was much influenced by his older friend, but he, too, rejected many of Leontiev's philosophical theses. For Rozanov the two religions were those of the ancient Egyptians and the Hebrews of the Old Testament. The wise men of the Orient had stressed the importance not only of the moral but also of the sexual behavior of the faithful: they had sanctified the holy "Tree of Life," which the gloomy Christians tried to cut down. "The world became a bitter place in Christ," said Rozanov, "deprived of all the joys that God too had once blessed." Rozanov accepted Leontiev's one-sided interpretation of Christianity only in order to reject it completely. In his opinion Leontiev had approached the Optina elders because he was afraid of dying. But actually Leontiev had always remained an unrepentant "pagan" with the "appetites" of an arrogant Alcibiades. It is interesting to mention that Rozanov, at the end of his life, rejected all his "heresies" and died reconciled with the Church on the outskirts of the Trinity Monastery (Zagorsk), where Leontiev had died twenty-eight years before him.

Vasily Rozanov, who is now still taboo in the U.S.S.R. and rather neglected outside Russia, may also be called a "Russian outsider." He was a man of genius, I believe, a master of the colloquial idiom who, along with Ivan Bunin, may be considered one of the greatest Russian prose writers of the twentieth century.

There are some other admirers of Leontiev who rather disapproved of his ideas but were puzzled and fascinated by his controversial personality, his brilliant paradoxes, his ability to dramatize ideas, and, finally, his original style. Among them were Lerner, the Pushkin scholar; G. Adamovich, the leading emigré critic; B. Filippov, his latest editor; Evel Gasparini, the Italian Slavist; and Kosta Lassithiotaki, the Greek archeologist.

V

As a literary critic, Leontiev was highly appreciated by some of the Russian Formalists who emerged on the Soviet literary scene in the 1920's, and also by the American Slavist Donald Fanger, who said that Leontiev anticipated Lionel Trilling's notion of "manners" as "a culture's hum and buzz of implication, the whole evanescent context in which its explicit statements are made."

In his essays on Dostoyevsky and Tolstoy, Leontiev did not limit himself to discussing only the ideas of these writers whom he considered to be pseudo-prophets. He also analyzed the stylistic devices used by various "realists." While the sentimentalists of the eighteenth century exaggerated the nobility of their characters, Leontiev argued, the "naturalists" and the "realists" tended to overemphasize the ugly aspects of manners and thoughts. Gogol's grotesque novels and even Tolstoy's great epics are spoiled by the disgusting details and the suspicions which he called the "dirty flies" of the Naturalist School. Leontiev praised *War and Peace* and *Anna Karenina* but he still accused their author of degrading some of his characters; for example, Pierre Bezukhov and General Kutuzov. According to Leontiev, Tolstoy was not only afraid of idealizing his heroes but also somehow enjoyed the very process of debunking them. Leontiev also made use of naturalistic details and colloquial expressions in his Russian novels; but, when he later depicted the way of life in the Balkans, he tried to avoid both "vulgar naturalism" and depth psychology as Tolstoy had sometimes used it. Leontiev preferred Pushkin's almost ascetic prose style and objective manner of narration. Leontiev even thought that Pushkin could have written another novel about the Napoleonic age or another *War and Peace* if he had not been killed in a duel in 1837.

But Leontiev himself never attained to such simplicity. In the best of his long novels—in *Podlipki,* in *Odysseus Polychroniades,* and in *The Egyptian Dove,* his narration is often capricious, elliptic, impressionistic, and full of lyrical digression depicting the vague moods of his superheroes, who express his own narcissistic ego. His style in no way resembles either Pushkin's or Tolstoy's. To some extent it is rather like Turgenev's. In any case, in the second half of the nineteenth century, when the majority of Russian critics were mainly preoccupied with the social problems reflected in works of fiction, Leontiev in his essays analyzed literature as literature and also examined the various devices employed by the realists and the naturalists. In their essays on Tolstoy, the Formalist critics B. Eikhenbaum and V. Shklovsky accepted and developed the purely analytic methods used by Leontiev. But, in contrast to Leontiev, they were not at all interested in the aesthetic evaluation of particular works of art.

VI

In conclusion, I should like to say again that it is hard to believe now in the threefold natural law which Leontiev established and applied to history. But his strict counterrevolutionary criticism of modern technological civilization, so destructive of beauty and so leveling of individuals, has not lost its significance even now. In some aspects of his thought Leontiev coincides with certain other contemporary philosophers—with Nikolai Berdyaev or Ortega y Gasset (*The Revolt of the Masses*), for example. Few critics will agree with Leontiev's arbitrary rejection of Dostoyevsky, but his analytic approach to stylistics is still illuminating.

Leontiev hardly succeeded in defending or even in defining his ideal of beauty. But he obviously succeeded in portraying things of beauty in Russia and particularly in the Balkans, as well as in history. This gloomy Cassandra of Western civilization expressed a genuine *joie de vivre* when he described the heroic struggle of the distant past and the picturesque way of life of the Albanian bandits in the Epirus or the Russian Old-Believers in Moldavia, or the "paradise" of a Turkish harem. There is also the more refined and somewhat decadent delight he experienced in his semi-terrestrial, semi-celestial eroticism. Moreover, their is rapture in the fanciful moods of this rapacious aesthete who was also a romantic dreamer at heart, an amazing Narcissus in love not so much with himself as with the variegated world reflected in his enchanted eyes.

Leontiev may have failed to reconcile his aestheticism with his austere theology, but this very tension between an adventurous Alcibiades and an ascetic monk fighting for the salvation of his soul was dramatized both in his life and in his writings. The great Russian theologian S. Bulgakov, who had already condemned Leontiev for his one-sided and fallacious interpretation of Christianity as a black religion of fear and death, nevertheless admired his integrity and independence, his peculiar style and, as he stated, the "tragic rhapsody" of his life. We may also admire the intense sensibilities and the vision of beauty of this *other Russian,* who made absolute demands on the real being, the "living life," although his demands were very different from those of his more famous contemporaries.

Leontiev demonstrated his first commandment, "be beautiful" *here* better than his second commandment, "save your soul" *there*. One can only guess that his antinomy has already been or will be resolved.

In his theoretical writings Leontiev was sometimes too loquacious. The composition of his essays frequently lacked balance, although he was logical enough to demonstrate his main ideas. As a philosopher and stylist he expressed himself best in paradoxical aphorisms, in brief notes sparkling with wit, or in lyrical digressions. Therefore, in this volume of Leontiev's selected works, we do not include entire essays or reminiscences, but only selections from them, sometimes only small fragments which are more representative of his ideas and moods than his longer writings are.

The book is divided into three parts: *Experience,* which includes not only memoirs and letters, but also some excerpts from his semi-autobiographical novels; *Philosophy*; and *Literary Criticism*. Also included are a short chronology of his life, a selected bibliography, and an index.

GEORGE IVASK
University of Washington

Against the Current

 # EXPERIENCE

to his funeral together with our (the Shchelkanovo) parish clergy. At the time they said, "We must send for his confessor." I was then eight (or nine) years old. I paid little attention to all this, because I was absolutely indifferent to my father and his death. The only thing that made a fairly strong impression on me was that this priest's chasuble at the funeral service was of various triangular silk pieces sewn together in the manner of a patchwork quilt—plus the fact that I had never before seen so many fine wrinkles as crossed the forehead of Father Athanasius (that, apparently, was his name). For a long time, my father had been living a detached life of his own, apart from us, in a small, meagerly furnished wing of the house. He had fallen ill there of a terrible disease (*miserere*), had died there, and had lain there on a table in a very narrow room. It was in the winter, and since they wished to bury him in the Meshchovo monastery, the preparations took a long time; he lay there for about a week with troughs full of ice standing under the table. During the requiem mass the clergy crowded round this table, treading on each other's toes and pushing one another. The Shchelkanovo deacon, whose face struck me as being very coarse and even wicked, like a bandit's, at least twice very rudely shoved the Chemodanovo Father in the patchwork chasuble; and this priest, turning round, gazed so sadly and pitifully, and the wrinkles on his forehead grew so numerous, that I felt a great pity for him. And my relatives said with compassion, "What poor vestments that Chemodanovo preacher has! It makes your heart melt to look at them!"

That is all I have preserved in my memory about my father's funeral. My aunt and sister took his body with them to Meshchovo for burial; Mother and I remained home, and I remember very well that I did not grieve in the least or weep. As regards Father's religion, I recall two further instances. One of them is quite insignificant, the other more important. One summer day the miraculous icon of St. Nicholas was brought to us from the village of Nedokhodov. We all went out to meet it. My father was the first to kiss the icon, stooping with great difficulty as he passed under it, because he was very large and stout. I remember the multi-colored Caucasian coat he wore and the way the wind blew his white hair about over his bald patch. Afterwards, all of us began to pass under the icon, and for some reason this gave me much pleasure. I do not recall whether my mother also passed before it: she was not fond of observing all the details of ritual. It seems to me, she did not. If she had gone by, then surely I would not have forgotten it; I loved her so much and was so eager to admire her! (She was incomparably more elegant than my father, and because of an inborn instinct, that was very important to me.) I recall this incident because it was the only time I can remember my father observing a ritual. That my father had sometimes gone to confession was evident from the fact that a Father confessor of his had appeared at the last minute. But my memory has preserved nothing more concerning my father's religiosity. This is, perhaps, because I was very indifferent and paid little attention to him. Meeting him in the morning, I would kiss his hand; in the evening, I would approach him to receive his blessing and also to kiss his hand, and nothing more. And he showed not the slightest concern either with me or my bringing up.

Another circumstance was a little more important. When, for the first time, I went to confession at the age of seven with Father Luka (from Bykasovo) in our large reception hall and my aunt commanded me to ask everybody's forgiveness, I went up to Father first of all. He held out his hand, kissed me on the head, and, bursting out laughing, said, "Well, brother, be careful now. As a penalty for sins, the priest rides round the room astride of people!"

From all of this, it is evident that my father was one of those frivolous and easily distracted Russians (and gentry, especially) who reject nothing and uphold nothing rigorously. In general, it may be said that my father was neither very clever nor very serious.

MOTHER

MY MOTHER had long ago complied with my request, and, during her lifetime, some of her notes were printed in *Russky Vestnik* * ("A Holiday in the Village of Pokrovsky," notes on 1811–1812, and so on). She had written a great deal more that was interesting, but all of this, it is to be regretted, was lost with the trunk that went astray between Kaluga and Moscow towards the end of the sixties. I have preserved very little of all this material, but it includes the accounts of how my two elder brothers were accepted without any proper claims to it into the Corps of Pages as a result of the special favor and solicitude shown by the Empress Maria Fyodorovna. Our father not only did not have the rank of general but also had been discharged from the Guards at the beginning of this century for his part in some riotous incident and had resigned with the rank of ensign.

The wife of the retired ensign, who had moreover been dis-

* *The Russian Messenger.*

From REMINISCENCES. WORKS, *vol. I, pp.* 36–46.

charged from the Guards for riotous behavior, was the proprietress of a small estate in the province of Kaluga. What right had she, my mother, to expect her two eldest sons to be placed in the Corps of Pages? None, of course.

But while still a schoolgirl, at the Institute, she had attracted the attention of the Dowager Empress; and *fifteen years* after she left school, the Sovereign Lady had not forgotten her and granted her request in the year that Nicholas Pavlovich * ascended the throne.

In our dear Kudinovo, in our spacious and cheerful house, of which no trace now remains, there was a room with windows facing west onto a tranquil, densely grown, and far-flung garden. Our house was elegant and tidy throughout, but this particular room appealed to me most of all; there was something mysterious and inaccessible about this room for the servants, for strangers, and even for our family. It was my mother's study! To reach it, one had to pass through a long corridor, and her dressing room and bedroom, and this entire half of the house was very often under lock and key. My mother loved solitude, silence, and reading, and followed a strict timetable in her occupations. When I was a child, when "all the impressions of being were new to me," I found my mother's study a great delight.

And in reality this study was very original and charming. At that time we had not yet grown accustomed to upholstering furniture with variegated satins, and I do not even remember ticking in bright colors, though in early childhood I had driven more than once with my mother to the capitals and had noticed with attention a good many things; but my mother had a strong imagination and very fine taste; she wished to arrange this room for herself in the form of a multicolored tent, and she gave orders for some sort of cotton material to be sewn with wide stripes—dark green, bright rose, and white—and with it decorated the walls and ceiling; above, it was gathered in the middle in folds into a large rosette, in the center of which was inserted one of those round

* Nicholas I.

bronze figures which are used for supporting window curtains. In the winter a large white carpet with dark green velvet designs was spread over the floor, and this was very appropriate and very handsome. Mother managed to put to best use a sort of dark box-room; above it a staircase led to the mezzanine, Mother did away with the box-room, shifting the wall further back into the corridor; instead, she set up several small wooden columns there and upholstered them with canvas. She gave orders for the canvas to be painted with white oil paint and then spirally around the canvas-covered columns she pasted a flowery border of the kind used for pasting at the top of wallpaper. The result was that instead of a dark box-room for firewood in the corridor, we now had behind the columns in the study a sort of niche, a very cozy and beautiful niche; and the curtains, which could be drawn, and the divan itself and the Turkish cushions upon it the whole length of the niche— all these were of the same material as had been used for the walls and consisted of the same three colors, dark green, pink, and white.

All this cost very little (because my mother was poor rather than rich), but everything was bright, neat, and fragrant. In the summer almost everywhere there were flowers in vases—lilacs, roses, lilies of the valley, wild jasmin—and in the winter there was always a delicate perfume of good scents. Mother had, I recall, a special small carafe of cut crystal, very beautiful to look at, filled with scent and with a sort of gadget attached, the function of which I did not understand then and cannot explain even now. It consisted of a sort of twisted wire and a wick, which could be ignited; the wire grew red hot, and a tenuous, subtle fragrance spread through the house, steadily, evenly, and for a long time.

There was not much furniture in this room: the room itself was not large. By one window stood a spacious writing table of ash wood with shelves for books; in front of it was an antique armchair with a semicircular back, adorned with two carved sheep's heads; near the table, on the other side, was a large, deep Voltaire armchair also of ash wood, and in another corner by a second window were another armchair and a folding table. But the room did not seem at all empty, thanks to the tricolored drapery and the divan behind the columns in the mysterious niche.

There were no landscapes on the walls; the large family portraits hung in the drawing room; in Mother's study there were only the portraits of her seven children and of four other persons, whom she regarded as her best friends or even benefactors.

The children's portraits were hung in a row behind the columns in the niche and had been executed at different times in various media. Pyotr, my eldest brother, who later became a Guards officer, was recorded very well in crayon as a handsome, pink-cheeked youngster of about sixteen, wearing his page's uniform. The portrait of Anna, my eldest sister, as a girl of about twenty, of a beauty that was somewhat serious and regular but not particularly pleasant, wearing a high ornate comb in her large, high-piled braid—this portrait had been for some reason engraved on stone, as had also been two other portraits of the younger children, a son and daughter; theirs were most charming little Russian faces, irregular and appealing; the boy wore a cute, sleeveless Turkish jacket, and the girl had a large braid wound like a wreath around her head; a silhouette, a black one of course, a good likeness, had been taken of one of the middle brothers; and the icon painter, a serf of my grandfather Pyotr Matveyevich Korobanov, had done a fairly successful aquarelle of another pale and dreamy child.

I was the youngest, much younger than any of the others; and soon after my birth the very same serf-artist had depicted me in oil paint in the ideal aspect of an incorporeal cherub with wings. When I grew up and nothing innocent or angelic was left in me, my mother gave away this fantastic portrait to one of our devoted servants. Returning from abroad twenty years later, I found it in the kitchen in the possession of an old cook of ours; the cook could in no way prevent the village women from praying to this cherub when they entered the kitchen.

As I have said, all these children's portraits hung in a row behind the columns in the niche, and they were all adorned at the top with rosettes of the same three colors as the divan and the curtains and the walls; on all the seven rosettes the colors had been deliberately arranged in varying order: on the first to the right, the white was below, then came pink, and the button was green; on the second, the white was below, then came green, and the button was pink, and so on. When a small boy, I used to sleep on the divan behind these columns, and this symmetrical variety of rosettes, which I studied on awakening in the morning, furnished me with many delightful moments.

I beg to be forgiven for all these perhaps superfluous details, but it gives me such great pleasure to write about all this! And besides, my memories of this charming maternal "Hermitage" are so bound up in my heart with the very first religious impressions of my childhood and with my early awareness of the beauties of surrounding nature and the precious image of a beautiful, always graceful and noble mother, to whom I was so much obliged, without being able to repay it, for everything (the lessons of patriotism and feeling for monarchy, the examples of a strict order, constant work and refined taste in everyday life), that I cannot contain myself; and it always seems to me that even a simple account of my mother will become far more vivid if I tell more about her individually and even about those objects with which she surrounded herself, not by chance, but fully consciously and according to her personal choice and creative instinct!

In this room and the one next to it, I was taught to pray in front of a corner image case. For several years in succession I slept in Mother's study behind the columns on the tricolored divan; and how often, awakening on a wintry morning, I would prolong my state of indolence and, lying on the divan, would listen attentively to my sister, home from the same Institute where my mother had been educated, reading aloud the morning prayers and psalms: "Lord, have mercy upon us. . . ."

My sister read, my mother prayed. In the bedroom on the other side of the wall a morning fire was burning with "a merry crackle" in the fireplace. Without rising from the divan I could peer through the windows at the immaculate snow on a flowerbed —the mute, peaceful, immobile beauty of winter. I could see the grafts wrapped in straw, the bared apple trees, and the large maples of the two straight alleys. These "Kudinsk" apple trees, almost all of them standing in the flower garden in front of the house, like people that are familiar and even memorable to me by the very peculiarities of their appearance, have long been stricken by frost and have perished. My mother and sister have long been in their graves, and the beautiful maples may be chopped down tomorrow to "make bast shoes" by the peasant Ivan Klimov, to whom, like so many landowners, I *was obliged* to sell, after a protracted resistance, all of this holy patrimony of mine!

Many years have passed since those winter days when I used to wake up on the striped divan, and I have experienced many new joys and much unexpected grief; yet those morning prayers still remain quick in my memory and heart. Many profound changes have taken place in my life; there have been painful breaks in the form of my thoughts; but nowhere and at no time have I ever forgotten those words of the psalm which then (why, I myself don't know) particularly astonished and inexpressibly moved me: "Therefore is my spirit overwhelmed within me; my heart within me is desolate." To this day I can never recall my mother and my native land without also remembering these words of the psalm; to this day I cannot hear them without remembering my mother, my young sister, our dear Kudinovo, the beautiful spacious garden, and the view from the windows of this room. This view—not only in the summer, when so many roses bloomed in the round flowerbeds before our windows, but also in winter—was replete with inexpressible poetry which could only be fully understood by someone very close to us!

In this same room, when I had grown up, I heard my mother tell so many stories of old times: about Louis XIV and his so strikingly different mistresses; about the bloody acts of the hateful Convention; about our struggle with France and the horrors and heroic deeds of the year 1812; about Nicholas Pavlovich, whom

Mother worshipped—and the fragments about the Empress Maria Fyodorovna from this very same story, which I heard more than once by word of mouth before seeing it in writing!

I have already said that, besides the children's portraits, Mother had allowed into her study representations of four persons only, whom she had cause to regard as her closest friends or even benefactors. Even now I have all these portraits preserved intact. One of them, a lithograph, depicts a young general in a cuirass, with decorations and thick epaulettes; his face looks extremely energetic and pleasant; his mustaches and beard have been shaved off in the habit of all the military men of the first quarter of this century. This is the portrait of Ivan Sergeyevich Leontiev, a first cousin of my father. He did not live long, leaving a widow and an only son. He had been on very friendly terms with my parents, and, as a wealthy man, he had done them a lot of good, it seems. His cousinly affection apart, Ivan Sergeyevich greatly admired my mother's intelligence and beauty, and in Kudinovo many pleasant traditions have been preserved concerning him, his generosity, his affability and cheerful energy. On my bookstand there stands even now an old, broad, white marble vase, long since mended in places. On it were inscribed the following French words:

Elle ne s'etteindra
qu'avec la vie.

Into this vase, a gift from Ivan Sergeyevich, a flat candlestick of unusual make with long handles and a short wax or stearin candle, was lowered in my mother's presence. Then this inscription about the eternal flame of an elegant friendship could be more clearly discerned on the transparent marble of the vase, and the whole room would begin to glow with an enchanting, romantic half-light. I loved it so much when that invisible candle was lit, and respected my mother greatly for her poetic tastes! In her album, which I have preserved, an album bound in red Morocco with a bronze clasp, there was a couplet written by my grandfather Mikhail Ivanovich Leontiev on the subject of this vase. Here it is:

Art is silent here, but friendship says,
"This flame I've lit will burn forever."

The water color by Sokolov * depicts a man of thirty, perhaps slightly more. He is wearing a fashionable light brown frock coat of the thirties and gold-rimmed spectacles. His face is extremely refined, handsome, tender, slightly pink; his light brown hair curls about his forehead and temples, like that of all the dandies of the day when Byron was dying in Missolonghi and Pushkin's fame was beginning to grow in Russia. This Russian "gentleman," this "baron" of diplomatic aspect, transposed so successfully and vividly on paper by Sokolov's fine brush, was also a close and faithful friend of the family, a neighbor because of his nearby Meshchovo estate and a very wealthy man, none other than Vasily Dmitrievich Durnovo.

The copy from Gau † (of an altogether different brushstroke, no less beautiful but somehow more labored, more *punctuated*, if it is permissible to say so) shows an *elderly* lady in a white batiste dress and a white mobcap with *pink ribbons*. Yes, an elderly lady with pink ribbons! But even in her old age this lady looked so charming and beautiful that not only in the portrait but in actual life these pink ribbons became her perfectly. I remember her very well.

This was Anna Mikhailovna Khitrovo (or, as they used to say in former times, Khitrov*a*), born Golenishcheva-Kutuzova, one of the daughters of our famous Field Marshal.‡ My mother already had a nodding acquaintance with her in childhood and was obliged to her for her admission into the Ekaterinsky Institute.

All these portraits of friends hung in a row, and above them, as in a special place of honor, was nailed a small lithograph portrait of the Dowager Empress Maria Fyodorovna, of whom Mother could never speak without the deepest and sincerest feeling of rev-

* Pyotr Sokolov (1791–1848), painter.
† Vladimir Gau (1816–1895), painter.
‡ Anna M. Khitrovo, the grandmother of our present Ambassador to Bucharest, M. A. Khitrovo. (K. L.)

erential love. The Empress is depicted, if I am not mistaken, in mourning after the decease of the Emperor Alexander Pavlovich, in a black dress with a wide collar and in a black tulle toque. Listening to my mother's stories about the Empress, I often gazed attentively even in childhood at this small lithograph, and already at that time the appearance of the now deceased Empress pleased me very much; her somewhat rounded, full face was so expressive and tranquil, so generous, dignified, and firm. The lines of her lips also conveyed great refinement and authority.

I shall not try to pretend or to convince you that I often thought about the Imperial family and loved its members quite consciously even in those early years when the tricolored draperies in mother's study had not yet faded and been replaced by light blue wallpaper. No, of course that was not so; but I can affirm that our house in Kudinovo was redolent of the monarchical spirit and that my extremely strong love for my mother, who was elegant and noble in the highest degree, not at all affectionate or tender, but on the contrary strict and angry, made me regard as sacred those people and those objects she loved and honored.

Later on, as a young man in the fifties, I too paid my tribute to European liberalism. But I can say with pride that even in this confused period of my life I did not once insult, either by a blasphemous sarcasm or by the too insistent and abrupt conclusions of a bad liberal philosophy, those personal feelings and those ideals which my mother had inalterably carried in her heart to her grave.

I even recall one dispute. Mother was unfortunately too quick-tempered and immoderate in certain ways of expressing herself when something upset her. One day (I was already past twenty) she offended me greatly. I was in love; Mother disliked the girl of my choice, because she was older than me and, in Mother's opinion, scheming and not at all pretty. Refusing to confine herself to reasoned parental warnings and counsels, Mother began to deride both the appearance and the spiritual qualities of this girl, whom I had loved with all my heart for a long time.

Irritated by these really inappropriate escapades on the part of my too impetuous and authoritative Mother, I stopped her tirade and addressed her thus:

"Listen! Why do you so imprudently demean that which is so dear to me? Can you recall that I have ever scoffed either by hint or in jest at anything you held sacred, anything that constituted the poetry of your memories, of your youth? On the contrary, I love these memories of yours. I remember your stories almost by heart."

Here I paused and thought—what example should I give? I found nothing better than to point to the Empress Maria Fyodorovna:

"There, for example, I know that you love the Empress Maria Fyodorovna. I know that you love her not only for the generosity she has extended to you but also because you were brought up on monarchical traditions and because you find poetry in them. Have I ever questioned these feelings of yours? Have I ever scoffed at them, tell me? But, as for me, perhaps I prefer the republic?"

My mother understood I was right; she stopped talking and even felt ashamed. And I felt so sorry for her, when I perceived the *honest* confusion of this beautiful, energetic, determined, elderly parent of mine, that I immediately began to kiss her, and we made peace.

Of course, it was not without some justification that I blamed my mother for her indelicate and tactless ranting against the then object of my adoration (all the more so since now, forty years later, I can assert that this girl was entirely worthy of love and respect). But as for "the republic"! "The republic!" That is where I proved so intolerably stupid!

I did not even suspect that I myself, like my mother, *was growing up in the midst of monarchical traditions* or secondly, that I had not the least need of "the republic," that all this was nothing but a youthful impulse to praise what we do not have and, in particular, what was *then*, in the days of the Emperor Nicholas I, not too safe to praise.

Recalling now attentively and conscientiously my various "psychological moments," I am convinced that what I liked about republics even then were not those elements that distinguish them from the monarchies, that is, not equality and not political freedom, but on the contrary those aspects of the great republics which they have in common with the great monarchies, namely, strength, the differentiation of characters that is worked out by a conventional order, the conflict, the battles, the picturesque aspects of life, and so on.

In this *aesthetic instinct* of my youth there was far more *statesmanlike tact* than is usually admitted; for one can find a great deal of everyday and every other sort of poetry only where there is a great concentration of state power and social strength. State power is the hidden iron framework upon which the great history-the-artist molds the elegant and mighty forms of cultural human life.

Thus I repeat again, without suspecting it, I myself, was growing up in the traditions of monarchical love and genuine Russian patriotism, and, as I have already said, I had no business with any "republic." And for those good principles—which began to assert themselves not too late, but at my very first encounter with the extremes of our "democracy" of the sixties—I am obliged to my mother, who, since my early childhood, had sowed good seeds in me.

NARCISSUS I

I HAD A feeling of revulsion, of terrible revulsion at the mere thought of my spiritual poverty! These two creatures, these two selves, who were just beginning to grow up before my poverty-stricken soul—they, both of them, repudiated me. What need had I of my quarters in the wing, of my dressing gown in the new style? A breath of deadly chill assailed me from these dumb walls, from my whole family, from the outside world, from my own self. Did I really wish to introduce into this abode, deliberately lonely and deliberately tumultous, the person whom my conscience, pining from impotence, now beheld? No, neither the contemptible young boy nor the man grown suddenly senile without ever properly maturing. . . . My Volodya Ladnev was no such person! He was modest in his thoughts, careful and firm in his affairs, and fierce as a tiger in the cause of good and in defense of the weak. Of

---

From the autobiographical novel PODLIPKI, 1861. WORKS, *vol. I, pp. 229–230. In* PODLIPKI, *Leontiev is concerned with his adolescence and early manhood, his spiritual development and his aesthetic tastes. Ladnev is the hero of this novel.*

17

course, he loved himself—that's nothing. But he was not mean; he was quietly proud; underneath his apparent carelessness he concealed a fiery soul and a lofty mind; he understood "the murmuring streams, he clearly saw the book of the stars," and although he had no "sea wave" near him,* he was yet able everywhere to penetrate into the secret life—and the green mold of the pond breathed before him. O my Volodya, my Volodya! My dear Volodya! Where are you? And hardly had the door of life opened before him, hardly had the fresh breeze of love been wafted upon him, when he crumbled to dust like an old corpse, which had long been lying motionless in a vault! And how could I entrust myself to those frivolous people, whose blunders were completely devoid of meekness and whose undignified suffering only brought a smile to my face?

* From Baratinsky's poem *On Goethe's Death* (1832).

NARCISSUS II

SOMETIMES, when blissfully happy and full of self-admiration, I used to compare myself to a lilac-colored flower; and this is why I did so. Not too far from us, on the corner of a quiet cross street, stood a not too large house behind a cast-iron railing and a front garden; it was a white, stone, one-storied house, and it was inhabited by an acquaintance of the same age as myself—he had lived there first with his father and mother and then, when he turned nineteen, all by himself. I liked the front garden even in the winter—the vegetation wrapped in matting, the clean snow, showing no traces, on the ground, on the semicircular terrace, on the white vases of the balustrade. In the evening, behind the Gothic windows, heavy curtains were drawn; in a corner by the terrace grew a young fir tree, so dense and velvety-looking from a distance that it made me sigh each time I drove past. Yanitzky was ugly and sickly-looking, but he was well-built and supple; gazing at his somewhat African profile, at the kindly expression on his ani-

From PODLIPKI. WORKS, *vol. I, pp. 222–224.*

mated face, at his curly hair, I often recalled either Pushkin or Onegin. For a long time I could not decide who was more like Onegin, he or I. His study and bedroom looked as if arranged by a woman's hand. There was not a shade of disorder, no trash, nothing crude, not a single ponderous object! Expensive furniture, carpets, French books in Morocco and velvet bindings with gilded edges.

> A table laden with bronze and porcelain,
> And the exuberance of pampered senses.
> The scents in crystal flagons. . . .

In his abode one involuntarily whispered these verses.

A marvelous life! He used to dine at five; if one called on him in the morning, he would be playing on an excellent grand piano; his mother, appareled in velvet and ermine, would walk by in the distance through spacious rooms. His father would drop in; how polite he was! how handsomely gray! what a healthy glow in his cheeks! On his black dress coat a Kulm cross and star, boots of soft leather, his smile even softer. He would press my hand, chat with us, and depart.

In Yanitzky's company, I did not have to think; instead, there awoke in me such light hopes, such ethereal thoughts!

What did we talk about?

"Good day!"

"Good day!"

"You were *there* yesterday? Did you see *her?*"

"Come and dine with me tête-à-tête. . . ."

"I'll show you a statuette, which they have just brought me from Paris."

"Let's go! Let's go. . . ."

All facts, nothing but facts! I would get tired of them at last and would go to Yuriev's.

"Why," I thought, "can't I find a single man who would be a combination of Yanitzky and Yuriev? Where is there a man like that? Am I not myself that elect one? Of course, I am not as intelligent as Yuriev and am not as brilliant and not as spiritually gracious as Yanitzky. . . . What of it? So much the better! If they are taller than me at both ends, then I am stouter than they are! I am like the lilac light—a mixture of rose and deep blue!"

CHRIST

OTHER feelings were also mingled with the sadness of solitude, with the fear of being punished beyond the grave, with the hope of finding succour while still among the living. On the one hand, the memory of childhood images was inseparable from prayers and hopes; in my imagination I saw my aunt's image case and icon lamp. Whenever I remember it, my aunt in person, her bedroom, her rug, my carefree happiness, my soul is drawn homeward and heavenward! When I happened to leave church earlier than I should have or to drop the crumbs of a communion wafer on the floor, I saw myself as one who had rudely abused something innocent and indulgent. At times I also loved to read the Holy Scriptures; and when, toward the end of the Old Testament, in its concluding chapters, I somehow had a sense of emptiness and peace, and the strict Romans were already present, a feeling of barely audible, barely noticeable, sweet expectation stirred within me. The dawn of a better life seemed to be awaiting the whole world.

From PODLIPKI. WORKS, _vol. I, pp._ 74-75.

There was no light as yet, and one felt both sad and relieved. Then a poor child was born in Bethlehem. . . . How good it is in these dry deserts, where only palm trees grow and people walk about barefoot in light robes! And already Peter was weeping in the night when the cock crowed, and I wept with him; all grew dark, the dead rose out of their graves and walked into town, the curtain in the temple was rent. . . . Before me is a picture. . . . Christ manifests himself for a minute to a couple of disciples, who were on their way to Emmaus. Some poor little town, this Emmaus; three smallish men are hurrying out of some valley, their robes blowing behind them; to one side are rocks, and in the distance looms an agglomeration of small houses with flat roofs. How deserted it all seems! As though after dinner when it is no longer hot, you might enter a large green garden which no one is using and where the shadows cast by the trees grow more and more elongated. As though the person closest to one had departed from the house and from this garden, in which he could have strolled had he wished. And something new was about to begin, was about to glimmer. . . . But what was it? Even then I could not explain it, nor can I do so now.

A PRIEST'S DAUGHTER, POOR GIRL

THE TEARS shed over the grave of my relatives moved me, and the proximity of death reawakened once more my thirst for enjoyment.

At the same time I perceived a mute reproach on all the familiar objects, which came into view as I drew nearer the estate from the north, where groves of trees kept it long hidden from sight. The oak was bending over the hilltop by the pond; the hay, a second mowing, lay in tranquil rows upon the green grass that somehow looked rejuvenated after the mowing. Felka, the washerwoman, was busy wielding a battledore as she stooped over the water on the spot where stood our elms. The postprandial emptiness of the courtyard! All these silently called out to me, "Why did you abandon us for vain amusements? And because you preferred an alien life to the one that was always native and even subject to you in many ways, for this God has punished you!" We rapidly

---

From PODLIPKI. WORKS, *vol. I, pp. 248–255, 260–262.*

drove into the courtyard. Olga Ivanovna in a white housecoat was working on the veranda; beside her sat Pasha. They both got up and came down from the veranda to meet me. All their faces were smiling! Here I was king!

I kissed Olga Ivanovna, greeted Pasha, and dashed off to find my aunt. Over tea they insisted on my telling them everything in detail; and I began telling them, but omitted to mention my losses. Shortly afterwards, as I was walking down the corridor, I met Pasha and stroked her head in passing, and she seized my hand and kissed it passionately.

At this very moment I fell in love with her.

We went our ways, but I was distraught all evening and made very random replies to my aunt. She even scolded me in a maternal way for this and threatened to "bang my forehead."

And how well her small braids suited Pasha that evening! My darling Pasha! I could not fall asleep for a long time!

Finding her alone next morning at the embroidery frame in the divan-room, I begged her to meet me in the alley that night.

"I'd be frightened," she replied. "Didn't you hear the owl hooting all night long? It has a child in the hollow, in the apple tree on the right."

I promised to kill the owl; I loaded a rifle, and, failing to find the owl itself, I pulled out the owlet, set it on a branch, and, without any real necessity, shot it at ten paces.

Pasha promised to come out into the alley. I was burning with impatience and, to shorten the time between tea and supper, went horseback riding. The moon was shining brightly, and when I returned home, the air was very fresh and melancholy all around.

Another hour remained till supper.

My aunt, Olga Ivanovna, Pasha, and Fevronyushka were all sitting on the veranda.

In the garden the old owl was hooting in a heart-rending voice. I went off to my room and, unable to write verses, expressed I know not what in prose!

I had recently been reading Chateaubriand and remembered

the nocturnal song of the young redskin, who says that he will fertilize the womb of his beloved (*je fertiliserai son sein*).*

The owl, the moon, and the dampness, Pasha and her mother, the perfidious Sonyechka and her mother—all this fluttered around me. I sat down and began to write as if the girl were addressing me.

The sheet of this manuscript has survived to this day, and contains almost no corrections. I could never decide either to burn or tear it up.

"My friend! what is that pale cloud doing on the edge of the sky?

"It is already dark, and the air in the fields is full of moist chill.

"My friend! my soul is gnawing within me!

"I have gone far away from my people, have left the house and gone into the fields, and my soul keeps gnawing within me!

"How shall I describe for you, my brother, how shall I describe the feeling that thrills me?

"I would have called it the music of distant death, my darling; but my hands are so chill, such a cool breeze is blowing upon my cheeks from yonder grove. . . .

"What am I to do? I have no words!

"All last night the owl hooted in the garden. . . . My brother, why did you kill its offspring, a still innocent child, my dear brother? . . . Do you remember? Your mother, too, was harsh and unloved by people, and why did you sigh so deeply when you heard last evening the pitiful laments of the owl above the apple tree, beneath which lay the blood-shattered body of her fledgling?

"I heard you sigh, my friend; forgive me my words, the poor words of your lonely sister. . . .

"Yonder, do you see a glimmer of light through the faded autumn bushes? That is my house, dear brother mine.

"Come to me! It is chill in the fields!

"I shall warm you by the fireplace, and the breath of my love will drive away the chill of your hands. . . .

* Vicomte de Chateaubriand, *Atala*, 1801. *Oeuvres*, vol. XVIII (1836), p. 21.

"Let us go, let us go, my chosen one. Let us go; my soul is singing! There we shall be alone for a long time in a bright room, while it is so dark in the fields and all around us outside are only dampness and night!"

I lay down in a state of anxiety. I was still patient while everything was moving in the house; but soon Stepan stopped clanking in the pantry; in the distant women's quarters not a sound was to be heard. Then I became all ears, began to tremble, jumped up. . . . A door creaked in the distance and was silent again (by the sound I knew which door it was). I was expecting that door to creak suddenly and briefly at last, because Pasha would soon grow tired of indecision. In a minute indeed this came about. If she had gone boldly at once through the women's quarters, then I would have heard the click of a lock following the familiar creaking, the whining of a pulley in the passage; but apparently she was taking every precaution; so much time elapsed between the first sound and the second that I began to think, "It's probably not her!" God alone knows what a torment it was to me, but I was prepared in any case. At last the lock clicked, the door in the passage whined and banged . . . I had no doubt now that it was she! She had dashed quickly past the maids' quarters so that no one, awakening, might recognize her. I seized my cap, opened the window, jumped into the garden, and hastened along the dark alley towards the orchard. Pasha appeared on the little bridge outside the gates; she was wrapped in a large shawl. I waited for her in the darkness of the alley, and she threw her arms round my neck.

"Ah, my darling, it's you! I was so frightened of the doors, they creak so loudly! It's sheer craziness!"

We decided to walk into the fields, towards the hillocks where the brick shed stood. It was not far off, and deserted, and one could hide in the shed, whereas there were watchmen in the garden. Pasha was frightened and cold but was agreeable to everything. How charming her submissiveness seemed to me, her childlike meekness, the respect she showed me, which I noticed in her words and the timid way she looked at me. All this pleased me so much after the coquettishness and the deceitfulness of Katiusha, after the caprices and tastelessness of Klasha, after the impudence of Sophia! When Pasha and I walked along the deserted road past the marsh and gazed at the vast fields covered in mist, the poor, pale child became, as it were, an object of reverence to me. My very sensitivity was penetrated with such sincere tenderness, with such tender emotion, that I suddenly felt no desire to part from her even for a minute; I wrapped her in my coat, and we soon reached the brick shed. Here, embracing tightly, we sat for a long time on the hillock without saying a word. I gazed at this gentle, adolescent face, at the child's mobcap she wore, at the fair braids which stuck from under it; I looked into her eyes, which kept switching their attention from the mist and the fields back to me and again from me to the mist and the fields, and was still unable to utter a word. What should I tell her? "I love you!" Yes, at this moment, I loved her with all my soul. And what then? And the sacrifices I would have to make? I had already rejected them in advance. O Pasha, darling Pasha! You do not realize with what precise calculations I began courting you, the man with whom you are not afraid to go out into the fields!

However, I squeezed her hand and, in spite of myself, said with an effort:

"So, Pasha, you are agreeable to love me wholly. . . ."

"How wholly? I am simply amazed how it is even possible to love a strange man the way I love you!"

I was afraid to utter an abusive word or to permit myself a mute liberty.

Pasha understood, however, and grew thoughtful.

"So that's it," she began after a pause. "But what will happen? It's fearsome to think of it, dear soul. My mamma, as you know, is so strict. She does not love me, I don't know why. Just recently, when we drove into town, she did nothing but repeat, 'You spoiled brat, you never make any sense.' Why hadn't I pleased the prospective bridegroom?"

"And you would have gone with him if you had pleased him?"

"Of course I would have gone. How could I not do so? Even if he were vile, very vile, what's to be done? I would have gone! Please wrap me closer, it's so cold. . . ."

Sighing deeply, Pasha continued:

"Yes. I don't know why mamma doesn't love me. My deceased father—he did love me. He would take me on his knees and fondle me, and I was not afraid of him at all. One day Mother got hold of me and locked me up in the lumber room, I forget what for. O Lord! what a fright I had, dear soul! It was dark; the rats were squeeling and scuffling. And I sobbed, how I sobbed. Only Daddy returned from church, heard about it, and unlocked the door. 'Don't cry, Pashenka,' he said. And I stopped crying. And Daddy was so pale himself. He pitied me greatly. . . . What are you thinking about?"

What was I to say to her? What was I thinking about! I was in a state of unutterable confusion; I stared at the misty fields; they were the same fields over which, behind the impassable winter garden, *once upon a time the bridegroom had walked at midnight.* Once upon a time! When I believed with all my soul, when Father Vasily sang in our house in the evening amid clouds of smoke! And I would defile this pure image with my instable passion? I would deceive him? No, I would not do so! I rose and said to her, "Let's go home." "Let us," she replied, sighing. And we went back. She was reluctant to part from me so soon; she accompanied me into the alley, and here we bade farewell and embraced each other in the darkness. The owl, as it had done the day before, was hooting in a plaintive, terribly plaintive voice. Pasha was walking away to the rustling of dry leaves. My eyes followed her; she also stopped at the end of the alley, in front of the orchard, and in a lighter place between the trees I could once more distinguish her checkered shawl and her little girl's mobcap.

"Goodbye, darling, goodbye!" she called out from there.

I could not fall asleep; I lit a candle and paced up and down the room for a long time, but it still felt stifling; I walked out into the drawing room and paced up and down there.

What was I to do? Leave her? But how leave her when she was always present before my eyes? A cooling off. . . . Promise security—was that all? . . . And all the awkwardness, the misunderstandings, the false words of a lover fallen out of love? . . . I felt terribly sorry for her, but this compassion in itself only doubled my desire to possess her. My poor Greece, where are you? Where is that blessed corner where I can find a lover without reproach and without debauch, an unselfish and fearless priestess of love? Does my life have to follow the same course as the life of all the others? In that case it would be better had I never been born! Better a vice of passion than vile mediocrity! A vice of passion—so let it be! But what if a liaison with this poor girl would merely lead to another sort of vile mediocrity, to senile uncertainty of feeling, to the repressed breathing of one who fears a vile act, a victim's fear? If I should be fated to evoke in somebody's soul, at some distant time—if I were destined to evoke contemptible pity, would it not be better to reject everything at once, reject Greece, reject life itself? Could I bear the full weight of the answer? To marry afterwards? It would be stifling! How terrible is a woman's exhaustion after giving birth, the blue veins on her bloodless hands; but all that would not be as terrible as my own weakness. . . . But if I am fated—having satiated myself at once with both lust and compassion, having enjoyed both her adolescent body and gentle soul —if I am fated to hear somebody say about me, *"Yes, he only thought that he loved; he merely loved his own imagination, not her!"* O Lord! is it not better to become a hermit or a monk, a dedicated, luminous, perceptive one, which is what the soul wants —to be free and clear as a cool autumn day? Is a bright, solitary life not better than a stifling marriage, where pity and boredom must mix so tragically, as well as the faint glimmers of the last fading love, and children and monotony? . . . Would it not be better to marry, to offer one's name, and then leave the woman afterwards? Then one would be alone again and free! But everyone censures this, and perhaps this is really vile. And is all life really like this? Or only mine? But whose is better—whose? Wherever I turn, everywhere I see tears, tears vulgarly wiped away, and again tears. . . .

And how stifling it is everywhere! Even great men—what was their end? Death, only death. . . . What did life bring them? How vivid is the picture I see of Napoleon in a broad round hat and a frock coat standing there, with his hands behind his back! Facing him are a lady and a negro bearing a burden. How bored he looks! And here is another picture: Madame Bertrand with a Spanish comb in her hair, cancer inside her, her mouth open—and death! I also see Goethe in an old-fashioned frock coat, the old Goethe, married to a cook; how stuffy it is in his room! Schiller, worn out by his nocturnal labors, dies early, Rousseau, the husband of Teresa, who does not understand who her husband is. . . And these were all great men! Is that not horrible, horrible in all its aspects? . . .

I seized my cap at last and dashed out of the house; I walked and walked and walked to the river on the road to the village, strolled about the river bank in the cold mist, and returned home tired and chilled; but on the way I was fortified in my intention to make a first, true trial of will power by disavowing Pasha. I would tell her she must go away from here! . . .

Little by little my soul grew calm, and I fell asleep. . . .

All of them deceived me, disillusioned me in some way or another. Pasha alone remained forever in my mind as a flaxen-haired, gentle, and innocent child. She did not long survive our meeting.

THE MEDICAL STUDENT

FOR THE first two years, my medical studies weighed rather heavily upon me, although of course there were moments when my interest was stimulated by something during the lectures. To begin with, general scientific conclusions attracted my attention more than details. The details began to appeal to me later, in my fourth year, at the bedside of a patient, and even more in the military hospitals, where I was already my own master and manager. In the course of time, I began to cure my patients fairly well and not infrequently in a very happy way. It seems to me, however, that I began to understand more and more deeply such questions as "whether to prescribe in this case opium or *aqua laurocerasi*" and "to bleed or not to bleed", not because of any love for science or out of mercenary considerations, but rather out of a somewhat romantically tinged love of mankind. However, more of this later. In short, having been obliged by circumstances to enter the medical faculty, I still could not take to medicine with all my soul.

From REMINISCENCES, 1888. WORKS, *vol. IX, pp. 69–72.*

Science, then, could not console me at that time, and especially not in my second year, when I had not yet been confronted with *living sufferers,* who might excite my sympathy, my fervor, my self-esteem, but only with the sprawling bodies on the slabs of strangled old men, drunkards frozen stiff in the streets, murdered wantons, whose corpses the students tore to pieces, laughing and blaspheming in all sorts of ways.

I was not amused by the crude merriment of my comrades. Evidently there was almost nothing they worried about or gave any thought to except their exams and their careers. As for myself, I *thought* and tormented myself about everything from morning till night.

I then lost for a long time my childhood faith; I had just ceased to agonize; at that time I could not yet rely upon some sort of vague deism, aesthetic and libertarian, upon which I came to rely not very much later. I was tormented by lack of faith, having to live with my family, sicknesses, lack of money, repressed self-esteem, and my university studies, which I disliked and which I forced myself to pursue in order to complete at all costs a course in an establishment of higher learning. I almost made no acquaintances among the other students; it seemed to me they did not understand anything, and, for that reason, many of them had unpleasant faces; but I always loved elegance, even in my comrades. At the lectures I talked with almost no one and was wary of everyone.

I only had one friend, Alexey Georgievsky.* He was also a student, two years my senior, the son of a very indigent petty official with a large family in the remote little town of Borovsk in our Kaluga province. For about two years in succession I loved him madly, but I experienced more sorrow and injury than joy from him. He represented to me what Mephistopheles was to Faust. But his irony and negation were not so much the result of a lack of poetry or idealism in him as the expression of his anger against a life which gave him nothing. The majority of the students paid

* Yuriev in the novel *Podlipki.*

no attention to him and regarded him simply as an eccentric; but those few who were more intelligent and more developed, whom he frequented, immediately submitted to his intelligence, or, to put it better, to his genius.

He *poisoned* himself in '66. I had lost sight of him altogether since '54; but already in '51 I had broken off all relations with him, because he had by then become intolerably jaundiced and unjust. One could write a great deal about him alone, and even here I want to say a couple of words about him, if only because he exercised, through his counsels and opinions, a considerable influence on my literary studies; and over and above this, my comedy *Marriage through Love* would not have been written without him.

In those student days I found it very hard to live in this world. I suffered then from everything—from need and worldly vanity, from having to live with my family, which I did not like in many respects, from my work in the anatomy theater on the putrid corpses of various unfortunate and forsaken people, from bodily ailments, from lack of faith, from fear that *I might fade before I had time to blossom*, from fear of dying early, "sans avoir connu la passion, sans avoir été aimé!"

I was, then, like a man who had been skinned but who was still alive and who experienced more acute and terrible sensations than before. For this reason I could not long bear the irony and the mental acerbity of my disillusioned friend; even his jocular remarks had the same effect as caustic upon a raw living body.

In '51 I finally felt so dejected and pained that I ceased altogether to understand light verse, humorous sketches, and so on. I only understood works that were full of suffering and morbidity. When Turgenev published his *The Diary of a Superfluous Man*, it seemed to me that he had divined *my state of mind* without ever seeing me. Opposite the university was the tavern Britannia, which I frequented in order to read newspapers, listen to the organ, and drink *tea* (I did not venture to *lunch* very often, because I was short of money).

What was I to do when I was obliged (I say so without exaggerating) *to weep* in the tavern over the story of this "superfluous man"? I hid behind the book in a corner and wept. Thank God, nobody paid any attention.

There was in Moscow a certain young woman, Z. K——va. Our relationship lasted for five years on end, assuming various forms ranging from friendship to the most flaming mutual passion. *But the good time* was to come later; in '51 this relationship was still somehow indeterminate, vague, instable, and it even caused me greater pain than joy. There is a poem by Kliushnikov which has the lines:

> *I do not love you, but if I were to love another,*
> *I would despise myself most bitterly.*

At the time these lines were dearer to me than all other poetry, closer than Pushkin, Fet, Lermontov, Koltzov, dearer than anything else in the world. "*I do not love you*"—I found untold delight in repeating this line both to her and to myself. Yet it was hard for me to miss seeing her for one day.

TURGENEV

ONE EVENING I called upon my relatives the Okhotnikovs, who lived on the Prichistenka, and sat down at a round table under a lamp and chatted with a young woman. A newspaper was lying on the table. I did not like newspapers and did not read them, but on this occasion things turned out differently. I was talking with the young woman about some of my problems. I spoke of Turgenev and accidentally opened the paper. There I suddenly saw an advertisement: "Nikolay Sergeyevich and Ivan Sergeyevich Turgenev call upon the debtors and the creditors of their lately deceased mother, so and so, to present their claims; *Lomakovskaya's house, on the Ostozhenka.*" This house was almost opposite my apartment. I went home, and the next morning at about nine o'clock, with a contracting heart, I carried my manuscript to Turgenev.

A servant went off to report my arrival. Turgenev lived in the entresol. However much I may have been preoccupied with the matter in hand, my ever-present sense of objectivity did not for-

From REMINISCENCES. WORKS, *vol.* IX, *pp.* 77–79, 106–107, 133–134.

36

sake me even then. I was not familiar with either Turgenev's appearance or his social position and was terribly afraid to meet a man *unfit to be a hero*—a plain, unassuming, modestly situated man, in a word, one of those wretched toilers, the mere sight of whom was already then adding poison to my inner sores. Although I then considered myself to be an extreme democrat, from my early years I could not bear anything colorless, boring, and bourgeois plebeian. Turgenev's heroes were, all of them, so modest and pitiful. At the time he had not yet created either Rudin or Lavretzky. However, I was soon called into his presence and received a pleasant surprise. Turgenev rose amiably to meet me and, holding out his hand, asked what I wanted.

He was almost enormously tall and broad-shouldered; his eyes were deep, thoughtful, dark gray; his hair was then dark, thick, somewhat curly, if I remember correctly, slightly grizzled; his smile was enchanting, his profile a little coarse and sharp, but sharp in a gentlemanly and handsome way. His hands, as befitted him, were beautiful, *"des mains soignées,"* large and virile. He was slightly over thirty then. He wore a dark raspberry silk dressing gown and fine linen. Even if he had received me badly, I would have still loved him because of his appearance. I was terribly glad to discover that he was far *more heroic* than his *heroes.* Saying almost not a word, I sat down opposite him in a large armchair and began to read my composition to him. He covered his face with his hands and listened for about a quarter of an hour; but then he interrupted me and asked me to leave the manuscript with him; it would be better for him to read it and think it over. He made an appointment for me to call next morning, asked me a few more questions about the university, about how long I had been studying and how long I had been writing, and so on.

I called next day, but was told that he was very ill, having had a heart attack, and that Inozemtzev in person had been to see him. The day after, he felt better and received me. We had a long chat.

It may be appropriate here to recall his own impressions; later, friends in common told me laughingly about them.

"I was sitting one morning at home," Turgenev told them. "On the previous day an army officer I did not know had brought me a drama he had written. His paper had a strong smell of Zhukov. There was some sort of countess and a seducer and such a very noble officer—the author must have been describing himself. The thing was worthless. The second time I did not receive him and sent down a note saying that in my opinion the drama could not be printed. He grew terribly angry in front of my servant, tore up my note, and departed. As soon as he had left, I was informed that a student had called. There entered a very young man, flaxen-haired, in a parade uniform and tricornered hat, holding a manuscript. He said his family name was Leontiev, shook my hand, apologized for not having his sword with him, because he had given it to be repaired, sat down, and began to read. He did not read very well, and for that reason I preferred to peruse the manuscript myself. And I perceived at once that it was not at all like the officer's." To me personally Turgenev also said many encouraging and flattering things.

One day, I recall, Turgenev was sitting on a table in his handsome hotel room; I was standing close to him and, admiring his broad shoulders and his expressive, noble countenance, I said:

"I don't know what is having this effect on me—whether it is my medical studies that are developing in me the need for a strong physiological ideal or whether it is my artistic inclinations (for I have taught myself to draw not too badly, it seems)—but I awfully love to gaze at people who are strong, healthy, and beautiful. When I went to see you for the first time, I was terribly afraid I might discover that you resembled either your consumptive 'superfluous man' or, even worse, your 'Shchigrovsky Hamlet.' Even though the 'superfluous man' fought Prince N. in a duel and wounded him and even though your 'Hamlet' sniffs tobacco, I find them terrible! But when I saw that you were so large and healthy, I was overjoyed. I especially detest it when literary men are abject in appearance—it pains me and makes me feel sad."

While I was saying all this, Turgenev's face changed completely: it turned gloomy; his eyes grew thoughtful, even sorrowful. I thought that for some reason he did not wish to prolong this conversation, and I fell silent.

Afterwards, our common friends informed me that he was a very sickly man, not at all strong, and that he was frequently ill. Therefore, one of two things: either my words—"strong, healthy" —reminded him of the ailments assailing him, of which he had no desire to speak, or, on the contrary, my speech pleased him so much that he found it necessary to hide his pleasure from me.

If the latter was the case, he disguised it very well. I shall never forget the sad, severe, deep shadow that suddenly passed over his face, so expressive was it! But his motive has remained an enigma to me to this day. One may suppose anything at leisure, but how prove it?

On this occasion Turgenev and I discussed literature in general and Russian writers in particular.

I cannot remember everything we said; but what I do remember, I remember faithfully and firmly.

Turgenev tried to persuade me not only to read Pushkin and Gogol more often but even to study them very closely.

"As for all of *us*—myself, Grigorovich, Druzhinin, and so on— you can do without reading us, perhaps," he added.

As regards Pushkin, this is what I myself have to say. Just about this time it was Lermontov, the sharper, more passionate and gloomier poet, who began to appeal to me more strongly than the luminous and conciliatory Pushkin. At this time *everything I came across in Pushkin began to seem* to me too light, seemingly superficial, *and far too familiar* and simple. This happens, however, to many inexperienced young men who feel all things very violently. Their need of violent, *soul-rending* impressions from poetry is not easily satisfied.

Turgenev's authority, which did not convert me at once, obliged me, however, to cogitate once more over Pushkin, who had only a couple of years back still reigned over all the other poets in my adolescent heart. My then, as yet unspoiled half-childish feeling proved to be more true in the end than all the more refined definitions of my subsequent critical taste, which did not redis-cover the right path for a long time to come.

As regards Gogol, he was still alive at the time of these meet-ings between Turgenev and myself. I knew he was in Moscow, but I had not even the slightest desire to see him or to be introduced to him, because I was almost personally predisposed against him on account of many things. Incidentally, one was his *Dead Souls*, or, more precisely, the crushing, hopelessly prosaic impression this "poem" produced upon me. Let us assume that I was already be-ginning to recognize the faultless and impressive artistry of this work; Belinsky in his articles and Georgievsky by his oral criticism had confirmed me in this latter concept; but what was I to do if I nourished in me that ineradicable, vital, aesthetic feeling which at-tached more value to *the poetry of actual life than to the artistic perfection of its literary reflections!*

I have never particularly liked extremely cruel caricature, satire, or comedy tinged with malice; and having fully suffered them on my own account and that of others, I even hated all these things— and Turgenev was obliged to remind me of Gogol's *Taras Bulba*, of his sketch *Rome*, and of the mighty poetry of his tale *Viy* in order to reconcile me with the genius whose latest and most ma-ture but nevertheless dry and malevolent works (*The Government Inspector, The Gamblers, Dead Souls*) almost shut off for me all these other admirable novellas of his—admirable not only in their form but also *in their content*, in the choice of the author's Weltanschauung.

Turgenev repeated approvingly Herzen's opinion that Gogol was "an unconscious revolutionary" because he depicted Russian life from the most vulgar and revolting point of view. However, he approved of Herzen (I remember this well), not in the *political* sense, not in having any direct sympathy with either the radical re-forms or the popular revolts he advocated, but only in holding that Herzen correctly understood the *sort of* influence Gogol's works might exercise by the way, independently of the author's original intention and unexpectedly for his consciousness. This, to me, completely new idea amazed me but left me somehow unconvinced; in my opinion, it only did a certain amount of damage to Gogol and nothing more. I loved too many aspects of Russian life; I knew of *no other* life at the time, except from books. Too many things gave me pleasure in this Russian life surrounding me for me to desire any radical changes; I only wished that the landowners and the officials could be as kind as possible to the common people and nothing more. In those years I did not reflect on *problems of state*. I did not even understand them at all and did not seek to understand them; I reduced everything to questions of either personal happiness or personal worth or to the poetry of encounter, conflict, adventure, and so on. Thus I did not regard revolutions in foreign countries as a form of *reconstruction* of society, but only as dangerous and interesting *insurrections*. I regarded all like manifestations, not from the teleological standpoint, but from that of their *dramatism*. For this reason, I found poetry wherever I could, *in one party or another*, depending on the man and the circumstances. For example, the Revolution of 1848 pleased me for some reason I do not now understand; and when later Napoleon made his *coup d'état* at night and then rode through Paris on horseback, wearing a uniform and pomaded mustaches, I also liked this very much. I suppose, however, that the Revolution of 1848 pleased me only because the French *Illustration*, which my mother received, contained very heroic and interesting pictures.

Turgenev arrived in Moscow. I learned that he was at Madame Salias's * and drove straight to her place. There I found, besides Turgenev and, of course, Peoktistov, that blockhead Valentin Korsh. Korsh kept silent all the time and stared from a corner at Turgenev in holy terror.

Turgenev was wearing a dark green velvet frock coat. He was very cheerful and sarcastic. He spoke about Orel, declaimed the verse of Fet, whom he greatly loved, jested, and even mimicked several people.

I remember many things in his stories about Orel that were re-

* Countess E. Salias de Tournemire (1815–1892), a minor Russian novelist.

flected a couple of years later in his novellas *The Friends* and *Calm*.

I liked him awfully; everything in him and about him was on a large scale. I have never envied him and have always admired him. For a moment, however, I was obliged to feel sorry for him.

Half reclining on a divan at Madame Salias's and shaking his wavy hair while in a sort of leonine pose, he delivered himself of the following: "The most important thing for a writer is to know how to get out of the saddle in good time. It's difficult for him to mount a horse, terrifying, at first he doesn't know how to. Then he will master both the horse and himself. He's at ease. Then comes a more difficult time than that of the first assault; how will he understand that it is time for him to leave the stage with dignity?

"I am not speaking," he continued, "of those insignificant 'photographers' like my friend Panayev, but only of those men who possess at least a little artistry—Pisemsky, Goncharov, and myself, for example. This poor Apollon Grigoriev is still searching for the *new word*. I like him tremendously, because he can't stand me and for many reasons criticizes very fundamentally the things I write. He will wait in vain for a *new word* from me, Pisemsky, or Goncharov. Only two young men, from whom much is to be expected, are capable of uttering it—Lev Tolstoy and *this* one."

Without changing his lordly pose, he simply pointed his finger at me.

I did not even blush; I accepted this *as my due*. I already entertained so few doubts about this that when Turgenev once more praised my face *à propos* of something and, commenting about a certain Golytzin, said—"Leontiev is an extremely *joli garçon*, and Golytzin is even better"—this delighted me far more. Let Golytzin be *"even* better"; I was still a *joli garçon*. Which of us a woman might favor was a matter of taste.

I also remember my successful treatment of certain seriously ill patients, some tolerable success with a woman, the conviction I had acquired through my experience in the Crimea that I was fairly courageous in the face of death, the Order of St. Anne of the third and second class awarded me in Adrianople and Yanina, and some astute consular transactions—all these memories afforded me far greater pleasure than the recognition of my talent in *conversation*, in *spoken words* (I do not here refer to articles, which nobody ever wrote about me, except Shchedrin: see the bibliography of *Sovremennik*,* 1862–1863, regarding my novel *In His Land*).

* *The Contemporary*, a radical review.

REJECTING A BRIDE

WHEN O——v, who was a leader and much older than me, proposed to my cunning but loving Z.,* she wished to refuse him and said to me, "I shall wait for you. You must finish your studies first, but tell me now—will you love me as much in a year's time as you do now? I shall refuse him."

I stood before her. She was twenty-five; I was twenty-three. I thought of poverty, children, hasty work, of her losing her attractiveness very soon, of *Turgenev's muse*. And I said to her, "I love you now; but we have nothing to live on at present, and who knows what will happen in a year's time? Marry him."

She kissed my hand, went off, and immediately became engaged. Her future fiancé was waiting for her in her aunt's room, not suspecting that his fate had been decided that very minute.

I tried to be as firm as possible. I resolved to sacrifice love for freedom and art; and I was right, of course, but it cost me so much

* See also "The Medical Student."

From REMINISCENCES. WORKS, *vol. IX, pp. 142–143.*

suffering that I—I am somewhat reluctant to admit it—I cried and sobbed for two hours on end after this, quite like a child or a woman.

Let me add that my relatives and friends, who had observed our closeness for the past four years, thought that she had led me a *fine dance, "qu'elle s'est joué de ce pauvre garçon"*, and they pitied me in a distressing way, kept looking at me with cautious smiles, and for a whole week treated me in general as if I were something soft and frail. Some of the women condemned her to her face, saying, *"Voilà nous autres femmes! Nous prétendons être meilleurs que vous autres."* Then to me: "However, I remember that you always maintained in arguments that you were afraid of a poor marriage and children, and you said that a wife's bandaged cheek or a husband's rheumatism was more horrible than anything else in the world while she would protest and try to idealize; and now, out of calculation, she has married a man she does not love."

I beg anyone at all to place himself in the situation of the proud lover, a very sensitive and inexperienced twenty-three-year-old youth, and then ask himself how he felt. And what pains of every sort does such a victim recall while sacrificing a long-lasting passion on the altar of freedom and art?

And I am not yet revealing a hundredth part of the details! I must admit that my pride was crushed by the pity I felt for this noble-minded young man, who had been deceived by a coquette. But despite all my self-esteem and natural frankness, a sense of honor and another, even loftier pride forced me to keep silent and to conceal the flattering truth. Some four days after her engagement, Z. made an appointment to meet me in a certain park. Her sisters were with her, but in order to leave us alone, they went off boating on the lake. We spent a long time saying goodbye in an arbor, and this is what she promised me:

"I shall try to be a good wife to him. How is he to blame, the poor man! But if things become too trying for me, I shall write you, and then you must tell me the truth in reply. If you still love me as you did before, I shall simply arrive to live with you."

With the instinct of a man in love, her bridegroom grasped the truth with more certainty than anyone else. He grew pale whenever the "jilted boy" entered the room, and he did not conceal from her the anxieties his jealousy caused him.

ARMY DOCTOR IN THE CRIMEA

IN THE autumn I moved to Theodosia. Then, as a consequence of a quarrel with my chief, I was transferred in the middle of the winter to Karas-Bazar, where people were perishing by the hundreds from typhus, fever, and gangrene, where every half hour the church bells tolled for the dead, where only *two* out of fourteen doctors remained on their feet, while the rest were already lying in their coffins or in their beds. For a long time I only had a twenty-kopek piece on me; for a long time others fed me; I was in love, and my love was reciprocated; I almost died there. From Karas-Bazar I fled back to Theodosia, abandoning the sick, and it was only thanks to the efforts of my friends that I escaped a court-martial. I was attached again to a Cossack regiment. The steppe again; once more wine and vodka; again silence, leisure, a cavalry mount, and good health. Again a new assignment, to Simferopol this time, where there were very many wounded and sick. Again

---

From REMINISCENCES. WORKS, *vol. IX, pp. 148–153. During the Crimean War (1854–56), Leontiev served as an army doctor.*

47

hospital work. But more love than labor. On the way to Simfero-pol I carried off a certain girl * from her parents. At the same time a hussar carried off another girl. The military authorities confused us; we found ourselves in Karas-Bazar without passports; we were detained; they wished to hand over my poor girl to the police, but I showed so much energy and resolution in defense of her that no-body could decide to take the step; but for a whole day and night sentinels stood on guard at our door; a police sergeant accepted a bribe from me, my last five rubles; a certain drunken doctor, a married man who had sent his wife back to Russia and was now living with his quite plain "Natashka," lent me ten rubles. I was brought back under guard to Simferopol; having rescued my girl from the police, I now sent her back to her parents.

For three days I ate only black bread; hunger obliged me to en-ter a hospital, and for quite a while I deceived my medical col-leagues into believing that I was suffering from paroxysms at night. Because I was hungry, I ate the disgusting official food for a whole month; then I suddenly received a lot of money, both from the treasury and from my parents. Again good health, taverns, music, acquaintance with English Guards officers, porter and champagne. Again no money. Isolation in a quiet summer cottage "on the banks of the sprightly Salgir." An honest German family; a divine view from the vineyard on Chatyr-Dag; luxuriant gardens all around. Chats with the old German about the ancient past of the Crimea, about God, about nature! Two daughters, both widows; the second was young and favorably inclined. They wanted to marry her off to me.

But that was too modest! Within a couple of months I was again in a new world; I was at the other end of town, in a soldiers' settlement, staying in the small house of the widow Bormushkina. My runaway girl was with me again. We forgot the rest of the world and, like children, lived in bliss in this distant settlement. I stopped going to work and had no qualms. It was as though I were ill again. To tell the truth, it seemed to me that I was devoting more thought to my personal *development* than to the care of

* Lisa—later my wife. (K. L.)

other people. Having once convinced myself that I could really be a doctor no worse than other doctors in matters of medical direction and cure, I relaxed, and my amorous adventures seemed to me far more important and instructive than the *illusions* of our army medical practice. Here in the soldiers' settlement, one could not be deceived; here the *goal* could be attained. But in a hospital? My wanderings still had no end. In the settlement I was discovered by my old Moscow friend Shatilov,* who was a man of wealth. He learned that I had never visited the south Crimean shore, had never seen Yalta, Alupka, or the famous Ayou-Dag. He was delighted with my girl. He announced that we must all go together to the south shore. He gave me a hundred rubles for this purpose, and we all set off. Again we lived a life of bliss tête-à-tête amid the beauties of nature, of the southern coast and the mountains, which neither she nor I had ever seen before. We returned penniless, pawned our spoons, and separated again.

For a long time I stayed with Shatilov in the country.

The war had ended; for some time the ranks of the military had been thinning out; the regiments scattered in all directions with kettledrums beating and soldier choirs singing. The landowners were beginning to return to their estates. The hospitals were being emptied.

The battle scenes disappeared, one after another, like a mirage in the steppes, and the flowering, varied poetry of the peaceful and joyous Crimea became more visible and comprehensible.

For a long time I lived in Shatilov's estate in the steppes. A beautiful estate. For a yearly stipend, I treated his peasants and neighbors. Here medicine again became a pleasure; here I saw results; here there was less illusion. I rode on horseback, strolled about, read, occupied myself with comparative anatomy, and even practiced shooting. Here, finally, I began once more to write in peace. Nothing helps creativity so much as a regular life after a long period of trouble and wandering.

Unfortunately science in general, in which I was becoming in-

* Iosif Nikolaivich Shatilov (1824–1889), ornithologist and author of various books on agriculture.

creasingly involved here in my leisure hours, continued to vitiate my *style* and vital *spirit*. Any development on a high level is most difficult. A lot of crude rocks must be crushed before a vein of gold can be discovered; a multitude of rose petals are needed to produce a spoonful of expensive fragrant perfume oil. Even great writers, those whose ability is crowned with success during their lifetime, leave comparatively little of worth for the succeeding ages.

And how much has been written!

A practical life, an independent job—these were very useful for my independence, for new impressions, for my life, for that self-respect which the drab and stifling life I so much despised of the editorial offices of the capital had failed to give me.

Now I loved more, I respected myself more; I became formed and stood on my own feet. But such is the destiny of all terrestrial things that it was impossible to lead an active life without theoretical preoccupations; and theoretical studies trained me in realist methods that were too scientific, too *exact*, and these harmed the caprice of inspiration, through attention to detail distorted the simplicity of sweeping brushstrokes, and weakened my enthusiasms and the flight of my imagination.

The eternal fear of projecting oneself too much, the fear which I had caught from Turgenev and other writers of that day, had the effect of making me continue to prefer, out of a sort of *pruderie*, far less original and fresh subjects to the events of my own life, to do so out of a false shame that was perhaps laudable in a *man* but was nevertheless most injurious to art.

If one could only write a single work of genius, even though it were shamelessly sincere but beautiful. One would die, but the work would remain. But to do this, one would have to be either as young as I was when I wrote *Kireyev* or already tired and aware of the impossibility of communicating to the world even a tenth part of what one thinks.

At Shatilov's I applied myself a great deal to comparative anatomy and medicine. Moreover, Shatilov himself had some influence on me in this respect—whether for good or bad I am not certain! He was a passionate ornithologist and had an excellent museum of Crimean birds; even in school I adored zoology, and this was now a bond between us. At his house I read Cuvier and Humboldt, and it seems to me I was almost thinking of introducing into art some sort of new *forms* based on the *natural sciences*.

Zoology, comparative anatomy, and botany are all permeated with poetry when one delves into them. The variety of forms and the general laws, the temptation of new discoveries and new observations, my country walks and my closeness to nature with a scientific goal in view—all this I found very enjoyable. The poetry of scientific studies and the poetry of amorous adventures have this in common, that they distract one equally and materially from the pursuit of art. But they differ in this, that love and all sorts of adventures give food for future art and even exercise a beneficial influence on its *form*, for they supply an unpremeditated *content*; whereas science, by diverting the artist to present reality, tends to spoil the artist's *means of expression* even in days to come, and one would have to be almost a genius to *crush* or suppress within oneself this heavy load of scientific facts and data so as to avoid burying oneself in trifles, so as to burst out from these clutches of trivial though beautiful realism and soar into the area of broader statement, so as

> *To acquire a simple tongue*
> *And the voice of noble passion.*

At last the time came for me to return to my native land. Other doctors were returning home from the war, having enriched themselves by thievery and thrift; but I was returning home without any means, without any belongings, without a fur coat, without any military decorations or promotion. I traveled for eighteen days with a transport column from the Crimea to Kharkov, and in Kursk I realized that I would not have enough money left to get me to Moscow; and if I had not managed very adroitly to trick one of my traveling companions, I have no idea how I would have ever got there. He avenged himself on me by eating and drinking to his full for three or four days, while, except for a crust of bread and a morsel of lard, he gave me nothing at all, not even my tobacco.

Thus I traveled, living in poverty and enjoying the awareness of my troubles, for I was one of the very *few* who succeeded in leaving the Crimea without having to blush before the then nascent liberal and *honest* movement of minds; and over and above this, I had also become responsible for a certain destitute family,* which I had promised myself not to abandon and to support in the future.

I remember that I had a volume of Béranger with me. Having eaten with the peasants after covering fifteen kilometers, I would get into a cart. While I read Béranger there, the cart creaked and moved along at a walking pace through the endless steppe till nightfall.

> *Le verre en main*
> *Gaiement je me confie*
> *Au dieu des bonnes gens. . . .*

And raising my arms to the heavens, I exclaimed with pharisaical joy, "O Lord, I thank You, because You have created me different from those scoundrels and have granted me strength and honor enough for such a difficult struggle!"

In Moscow my parents paid the twenty silver kopeks I owed the cab driver who drove me home, and I settled down again in the house of the Okh_____s on the Prichistenka. *She* had not been living in Moscow for some time, and I preferred it so. Later on I met her and realized that she had grown accustomed to her husband and already had a multitude of children. . . .

I began to seek a post in the countryside, in the provinces.

Inozemtzov, who was famed for his ability to bring out young doctors, knew and liked me. He wished me to stay on in Moscow; others also advised me to do so, even tempting me with the prospect of my becoming a ladies' doctor, but I remained true to

* Lisa's family.

my original intention of going off again into the wilderness. Country life promised me better health, more leisure for thought and creativity, the possibility of seeing the common people more often and more closely, and higher society, too, if I came across any decent landowners. It always gave me more pleasure to know the common people, one of *les deux extrêmes*, than people of those middle, professorial, and literary circles in which I, according to my means, would have been probably obliged at first to move in Moscow. If I had wanted to ride on horseback, where could I have found a horse in Moscow? If I had wanted forests in the winter, where were they? There were so many things I wanted.

Apart from Turgenev, who was elegant, witty, worldly, tall, and a country gentleman of means, and Fet, of whom, if I had been a versifier, I would have said in verse

A *brave ulan, considerate and kind*

there was not a single literary man or scientist who attracted me personally for the purpose of social or everyday intercourse. Panayev and Nekrasov were both revolting, and so on. Goncharov was also an *épicier;* he was fat, and so on.

I had not met either Leo or Alexey Tolstoy. Maikov was a sorry figure. His wife wore glasses! Thus I looked upon almost all of the literary men and scientists as on an unavoidable evil, as on some sort of *sacrifice to the social temperament,* and I loved to live far removed from them, exploiting them only for my own ends. Perhaps this was the reason why not a single one of them paid any attention to me, and they all forgot me in my isolation, which was personally egotistical and artistically self-assured.

THE SURRENDER OF KERCH IN 1855

I CHANGED my uniform and sat down feeling blissful on the balcony of the hotel. But my state of bliss did not last very long.

While from time to time cabs dashed past in the street, carts crawled along, and Cossacks galloped by now and then, I continued to drink my coffee slowly and to smoke, thinking it might be a good thing if the bombs, grenades, and shells began to fall at this moment close to the hotel and I had the right as a private citizen and an artist to watch these tragic events from the balcony, to gaze, without avoiding in any way the possible danger, at this page of contemporary history which had suddenly opened before me in an interesting place. To be a mute witness and to be able to contemplate philosophically. A beautiful page this, not only of the history of mankind but also of the history of my personal life! Bombs flying, and I contemplating!

I was sitting there and thinking, "I'm a philosopher! I have no fear—I'm a stoic! I am smoking—I'm an epicurean!"

From REMINISCENCES, 1887. WORKS, *vol. IX, pp. 204–207, 213–217.*

54

But I was not blissful for long.

From the street on my left came again the loud thudding sound of wheels. A post chaise troika was galloping almost at full speed. Behind it came another. Yet another followed behind.

In the first post chaise sat General Wrangel himself; his adjutants galloped after him. Behind them rode a troop of Cossacks.

I barely had time to jump out of my seat on the balcony and salute. The general glanced at me from below and bowed. I had time to notice that his full, round face was perfectly calm.

Where was he off to? In a cart drawn by a troika? Driving out of town. Why? Had the enemy actually landed? That was no joke.

I left my coffee unfinished. Dmitraki ran down into the street, and in a thrice I learned the truth. When he returned upstairs, his face had changed: it now looked serious and troubled.

"It's true, there's been a landing," he said briefly. "The devil take them! They say the general has driven off to the Pavlovsky battery."

I decided that I must see someone in command as soon as possible or at least get hold of a horse at any cost and ride to join my Don Cossack regiment.

I left my new parade uniform in the care of Dmitraki and told him that I was going off to find Dr. L. or one of the staff officers, and that I would either drop in to pick up my parade uniform later or send my orderly for it. In any case, I took leave of him, saying, "And what shall I do about the thirteen rubles I owe you?"

"Show me your purse," Dmitraki suggested.

I opened my purse; there were only five rubles and some change in it.

"Well, what's to be done!" Dmitraki exclaimed benignly. "In a moment like this, you're in need of money yourself. It doesn't matter! Don't worry. God grant, we'll see each other again." (Actually we did meet again a year and a half later, and I settled my accounts.)

I thanked him and we said goodbye to each other. As soon as I stepped out of the hotel, I came across a good cabdriver; I jumped into the cab and we galloped off to the Theodosia gates, to the apartment of Dr. L., from whom I could receive all the necessary information.

First of all, it was essential for me to *know what I was to do,* where *I should go,* where *duty summoned me.*

Besides, my orderly and my luggage had remained at the doctor's.

From the moment I got into the cab and drove off, there was a sort of blank in my mind. My memory suffered from a lack of continuity such as I had not known till then.

I recall, for example, galloping back in the cab from Dr. L. I recall not finding him at home, but I can't remember what happened to my orderly or my luggage. We were galloping back somewhere along the street, thundering along! The street was quiet, silent, deserted.

We were thundering along. There was no sound of firing. Suddenly there was a terribly loud thundering noise—like a violent underground shock.

I wished to tell the driver to stop.

We stopped. Everything was quiet again, and we galloped off once more.

Later I learned that this had been an explosion—the Pavlovsky battery, which defended the entrance from the Black Sea into the bay of Kerch, had to be blown up.

It was blown up by our troops, so that the allied army, which had actually landed that morning some fifteen miles from town on the seaside estate, Kamish-Burun, of Mr. Olive, should be deprived of the use of the guns.

So that was where General Wrangel had been galloping in the post chaise under the balcony of the hotel, upon which I had so independently and meditatively settled myself down at a table with a cigar over coffee!

The general, however, who had glanced at me only cursorily it seemed, reminded me of this incident later. In June I arrived to ask him to arrange for me to draw half of my pay in silver rubles in advance so that I could outfit myself.

"Your Excellency, I left my new parade uniform in Kerch on the day of the retreat. . . ."

The general interrupted me and said, but without any trace of displeasure:

"A fine to-do! Your parade uniform would have been intact if you had not been drinking coffee on the balcony."

And turning to a staff officer, who was present during the conversation, he added:

"Just imagine, everything in town was upside down. There I was driving to the Pavlovsky battery, while he was sitting with a cigar on a balcony and sipping coffee like a gentleman! So he lost his clothes."

However, he gave orders for the money to be given me. But all the same, I did not have a new parade uniform tailored for me, but spent the money on some imaginary youthful needs and served the rest of the campaign in a soldier's topcoat.

What surprised me most of all that day was that the general, as he drove past at such speed along the street, had been able to distinguish, from the color no doubt, that I, on the second-floor balcony, had coffee and cream in my glass rather than tea or beer or some sort of wine.

He said it very bluntly: "sipping coffee like a gentleman!"

All this was said two months later. But what was happening now? . . .

It was such a beautiful day! The sea shone, shone so serenely and festively! And why should I not travel abroad as a prisoner of war at the "official" expense of the French, the Turks, or the English? Probably they would do me no great harm; perhaps they would even find me work somewhere as a doctor. So be it, so be it. I shall try to be pleasant and to please them. I would see two capital cities, of which otherwise (because of my lack of means) I could only dream or read in books; I would see them free and under exceptional circumstances. I would see Tsargrad,* the holy city of the Moslems; I would see Paris perhaps, *la capitale du*

* Tsar City—a Russian name for Constantinople.

monde. I would see the great monuments of the past—Nôtre-Dame, the St. Germain quarter, the Jardin des Plantes, with the monkeys which I love so much. O Lord! That would be lovely! All for the best! And finally, I was not an active officer, for whom it would be a disgrace to become a prisoner of war unless in a desperate situation. For I would not be surrendering out of fear. . . . Perhaps danger could even threaten a prisoner. . . . I was an army doctor. . . . Officers were indispensable for our country. . . . They are more useful at a time like this; to kill and be killed is more *real*, far more real, than helping to cure or save lives. There are no illusions during a battle; the more brave warriors we have, the more foreigners we shall kill and drive away. And as for medicine? I had done my duty in the hospital as best I could, but I had little faith in the serious outcome of our then medical practice. N. I. Pirogov's articles in the *Military Medical Manual* pleased me very much because in them I could often detect a great deal of scepticism. He evidently loved science, but he did not believe in it blindly and unconditionally. And if *he*, Pirogov, the great surgeon, thought thus, then of what significance was *my* contribution? What did one single young, little-experienced army doctor matter? There were plenty of doctors like me. . . . But there was something else in me: I was a *future novelist.* I would remain a prisoner of war and would then write a large novel: *The War and the South.* My hero would be a young man. Fair-haired? No, *châtain*, like myself. Only he would not be a military doctor. . . . Fie! a black-haired one in a long parade uniform with red piping and a three-cornered hat!

No, he would be a hussar. A young hussar, *châtain*, in an azure dolman. Slightly girlish-looking and even a little timid out of vanity. But he would show himself courageous in action. He'd be taken prisoner! Yes, of course! Fine! But the honor of his service would oblige him to make his escape, even on foot. . . . Honor, honor! And what about the novel? Goethe himself, the great Goethe, seems to have said somewhere, "If you have lost your money (or fortune), you have not lost anything yet."

"If you have lost your *honor*, then gain *glory* and everything will be forgiven you."

"But if you have lost your courage, your spirit, you have lost everything."

But where was there a horse? Where a horse? Yet what mattered most was my *mother!*

I loved my mother *very* much; I pitied and respected her very much.

The news of the capture of Kerch and Enikale spread quickly among us. Was I alive? Where was I? How could I send my mother a letter as soon as possible, informing her that I was alive, in good health, and even madly happy on account of all the adventures?

Would I be able to go and say to some brave French general, "*Mon général, j'ai bien bonne mère en Russie, une mère bien noble et bien tendre.* Please permit me to send her a letter through our advanced posts." But would the general consent to dispatch a letter of mine under a flag of truce?

And I remembered how I had harshly condemned one of my older brothers, who had also been so very much loved by our mother, because he had never bothered to send any news of himself, but had only written to our mother when he had *need* of her, of her help, of her financial assistance, and so on. This is terrible! From the fortress I had written to her regularly, though infrequently and forcing myself. . . .

And now, if I do not escape and remain as a war prisoner, what sufferings she will endure until she receives my first letter! For me even to resemble involuntarily *this* brother of mine, this insignificant and stupid brother, would cause me great pain and shame. . . . It was now the beginning of May; with us in Kudinovo it was still cool, perhaps; my mother might still be walking in the garden, perhaps, wearing her black Turkish shawl and carrying her umbrella.

From a distance of a thousand or more miles I could see her gray muslin summer dress with black flowers, her noble and austere profile, her large hooked nose, the round birthmark on the left of her chin, her stately gait and thoughtful appearance.

That was what was so terrible!

This very thought of my mother, this cruel thought alone, upset my bright mood all that strange morning.

Upset it for a time, yes. But the sun shone so gaily in the almost imperceptible ripples of the calm bay, and the familiar strait, shining, immobile, and blue, stretched into the familiar distance— and I don't even remember any sounds. Perhaps there were sounds, but I do not remember them.

I was immersed in meditation and contemplation.

Suddenly I heard behind me the ringing sound of horses' hooves on the cobbled street. I turned around; a Don Cossack reined in behind me—gaunt, plain-looking, with a red mustache, carrying no lance, only a sword. He had another riderless horse on a lead. This horse had the saddle cushion missing but carried the wooden base of the saddle, the *archak*, as the Cossacks called it.

Destiny! Yes, destiny. His epaulettes bore a number. *Number 45.*

Amazed at this, I hurriedly turned to him and asked, "So you're from the 45th Regiment of Colonel Popov? Where do you come from with that spare horse?"

"From Enikale," the Cossack replied. "Yesterday evening I accompanied a sick comrade from the camp. He had fever; I spent the night there; now I am taking his horse back to camp."

"And where's the saddle cushion?"

"He kept it with him."

I wished to say something else; but suddenly, from the left, from the quarantine battery, a loud cannon shot resounded, followed by another, and a shell, followed by another shell, shot half way over the bay and struck the sea with a great splash.

Smoke was rising above the battery, and we both stared at it in silence. And then, from the right, from the side right opposite the quarantine, from behind a high cliff that marked the passage into the open sea, the first enemy steamer entered the bay silently and majestically. It was not a large ship. From its mast fluttered the Union Jack.

"There's the Englishman coming in, your honor," the Cossack commented calmly.

A shot rang out from our battery, then another. The shells failed to reach their objective.

The "Englishman" did not deign to reply. It let out puffs of white steam and stopped without firing. In its wake another huge, splendid warship appeared. Our battery fell silent.

I stood as if spellbound and devoured with my eyes and soul these English vessels, from which perhaps I was also being stared at by those Jameses, Joneses, Walters, who were so dear, so attractive, and so familiar to me from the novels of Dickens and Walter Scott.

Perhaps they were wearing scarlet uniforms . . . and looked so handsome; young men like me . . . in love. . . .

And. . . . Oh, what stupidity on my part! Shall I say it? I was even inexpressibly grateful to them for providing me with all these strong sensations. . . . However, there was *duty*, there was *honor*, and there was my *mother!*

CONSUL IN ADRIANOPLE

I MUST admit that I love Oriental bandits, love them of course not in the sense that I should like to be captured by them or that they should remain unpunished, but in the sense in which one might prefer a wolf, hyena, or all the more a leopard to a domesticated pig or a harmless donkey. I had had my fill of observing all these domestic creatures in Petersburg, and I could well spare five piasters in order to see at such close range and in safety a real Arnaout bandit.*

At the time everything in Turkey was still new to me, especially in this part of Turkey; prior to this I had lived only six or seven months in Crete, where everything was different than in Thrace—nature, the climate, people, clothes, political interests. I had also spent four months in Constantinople at our embassy in Buiuk-Deré. Very eagerly and joyfully I grasped at every original

* "Arnaout" is a Turkish word denoting an Albanian.
_____

From RECOLLECTIONS OF THRACE, *1879.* WORKS, *vol. IX, pp. 256–257, 284–285, 294, 298–299.*

image, every phenomenon of native origin. Everything interested me at the time, everything pleasantly excited me, gave me ineffable pleasure—the songs of a gypsy driver, and a night spent on a hard bed with a locker as a headrest, in the company of half-wild, unknown men in the midst of an endless, deserted field on a dark autumn night, and the pale kaimakam with the sharp nose, and the bandit begging for mercy, and the dazzling rain wetting me through as in my native Russia, and the sunset which glowed red in the mysterious distance beyond the steppe to the right of the road we were on, and the Bulgarian shepherds in their lamb's-wool hats, and the green grass, and my thoughts as to how I was going to direct for the first time the affairs of the consulate, which we regarded as one of the most active and important ones. Incidentally, I was over thirty at this time, and with a feeling of joy I understood that, having lived only seven months in Crete, where I had almost nothing to do except supervise the activities of others, I would have to apply myself seriously and reasonably in Thrace. Aside from my civil duty, the noble and lofty burden of which I was prepared to bear with love—for my personal convictions and inclinations were at that time in the highest degree patriotic and almost national in a Slavophile sense—my self-esteem had also been aroused. I was regarded as a literary man, a poet, so to speak. It was necessary to prove that poetry does not interfere with business.

We arrived in Adrianople before it was light. On one side, on the Constantinople side, there were no silkworm gardens, no vineyards. Before we reached the suburbs, near the road, a multitude of marble and stone pillars gleamed white, crowned with turbans and other headgear of ancient days. This was a large Turkish cemetery. After we had penetrated into the suburbs, it was not far to the consulate. The town pleased me very much; within it and in the suburbs there was a multitude of gardens; and although the leaves had already fallen at the time of the year when I arrived, the multitude of bare branches around the buildings, with their slender, fantastic designs, which in the distance blended into a sort of light smoke, always gave me pleasure, even greater pleasure on certain days than the fresh and shady foliage. I also noticed that the town had a good many handsome houses painted over in many colors—pink, dark red, azure, brown—and many tall poplars and minarets. In places, Adrianople had a poverty-stricken and untidy appearance, but like Moscow it also had enchanting perspectives; there were beautiful corners, and there were houses that were comfortable enough and very beautiful inside, though like most Turkish houses they were not very solid. The inhabitants were dressed in a very colorful way.

How often, while living in Demerdesh,* I went to sit down in a certain overgrown, romantic courtyard and there ponder and compose so much that has never seen and will never see the light of day! How much thought I devoted to Slavism, to the destiny of Russia! I thought about our writers, who at that time never visited the Orient. . . . I imagined the following picture: A place like Demerdesh; a grayish field with, to one side, marvelous, whitish poplar trunks (not pyramidal, and rather dry trees, almost artificial, good to look at only from a distance, as they rise high above the sea of another green hue); at the foot of the poplars green moss, and as green, gay, and bright as possible. A young Bulgarian is thoughtfully handling a plow drawn by oxen. On his head he is wearing a dark blue turban; his *shalvari* and sleeveless jacket are of a dark color. Fair strands of curly hair fall down on his shoulders from under his turban. He is plowing up the new soil of life, without knowing what harvest it will bring. . . . And in the background stands an old mosque which has been abandoned because of a decline in the population; the Moslems are dying out. And these stones, this courtyard, so mute and so thickly overgrown, so mysterious! What soulfulness there would be in this simple picture, how much historical sense! If possible, I should also like to have a few yellow flowers growing on the moist green of the marshland and, somewhere near the ruins of the mosque, the brightest, reddest wild poppies blooming.

* A suburb of Adrianople.

Thus did I meditate, fruitlessly perhaps, but ineffably enjoying these dreams in this lovely Demerdesh. One of the blissful aspects of this place was that I was only very rarely visited by any member of any kind of "intelligentsia," whether hostile or friendly, and that was much the same thing from the standpoint of elegance! *really* much the same thing!

I must state that no government forbade its agents in Turkey to have "ideas" or even to express them from time to time; but no government, of course, *demanded* they do so. Our superiors constantly required of us two things: (1) to know very well what was going on and even what was being thought in the country and to report this in good time and (2) to behave in this country so as to make the populace remember that there was a *Russia in the world,* a Russia that was of the same faith as the Christians under Turkish rule. This was our general policy after the Peace of Paris: to support and defend the civil rights of the Christians and to moderate, as much as possible, their natural ardor and political aspirations.

One must agree that nothing more correct or moderate could have been thought of. With this clear and forthright aim in view, we opened throughout Turkey a great many Russian consulates following the Eastern war of the fifties * which had proved so disastrous to us.

Nature itself challenged me to a struggle! The river Maritza had overflowed its banks. All the lower quarters of Adrianople had been flooded—the Greek Ildirim, the Bulgarian Kirech-Hane, and so on. The water was rising higher and higher. On all sides one could hear rifle and pistol shots warning the inhabitants of their imminent danger. The poor inhabitants of the suburbs tried to save themselves on the upper floors, in the garrets of their buildings. Water was isolating them. It was frosty. People were without bread, without candles, without coal for their braziers. The wealthy Christians did send some provisions; but the Pasha, the

* The Crimean War.

Metropolitan, the French Consul Guize, the Greek Consul Menardo, and the Austrian Jew with a sabre were all inactive. Blunt *
was away; his brother Georgeaki, who in his absence was in charge
of British affairs, was a child; on Zolotarev's orders, he was serving
with me in the capacity of a nominal scribe for four liras, but he
cut quite a handsome figure in the saddle.

I had to do something. I assumed the responsibility for the expenses at my own risk!

There were boats on the water; more boats came from various
directions. On the one hand, some black monks were organizing
things; on the other, a tall Turk in purple clothes was giving
orders.

The boats carried bread, carried coal and tallow candles.

The orders were to make no distinction of race or faith, to consider only the immediate needs.

"Who sent the boats?" people asked. "Who's helping us in
misfortune?"

"The Polish Jesuits and the Russian consulate! Catholic propaganda and the Russian rebuff!"

All the other most influential bodies in town only realized what
was happening later.

All this, be assured, was both very difficult and pleasurable, tormenting and joyous. It was not just a service, but some kind of
admirable whirlpool of good and falsehood, poetry and coldness,
strict formalism and free enterprise, most subtle intrigue and military daring, European politeness and Tartar impetuousness, a
whirlpool, which, if one swirled expertly in it, brought decorations
and official gratitude.

Everything about this service pleased me enormously.

* John Elijah Blunt (d. 1916), the British vice-consul in Adrianople from
1862 to 1872.

CONSUL IN TULCEA (RUMANIA)

WHY DID I enjoy myself so much in Tulcea? Everything was fine then; everything was enjoyable! I was in good health and thirsted for life, movement, action; I also sought poetry and conflict in the practical world. And it was all there, all—poetry and practical conflict! But here I pass over the life of my heart. And my heart was living intensely then, as the human heart likes to live, boldly and tormentingly, cheerfully and meditatively, quietly and dreamily. And in front, ahead of me, I saw so many long years, so many successes, so much strength, so many pleasures. . . .

Alas! I shall now say what the German physiologist and thinker Carus* has stated in the preface to one of his fine books. At a certain age, he wrote, *"man wird sich selbst historisch!"* But he, the fortunate man, became *"sich selbst historisch"* at about the age of eighty, while I became so at fifty and a little more, while recalling

* Carl Gustav Carus (1789–1869).

From REMINISCENCES, *written in 1883.* WORKS, *vol. IX, pp. 328–329, 360–365.*

my life in Tulcea; and I am amazed and say to myself in the lines of Koltzov:

> Awake and gaze around you,
> At what you were and what you have become. . . .

Now, when I look at my portrait of those days, I see a young man, a trifle foppish perhaps, with a clean-shaven and rather sharp chin, with a mustache like Napoleon III's; when I remember my then pleasant, calm and at the same time impulsive self-assurance, my hopes, my ideals, both patriotic and personal, I smile in disbelief. Was that I?

I am ashamed to admit it. . . . No! Why should I be? Ashamed of whom? Why indeed? Even that slight foppishness pleases me now in that man that I recall, and I understand everything to the very subtlest shade—what he felt then—and since he is so far removed from me now, I am able to judge him impartially and am ready to condemn him and to praise him, whenever I can, without the least embarrassment; so remote has he become from me!

Already before the beginning of the Crimean War, when I was a student at the medical faculty in Moscow, my young, beautiful, and rich aunt, Anna Pavlovna Korobanova, in whose house I was then staying for several years in succession and to whom I was obliged in many ways, made my mother the gift of a very elegant and original little hanger for her pocket watch. It was round in shape and made of rosewood. There were two spiral, ivory columns of very fine workmanship joined above by a sort of figurine also of rosewood, and there was a hook on the figurine to hold the watch. When my young aunt, with whom I was on very friendly terms, died in 1859, my mother presented me with this small object, and it traveled safely with me to various countries under the most diverse conditions. But now, after my stay in Tulcea, every time that I glance at this object, there is added involuntarily to my recollections of my mother and my young and charming relative also the memory of a certain tall, broad-shouldered young emigrant, his small, light ginger beard, his old brown topcoat, and so on and so forth.

One of my ivory columns had become loosened. I sent this hanger with my young servant Yani Nikiforidos to a certain Austrian carpenter for repair. Yani returned in a state of fright, pale and with tears in his eyes; in his hands he held my family heirloom, all twisted and smashed to pieces. . . .

I went into a state of despair and mad rage:

"What's this? How did it happen? Where? Who did it?"

In a plaintive voice Yani told me the story:

"I come to the carpenter; I talk to him. Suddenly some *palikar*,* in a topcoat. . . . 'Whose thing is that?' he asks. 'The Russian Consul's,' the carpenter replies. 'Ah!' the other says, 'the Russian Consul!' He seized it from me and . . . one-two . . . broke in pieces. . . ."

"And you did nothing to him!" I exclaimed.

"Nothing," replied my timid Cretian, lowering his eyes.

I almost cursed him in the manner of Galub Tazit: †

> Get out of here. . . .
> You're no Cretan, just an old woman!
> You're a coward, a slave, an Armenian.
> Be accursed!

But instead I sent him to fetch the dragoman.

"Go at once to the Pasha and tell him everything that happened," I instructed the dragoman in a state of great agitation. "Tell Suleiman Pasha that I shall take independent action unless. . . . I'll pay some Greek sailors or some drunken Old Believers, and for a few gold pieces they will maim that scoundrel! I was just stupid enough to let out Dombrowski! Go quickly!"

Turkish governors are good in this respect, that one can almost always find them at home. They are busy all day, and all day long

* Fine fellow.

† Tazit—from Pushkin's *Poet* (1829–1830).

they receive people; sitting in an armchair or a divan the whole day, they try cases and rule like King Solomon or Sancho Panza on his island.

Suleiman Pasha was beside himself no less than I was. And hardly had the dragoman had time to return when the Pole in question had been arrested and incarcerated.

But that did not satisfy me in the least.

My precious little object, which had traveled so much with me and upon which, when going to bed, I had been accustomed every evening for so many years to hang my mother's antique gold watch —this little object was now lying broken on the table. . . . An object is sometimes more precious to our heart than a human being because it reminds us of people who mean most to us in almost invariably their best moments.

I confess with a feeling of repentance that I was very seriously considering at this moment what *to do* with this emigré Pole, and my rage (of course, on my just foundations) had reached the stage of calm consideration of all the possibilities and means of a cruel punishment and revenge. Actually it would have been very easy in this town on the Danube to hire through an intermediary some ruffians who would have beaten up and maimed the man who had insulted me. The Cephalonian Greeks alone were worth a lot! They would have been very willing and ready to serve a Russian, if only because of their Orthodox-political sentiment. There were examples: in Ismail six armed Cephalonians ran up to save (without being paid) a Russian from a huge mob of enraged Jews and in an instant had terrified and scattered the whole crowd of them.

I knew all that; and containing my rage, I paced about the room, *calculating*. I was worried only about the conventions of the service, about my career, and so on. I do not find it necessary to lie; I gave no thought at that moment to the "love of mankind."

Suddenly I was informed, "The *mother* of that Pole has come to see you. She is weeping a lot."

"His mother? But he ran away from Poland. Does he have a mother here?"

"Yes, here. She's even living in the same courtyard as we are.

She is serving as the cook to Mr. Metaxas, the Austrian agent of Lloyds."

"What's to be done? Call her in. . . . I don't know what she can tell me. . . ."

This mother entered; a stout woman, untidily and shabbily dressed, wearing the same sort of reddish *shushun* as our Aksinia (only Aksinia's *shushun* was far cleaner and newer). She entered and, weeping bitterly and drying with her soiled apron the tears on her rather ugly face, began of course to implore me to forgive her son. . . .

A *mother!*

I was accustomed to honor that word.

A pity!

"I can't forgive your son," I replied

She continued to sob bitterly.

This poor, stout, unkempt woman did not please me in the least; but I understood that I must have pity on her for this very reason. . . .

"Forgive him, he was drunk."

"That's no justification," I answered. "And he cannot restore the damaged object."

But this old Polish woman rejoined with an unexpectedly pleasant piece of information:

"Forgive only his impudence, Mr. Consul," she said. "He'll repair the object. He's a good turner, and he'll fix the little columns exactly as they were before."

I was unwilling to believe her, so pleased was I to hear this.

But I had to believe the old woman. I gave her the broken hanger and said:

"There you are. You're a mother and you are crying, but do you know I also have a mother, and that it was she who gave me this little thing as a keepsake? I shall order your son to be released from prison for twenty-four hours; but if these columns are not repaired within that time, then you must expect no further mercy from me."

The cook went away. Next morning she returned with her son,

who brought me my precious object beautifully restored, looking exactly as it had been. The son insisted on seeing me and expressing his regrets in person. I ordered him to be brought in.

My joy at the sight of the little columns, which now looked in no way different from what they had been originally, softened my heart.

This "proletarian" was far more handsome than Dombrowski, more imposing and more pleasant, and the expression on his face was at the same time more cheerful, more energetic, and more kind. I took a liking to him.

He excused himself in a simpler manner than Dombrowski, without any phrases in the "intellectual" style, and I let him go in peace, declaring however that this was my last condescension towards him.

His mother almost fell at my feet and wished to kiss my hand.

All this happened in 1868. In 1869 I was appointed consul in Yanina, and in the spring of 1871 I was transferred to Salonika. I journeyed on horseback from Epirus through the whole of fruitful Thessaly and through the southern part of seaside Macedonia, and in the month of April I was riding up to Salonika with a small retinue and packhorses along the highway coming from the north. The highway passed between cottages, small gardens and some sort of houses.

We were riding at a walking pace. The Turkish gendarmes rode in front and behind. I glanced to the left—there were a good many tables and chairs by one of the fences, and behind the fence were a white house, a palisade, and a sign, "A Café Excellent In All Respects." At one of the tables stood a fair-haired man of tall stature dressed in European fashion. He stood there, staring closely at our mounted detachment.

It was none other than the Polish turner from Tulcea. He recognized me, and his face suddenly lit up in an expression of joy. He began to wave his hat and to shout in Russian:

"Greetings, greetings, Mr. Leontiev!"

Greetings!

And then he dashed off at full speed along the highway to-wards the city gates ahead of us. I could not understand why and where, but that was soon explained.

In a little while we saw a rider on a raven horse, wearing a round lamb's-wool hat; the rider was galloping to meet us; when, reining in his mount suddenly, he appeared before me "like a leaf falling on the grass," I learned that he was the Bulgarian Nusho, who was the courier to our consulate in Salonika. We rode a short while longer, approaching even nearer to the gates of the fortress wall, and perceived coming towards us on foot a bearded, middle-aged man with a cane and in a formal service cap. It was Mr. Dershvo, the dragoman of our consulate, who had been born in Odessa.

My Tulcea emigrant had roused them all to their feet. He had come running to the consulate, shouting enthusiastically:

"The Consul's coming! Our Consul from Tulcea!"

He had unselfishly taken all this trouble, and afterwards he never came to see me or to ask for any reward or gratuity. We never even met after this.

I have forgotten the name of that young Pole, but the beautiful hanger serves me even now for hanging up my mother's watch. Destiny is strange: whenever I happen to glance as this object purchased some *thirty years ago* and remember either my severe and beloved mother or my young, rich, and pretty aunt (whom I most often love to picture attending a ball of the nobility in a white silk dress with a purple velvet headdress on her black hair)—when, as I have said, I happen to remember these two women so dear to me, I also involuntarily remember *him*, the turner from Tulcea, *and the poor, unkempt Polish woman weeping for her son!*

And I always remember him with a kindly feeling.

CONSUL IN YANINA

1. *Ali Pasha** (*pp.* 379–381)

MANOLI was followed by a stooping old man. Mr. Blagov suddenly came out in person upon the chilly gallery and exclaimed with a joyful look, holding out his arms:

"Ah, Captain Misho! Please come in, please come in. I'm very glad to see you!"

Misho was an old man of this kind: First of all, he consisted of only two colors, white and red. All his clothes—the *fustanella,*† the shaggy *flokata,*‡ the stockings—and his mustache, eyebrows, and hair were white. The skin of his face—that too was like wax, and

* Ali Pasha of Yanina (1741–1822), ruler of Epirus.
† A kind of Greek kilt.
‡ A white woolen Arnaout petticoat with wide open sleeves, worn in winter.

From the autobiographical novel ODYSSEUS POLYCHRONIADES, 1875–1882. WORKS, *vol.* IV. *Odysseus is the narrator in the novel. He serves in the Russian consulate in Yanina. Blagov is the Consul.*

74

even the pupils of his eyes were very pale. But his fez, shoes, which he removed as soon as he entered the door, the sash round his *fustanella*, his lips, and his aged eyelids, completely without eyelashes, were red. He had once been a servant to Ali Pasha and his children. When Ali Pasha was killed at the orders of the Sultan, his sons and followers, including the young Misho, were put in prison. Every day the Sultan's men came into the prison, took two or three of them, and cut their throats; the remainder awaited their turn; Misho too. But then another decision was taken: the prison doors were opened and all the rest were set free. Since then Misho has been living in Epirus, where he grew rich, married, became a widower, and continued to live in his old way, not poorly but austerely; he dwelt alone in his own rather large but already old and chilly archon's house. Everybody who scrutinized attentively this short and stooping old man with white eyebrows and pink temples, dressed in plain but clean and handsome Arnaout clothes, thought to himself, "The things this man has seen! The things he could tell us if only he were able to understand and appreciate what he has seen! He knew our gloomy hero Markos Botzaris and perhaps sang with him the monotonous and wild mountaineer songs to the sounds of the *tambura*. He probably knew *those very women* who threw themselves over a precipice on the Siliot heights. Perhaps Lord Byron himself (who celebrated our half-wild Epirus with fiery feeling), when visiting the satrap, walked past him as he was sitting in the courtyard of Ali Pasha with the rest of his brave followers (a mixed lot of Turks, Arnaouts, and Greeks, but all of them dashing fellows). Perhaps Misho spoke often with Ali Pasha himself; he perhaps washed his feet; he knew all of his wives, odalisks, favorites. . . . Who knows? Who knows the secrets of those times already so remote from us, those times so lustful and bloody, so pastorally simple and enthusiastically Christian? Perhaps this old man, who led such an austere, strict, and Orthodox life, who was so religious, serious, and taciturn, was once among those handsome adolescents and young men who, wearing short fur coats splendidly embroidered with

Yanina gold thread, amused the stout, senile, old man who was also a dreaded ruler—danced, embraced in his presence, and kissed the girls he had himself selected from his harem for this purpose. . . ."

This is what many people thought as they gazed at the gloomy old man. Blagov, of course, was thinking the same thing as he paid him every attention and respect and tried in every way to extract something from him. But the old man was not only sullen; he was unbearably boring in his enigmatic silence. And it was very difficult to make him talk about the past.

"There was a lot! Many different things!" was all he ventured to say, with a slight sigh.

And now almost the same thing happened.

Blagov made him sit down in the best armchair by the stove and sat down himself in order not to constrain or embarrass the old man (the old man would have suffered if he had been obliged to sit before a consul who was *standing*).

"What's new, Captain Misho? What's new in town?" Blagov asked him affably.

The old man smiled a little.

"Something new?" he questioned. "I have even forgotten the old things."

However, he did add (Blagov's attention had probably stirred even him in the end):

"I'm glad that you're such a fine fellow. Your predecessor was a good diplomat, a respectable man; we loved him; but he was one of our *kerkireitzi*, a Greek. . . . But I'm glad I am seeing a real Russian for the first time. . . . Don't yield an inch to anyone. Let them tremble. . . . You're doing well. Live and flourish because of that!"

2. A Public Execution (pp. 259–263)

ARISTIDE TOLD me hurriedly that this case was nothing very new, that it had already taken place before my arrival from Zagor.

Two young Turks, who were almost as youthful as Aristide and myself, had quarreled some five months ago and exchanged vituperations. One of them had struck the other in the face; the one who had been thus assaulted wished to frighten his assailant with a pocket knife, but the latter made a rash movement and the knife penetrated into his stomach. They were tried according to *Sheryat*,* and the parents of the murdered man refused to accept compensation and demanded "an eye for an eye" according to the ancient law. Aristide told me in addition that the father of the victim was a shopkeeper who sold inkstands, candlesticks, and other such articles at the bazaar; the father of the murderer was a good scribe. Aristide had already learned and gathered all the facts. He even knew that the murderer was called Saïd and the murdered man Mustafa.

It did not take us long to reach the edge of the town, and there we perceived that a great many people had already collected in the field beyond the quarter of Kanli-Cheshmé. Others were catching up with us.

Aristide and I soon pushed our way through the crowd and then I saw. . . . Ah, no! never in my life shall I forget the sight.

The executioner and his victim were ringed by a detachment of soldiers; their rifles were loaded, and with their rifle butts they kept pushing back the crowd; two officers with bared swords stood there in sullen silence, and only now and then did they look questioningly here and there.

Saïd, the guilty one, stood in the middle sobbing bitterly. He was no more than eighteen years of age. He wore a pair of tidy new *shalvari*, and his multicolored, quilted, sleeveless jacket was open and turned back round his shoulders and neck.

For a small fee a certain ragged gypsy water carrier had taken it upon himself to act as executioner; with his donkey cart he had been delivering spring water to various homes. He was very dirty and black and in rags. His face registered anxiety and sadness (it was the first time in his life that he was to use a blade against a

* The canonical law of Islam.

human being); in his old sash was stuck a large expensive yata-ghan, which he had acquired somewhere, they said, expressly for this purpose, and a small dagger.

In the circle around the officers stood the relatives of the mur-dered man—the father, an elderly Turkish shopkeeper in a striped robe and fez, a rotund, pink, gray-haired man; and two Turkish women, one of them his wife, the other his sister, the aunt of the murdered youth.

The father looked composed and sad; the women were scream-ing.

But can I really faithfully describe the sudden impact of all this on me? It was all so unexpected: the ragged, anxious executioner, the thoughtful father, and these women who were screaming and waving their arms in a terrible state of hysteria. All one could hear was, "Accursed one! Accursed one! No! No! You can't! Blood! I want blood!" This is what the two furies were screaming, their long, thin noses showing through their shawls, which did not prevent me from seeing their gaunt faces and their eyes glittering with the fire of hysterical rage. "Blood! Blood!" they kept screaming. The aunt seemed to behave even more hysterically than the mother. She would start the screaming, and the mother would take it up.

The officer said to them, "Stop! Let the man have his say!" The murderer's uncle was allowed to come out of the crowd into the circle. (His father had fallen ill with grief, and his brother had come to the place of execution in order to try his luck once again by offering to pay compensation, which the law permitted a mur-derer to do.)

The uncle was dressed in a frock coat and a fez; he was on the thin side and not yet old. His face had grown sallow from the horror and grief of the occasion. His hands and legs trembled. Entering into the circle, he hastily ran over to the victim's shop-keeper father, seized a fold of his robe, and exclaimed in Greek:

"Effendi! Effendi! Kind gentleman! In the name of the great God . . . Please agree. . . . You are a father, and my brother is a father too. . . . Look at this boy, he's only a child. . . . Twenty thousand piasters, all that we have! Take it!"

At this moment the boy also threw himself at the feet of the shopkeeper, but he sobbed so loudly I could not hear what he said. The only thing I could distinguish was the word "accidentally"!

The shopkeeper kept silent; dropping his head on his chest and with one arm behind his robe, he seemed to be plunged in deep reflection.

"Take it! Take the money! Take it, Makhmed-aga!" the crowd was shouting.

And I shouted loudly:

"Take it, effendi! Take it!"

"Unfortunate child! Oh! unfortunate one!" other voices, men's and women's, shouted.

Makhmed-aga turned to face the crowd and the murderer's uncle and said, pointing to the two women:

"I'm agreeable. Let them give their consent."

The boy crawled over the ground towards the mother of the victim and, trying to grasp her feet, said in such a ghastly voice that one would have thought even a stone would melt:

"*Hanum! Hanum* effendim! I'm afraid, afraid. . . . Mother mine, little lamb. . . . Hear me. . . . I'm afraid, afraid!"

And he tried to kiss her yellow slipper, wringing his hands, and threw his head back, opening his eyes that were full of tears.

Even Aristide, who was gazing on with his chin resting on my shoulder and his arm around my waist, exclaimed:

"Ough! What a *cold** thing!" and squeezed me with his hands as he suddenly shuddered.

I stood half dead from pity and horror, but I did not want to leave till the end, could not even do so. The crowd was pressing upon us all the time, and with threatening shouts and blows of their rifle butts the soldiers were constantly trying to widen the circle.

* A cold thing, a cold man—an oriental expression meaning revolting or unpleasant.

Everyone began shouting and howling; the officers and soldiers shouted at the people; the boy sobbed and screamed; the crowd began to roar with indignation. But louder than all of them rose the voice of the raving aunt. The officer finally gripped the gypsy by the shoulder and, shaking him, said in a menacing tone:

"Finish him off!"

The gypsy seized Saïd. I shall not attempt to picture the terror of the wretched youth. I am unable to describe with what hysterical prayers he turned now to the gypsy, now to the officers, as he dragged himself on his knees along the ground. It is beyond my ability to do so. But I would like you to imagine all this unbearable horror which was portrayed on his almost childlike face. And if you can imagine this, then I am not sure whether you can imagine what followed.

The gypsy did not know how to kill people; he was raising his hand, armed with a dagger, for the first time, and he was raising it against a hitherto innocent soul because he had been paid a few gold pieces. . . .

Finally one of the officers took Saïd under the arm and, lifting him up, said to him considerately:

"My child! Submit to your unhappy fate. So God wills. What can you do against the will of God?"

Saïd could only exclaim, "Allah! Allah!" and with a deep sigh he fell on his knees before the gypsy and stretched out his neck. . . .

What the gypsy did to him I did not see. My eyes dim with tears, I plunged into the crowd so as not to have to watch any longer. I heard only a piercing scream. I again heard the roar of the crowd and the officers' loud command, and then another scream.

A few more minutes and poor Saïd was no more.

The people were still uttering curses and howls of indignation. Suddenly someone yelled:

"Get the executioner! Tear that gypsy to pieces! . . . Curses on these old women! Get those old witches!"

I glanced around and saw that the soldiers were savagely beating back the crowd with their rifle butts and the officers were holding back with their swords some of the crowd who had pushed too far forward. A certain country *palikar* (I knew him; his name was Yani) had blood on his hand. he had been wounded slightly, probably because he was delighted to have the chance of laying this hand on a Moslem gypsy and a couple of old Turkish hags. . . . On a stretcher, covered with something white and bloody, Saïd's body was being carried away, and his uncle walked beside it. I glanced at him and saw before me a face so composed and sad that his composure struck me as even more terrible and pitiful than the screams of the unfortunate Saïd.

3. An Excellent Consul (pp. 417–419)

I SAW the chariot, a fine-looking chariot; I saw the raven horses strong as oxen, fast, well-proportioned and fiery as young stags, they were striking the ground with their hooves before the entrance to *our* house. I saw the young Arab driver (his *Frankish* jacket looked old, and I wondered why Rauf Pasha had not given him strict orders to sew up a large hole under his armpit).

Two mounted Turkish soldiers and our Kir-Manoli, also mounted, were waiting for the Consul to appear.

I saw Mr. Blagov come out differently dressed (I admired the way he constantly changed his vestments like the famous Tsarevich or a bishop). He was no longer wearing the velvet jacket in which he had been receiving the archons. He was now attired in a very long black frock coat with silk lapels (I had never seen the like before), and in his buttonhole he wore a tender ribbon of a decoration, light blue with red wings, which looked like a butterfly that had been flying, flying, and had then begun sucking into him as into a fragrant flower. He wore a high top hat on this occasion; his gloves, again quite new, were of the same light lilac color as sea appears sometimes in winter in calm weather during a gentle sunset. Tall, straight, and slender, he now looked to me very like a handsome bottle filled with orange blossom or rose water, such as we sometimes use to sprinkle on people when greeting them.

He took a seat in the chariot; the four oxen-stags suddenly dashed off and galloped him off through the courtyard towards the gates. Stavri all in gold leaped on the dickey like a young man; Manoli and the mounted Turks followed at a gallop through water, over grass, stones, mud, and snow.

Touched by this spectacle, I exclaimed through the window, "Zito* Russia!" and then quietly returned to my pleasant sleeping quarters.

Sitting there, I hesitated what to undertake first. Should I write a letter to my mother, as Father Arseny advised, or be inspired to compose some heroic verses on the occasion of Alexander Blagov's triumphal return?

For a start, accepting the challenge of the Muse, I attempted to write verse; but the inner choir of my varied sensations, solemn and joyful, Orthodox and demoniacal, serious and childish, false and true, did not pour out on paper freely, harmoniously and beautifully. . . . In vain I endeavored to write on the baize cloth of my new table. I proved unworthy of such a philosophical, diplomatic, or pietistic table covered with green cloth of good quality. I was too green myself for such a table.

"Boreas stirs!" "Boreas is blowing, blowing hard!" "Boreas is blowing, and the ice. . . ." "And the elders. . . ." "And the elders. . . ." "And now from the Northern power. . . ." "And greeting him he dances. . . ." "With fragrance filled and as graceful as a young palm tree!" I felt at last that, as in my dream the day before, a certain face vanished and became transformed into another, and a young dancing girl—la petite drogue, "my bitter fragrant herb"—instead of Blagov flew down unexpectedly upon me on the icy wings of that terrible Boreas! And even more (alas, alas!) I felt that a style less heroic, less strict, suited me better, that here the all-mighty Aphrodite herself was helping Phoebus.

* Long live!

I quickly put aside these verses and was about to begin writing a letter to my mother. This removed me further from temptation; this was more virtuous. And I began the letter:

"My much respected and much beloved mother, I shall inquire first of all about your precious health and that of our beloved grandmother, Mrs. Yevgenia Stilova—our governess and benefactress. Thanks to God, I am well, and, respectfully kissing your brow, my highly esteemed mother, and the brow of Lady Yevgenia, I desire to see both of you as soon as possible and to rejoice with you. At present, upon the insistence of His Excellency the Imperial Consul of All the Russias, Mr. Alexandrez Blagov, I have left Father Arseny and have moved to live in the said consulate for the purpose of our mutual correspondence at a most generous salary paid by the State Treasury and, I shall even say in all humility, incompatible with my tender age and my lack of sense; I cannot as yet determine the precise sum; but His Excellency was pleased to say that he would pay me several gold Ottoman liras on my completing a clean copy of the statistical data."

I was more successful with the letter than with the verse; even my lies about the Consul's insistence came out very well.

4. The Albanian Bandit (pp. 494–497)

DZHEFFER DEM was seized, brought to Yanina, and kept in custody for a time. But that lasted only a very short while. People were found to vouch for him, and the Pasha released him. No more than a week after he had been caught, Kolio ran into my office so precipitately that the door was almost torn off its hinges, gripped me by the arm, and, repeating "Dzheffer Dem! Dzheffer Dem!" almost threw me onto the balcony which overlooked a side street.

Dzheffer Dem was walking on foot with a single servant past the Russian consulate. It was the only time I saw him, but I could never forget him afterwards. And even if he had not been the hero of such a tragic affair, even if he had committed no crime, even if I had not known who he was, but had only seen him that one time walking along that street, even so I should never have forgotten him, just as one never forgets a beautiful painting one has gazed at closely for a short time.

Dzheffer Dem was still young and extremely handsome. His face was pleasantly round, very swarthy, and fresh-complexioned. About his whole person, in his huge black eyes, in his small black mustache that was twirled up, in his graceful carriage, in his smooth, unhurried gait, in his white hands peacefully held behind his back, there was so much that was inexplicable, of good breeding, calm pride, secret self-assurance, that I cannot put it all into words! He was dressed, of course, in a gaudy *fustanella*, and his jacket and the rest of his clothes were of black cloth embroidered with gold, which glittered like a newly minted ducat on his chest, back, sleeves, and the covering of his calves.

Behind him walked an elderly mustachioed servant, also dressed in the Albanian fashion; his face was one of those gaunt and fierce Arnaout faces, remembering which one begins to understand the events of the last few days in unfortunate Bulgaria—and one immediately sees a church courtyard filled with rotting corpses or triumphal arches built of the severed Christian heads interwoven with flowers, or the crucified or hanged bodies of priests, or again a Bulgarian mother, killed and bound to her violated daughter with ropes made out of their own skin!

Perhaps it was this very servant who had helped his young, handsome master to kill Pano and his traveling companions? Perhaps it was he who had taught him how to commit these atrocities?

When Kolio and I had leaped out like madmen on the balcony, Dzheffer Dem had raised his eyes without haste and stared at us. I should like you, dear friend, to understand just exactly how he had stared at me! Either his eyes were very beautiful, or thoughts about this terrible murder gave a special significance to everything that concerned him, but Kolio and I exclaimed almost simultaneously after he had walked away, "How he looks!"

But we were unable to put into words the exact way he had looked at us. He had glanced at us indifferently; there was nothing very noticeable about it; and yet we had both exclaimed, "How he looks!"

He had passed by, that young handsome villain. He had passed and disappeared, and I never saw him again. But so astonishing and strange does it seem to me still to this day that this tender and so youthful a man, full of dignity and elegance, had in person cut down Christians, had stained with warm blood his almost feminine hands which he now held so indifferently behind his back, had even lost the sheath of his sword in the struggle—so strange does all this now seem to me that if I only think of my early years and Yanina, one of the first persons to rise as if alive in my imagination is Dzheffer Dem with his black eyes raised indifferently towards our balcony, Dzheffer Dem wearing a white *fustanella*, which swayed a little as he walked over cobbles, with his hands behind his back—hands on which not a trace of Christian blood was visible. . . .

Kolio and I were not the only ones to pay attention to the handsome mien of this shameless murderer. People who had a far greater sense of "elegance" had also observed it.

One day the Austrian Consul dropped in informally (Blagov continued to like him better than most of his other cronies, and they often visited each other). Aschonbrecher admired the beauty of the young bey even more than we did. Indeed he said so. Kolio and I childishly thought it was our duty, so to speak, to pass over in silence if possible anything that might even slightly favor the Moslems, and particularly any Moslem villains. We did not dare reveal to each other what had astonished us and, though silently understanding each other of course, we merely said, "How he looks!" Aschonbrecher felt no need or necessity to conceal his impressions, and his praise was loud and enthusiastic: "*Quelle beauté! Ah! ce costume mirebolent! Mais c'est fabuleux! c'est curieux au plus haut degrés!* What a pity this young man is such a criminal, such a scoundrel!"

To this Blagov riposted gaily in our presence (he was always in good spirits when Aschonbrecher was there):

"I regret another thing. I saw him too, and admit the justice of what you say about his costume and appearance. I have appreciated all this so much that I have only one regret—that I am not an all-powerful satrap. If I were, I would first of all import a painter from Italy to do his portrait and then I would have him hanged. . . . I don't say I would have him impaled, because, as you know, this is no longer done, but I would have him hanged very picturesquely—before a large throng of Christians and Turks, so as to make the Turks more cautious in the future. And I myself would assist at this execution. . . . I'm not joking. . . ."

"Oh!" the Austrian exclaimed laughingly, "what a Neronian conjunction of artistic sense and bloodthirstiness! Oh!"

Blagov, blushing slightly, replied:

"Why Nero? His mother, perhaps. . . . That, of course, was something. But we cannot persuade ourselves that the fire of Rome was not beautiful. . . ."

"*Écoutez!*" exclaimed Aschonbrecher, "you're terrible today!"

And changing the conversation, he began to demonstrate that the Turks were absolutely incorrigible and that all the expectations put on them in Europe were vain: "They are a dying nation! They can exercise force only against the helpless and the weak, as in Syria, for example, and they do not wish or do not know how to punish crimes."

But Blagov, although he felt in good spirits that day, wielded a wicked tongue.

"Why then do you always assist them on the sly?" he asked unceremoniously with the same bright, triumphant look.

"Listen. What can we do against such a colossus as you? Your Russia is a sort of naïve baobab! It grows innocently like a tree. It does not desire conquests, is afraid of everything, but all things around it creak and crack like an old fence. Nobody can ever understand what your statesmen want. . . . *Voyons, soyez donc bon enfant. . . . Avoyez, que j'ai raison.*"

But Blagov rejoined to this as follows:

"It's a wicked thing you're saying there. You seem to imply that we Russians do not understand what we want. There are times this may be so, let us suppose, but not always."

5. *The Consul's Secret* (*pp.* 326–329)

"WHAT DO YOU SEE?" *

I was staring almost with fright. I had no idea even what I was thinking. . . . Perhaps I was expecting him to show me something magical.

"I don't see anything," I finally replied.

"Do you see the divan by the stove?"

"Yes, I do."

"Do you see the table in front of the divan and the armchair that rocks?"

"I see them. So what about them?"

"Just that I'm going to tell you, Odysseus, a great secret, because I love you very much and respect your father immeasurably. In the summer a *hanuma* sat here on this divan. And what a *hanuma!* Not a local one! A *hanuma* from Stambul! The wife of a *Meimura.*† She wore a fashionable *feredzhe* of blue satin. Yes, my Odysseus, just think of it! She came here at the greatest risk to herself, accompanied only by an Arab slave woman. I was dying to have a peep at her; I took off my shoes and tiptoed through the bedroom and looked in."

Manoli depicted with such warmth the *hanuma's* coiffure, her outer garment that had been thrown aside, and her purple dress with bouquets ("the size of my hand!" he pointed out) that I

* Manoli asks this question. Manoli is a *kavass*, an armed constable, servant, or courier.

† An official.

could picture her in person on this now empty divan smilingly leaning on the table.

"And what did you see?" I asked excitedly, almost horrified.

"Nothing! *She* was sitting with her legs stretched out on the divan in front of the table, propping her cheek with her hand thus, and she was laughing and talking. And the effendi was rocking in the chair and smiling as he listened to her. Then he rose, poured out some water from a carafe for her, picked up the jam, and served it all to her on a tray. Then he sat down again."

"He served it himself? Himself?" I asked in surprise.

"Yes! Himself. I saw it with my own eyes. But what they said to each other, I don't know. They were talking in very pure Turkish, almost in Hellenic." *

"Ah, how I regret all *this!*" I commented sorrowfully. "For that is a great sin. Why did he, Blagov, have to act like that?"

"What if it is a sin!" Manoli protested. "It's a kind of triumph for our side anyhow to put a pair of horns on one more Turk! All the same, it's our bit of trickery, not theirs! Do you hear that, my Odysseus?"

However, this explanation on the part of the frivolous Captain Manoli neither satisfied me nor set me at rest. My half-magical, pure, and strict picture of consular life was darkened for a time by a sort of unpleasant and terrifying impression. And I began to pity Blagov, as if I had arrived at the certainty that his death would be all the more terrible because he had sinned and was a man hardened to sin. And in my eyes I no longer saw him on an unattainable pinnacle or so superior to everything around him and to myself. "It doesn't suit him," I said to myself when walking home to Father Arseny. "It doesn't suit him. He's no Kusko Bey."

Yes! That's what I thought. And then the Father's farewell words uttered in the *han* † as he was leaving for Tulcea struck me all the more clearly and significantly: "If you have any sense, do

* The *kavass* implies by this that they were talking in the literary Turkish language, mixed with Persian and Arabian.

† A sort of road inn.

not throw away connections; visit good homes, learn from them useful examples of educated behavior and noble conduct; but whatever is unbecoming to your age and incompatible with the strict morality of a good Orthodox Christian—keep away from that. That is my fatherly advice to you. I have spoken, and you must remember it!"

However, little by little, little by little . . . my youthful thoughts. . . . Ah, my friend! It was not for nothing, of course, that the mallet wielded by so many of the Fathers of our church destroyed the beautiful statues of the pagan gods. Of course it was not for nothing that the struggle between the elegant but lascivious demons of Olympus and the austere and pure followers of the crucified Christ seethed for so many ages. The statues, the visible gods of evil and delight, were rendered powerless and no longer fearsome. They could be used to decorate ornate rooms without any fear that the presence of an idol would make one all the sooner believe in the invisible, corrupting ideal hidden behind a beautiful statue without fear of believing and revering it. But this same invisible ideal was both entrancing and false. . . . Surely it has not perished forever? Surely it is not every day, every hour, that we, dear friend, must quake with fear of it? And how but in the panoply of war, with which only the teaching of ecclesiastical asceticism (for it is not of this world) can clothe and cover us, must we go forth to take part in the noisy contest with the ubiquitously glittering and eternally exhausting life of this world? Dreary speeches about moral duty cannot alone dominate the restless heart of our youth and the stormy flesh of our younger years when there is no other law to govern our heads. When there is no such law that demands every minute a reasonable consent on our part (for, considering the inner mutability of even the strongest human soul, what then, tell me, can become affirmed in it?), but merely one that says to us, "Submit, for it is I have spoken!"

In the early years as a widower, Father Arseny spent some time amid the crags of the dreary Sinai desert and in the forests of Mount Athos. A simple man, inexperienced in many of the ways of the world, he was very knowledgeable and wise in the ways of his own thought and in the sphere of those sciences to which he had devoted himself.

One day, sometime later, I inquired of him at a difficult moment of my life:

"My elder! Tell me sincerely, I beg of you in the name of God, tell me what you think of this: why did the evil spirits appear before the eyes of people in ancient times, as the sacred tradition tells us, and why do they no longer present themselves before our own eyes?"

Father Arseny glanced at me attentively and keenly. In his eyes, as I recall, the flame of a certain joyous faith was suddenly kindled, and after pondering for a while, he answered me thus:

"In those days all men, even the pagans, had a great deal of faith. Now men have become powerless, and faith is weakening. The earth itself is growing old, and men are growing senile in both spirit and flesh. With the exhaustion of men's strength, faith has also become exhausted. Now it is more profitable for the spirits of temptation not to be seen by us. They say to themselves, "Things are well as they are!" Should a man of weak faith or a godless man see a demon before him and understand this, he would as a consequence begin to have a firmer faith in goodness.

Such was the excellent answer given me by my noble elder Father Arseny.

But this conversation of ours took place, as I have mentioned, at a much later time, in a certain year that proved a very trying one for me.

And previous to that? At that time my thoughts followed a less mournful direction and assume a less austere character. . . .

I soon forgot, not the Turkish woman in the mysterious study of the young diplomat, not her blue satin *feredzhe*, not her hair cropped round the temples, not her pose at the table, not her purple dress—not all this, of course not! I only forgot the first sorrowful impulse of my own heart, and I began again to wait about for Blagov with impatience, began again to wander in the vicinity of the consulate, if not in the flesh (because I had to learn my lessons and go to school), then at least spiritually, just as the shades of the unburied used to wander around the entrance to Elysium, the shades to whom the pitiless ferryman on the terrifying river Styx denied admission.

6. *The Consul-Sphinx* (*pp. 578–581*)

BOSTANDZHI OGLU relates that this same Blagov had apparently received a couple of years ago an inheritance of eight thousand rubles from his uncle and had spent them all within a month while on leave in Russia. Blagov had argued that such a negligible sum could not, as he understood it, provide for him, but that a month like that would leave him something to remember for the rest of his life. Eight thousand rubles! For me that represented a whole lifetime. A whole lifetime, unattainable as yet, but comprehensible. For me it would have meant a decent house in Zagori, trade in Thessalian bread or in fish, and Russian caviar on the Danube, a clean slate with the creditors of my hard-pressed father; for me it would have meant a happy marriage; it would have been the cornerstone of a large business or even a banking office in Galati, Smyrna, Bucharest. . . .

How did Blagov spend all that money? On *hetaerae*, on theaters, on an enormous *bakshish* to some servants so that they should flatter and hypocritically please him. . . .

Did he erect a school in his homeland to enlighten the enslaved Russians who wore their "shirts on the outside," shirts such as I had seen in my early childhood on the Danube, Russians who were thus described in the universal geography used in Greek schools: "The Russian common people are rude and enslaved, whereas the gentry class in Russia is highly educated"?

On what did he spend this money? On what? Bostandzhi laughed at my expression of horror and astonishment and asked:

"Do you think those noble Russians know the value of money?"

Well, was it this sort of nobility I was to imitate? Was I to learn to be a spendthrift?

Or was it that of which Coëvino had been talking on the balcony, yielding in everything so willingly and quickly to Blagov? "*Un gentilhomme doit avoir son epée toujours prête pour défendre son Dieu, son roi et sa maîtresse. . . .*"

Sa maîtresse! Yes! and not his legal wife. . . . To listen with solicitude to Blagov defining a legal marriage—a harmonious, friendly marriage, replete with tender and firm trust—as a *revolting thing!* And when he expatiated for so long about marriage, likening it to the necessary and compulsory recruitment of soldiers, he made not a single mention of the Christian illumination of marriage, which makes everything so clear, so good, so comprehensible. Yes! without that distant, infinitely distant, yet profound music, now so sweetly refreshing, now so loudly menacing, telling us somewhere about a halo or terrible, intolerable punishment beyond the grave—it may indeed be true that the song of marriage would sound boring and lifeless for certain people.

"For certain people"—this is what I say now. But at that time, when the sun of life was only beginning to ascend for me, I knew no other ideal!

A happy marriage with a beautiful and not impoverished girl, who would love me and fear me as a wife should fear her husband—that is what I was already thinking about in Zagori. To cross in good time, at an appropriate time, peacefully and unhurriedly the threshold of a hospitable *gynekeia* as a benevolent master, yet one who is strictly jealous of his honor, who will not lower himself an inch in public, but will raise himself still higher through this union if it is so possible—that was even my waking dream!

When in the street I caught sight of the as yet not fully mature daughters * of our archons as they hurried with eyes lowered to

* In the towns of Epirus, especially among the upper classes, girls on reaching their maturity are not allowed to see men until they marry. They even go to communion at night, but always accompanied by older women.

the girls' school with books in their hands and accompanied by servants, then I, like a hawk circling high in the air, would sometimes pick out with a smile from the crowd of them my future prey, admiring at the same time their tender youthfulness and counting the gold of their fathers.

And when a girl like that, when such an innocent and timorous cherub would approach me submissively to receive her orders and, in the presence of others, would kiss my husbandly hand carefully and respectfully the way they kiss the hand of a priest, but, when we should be alone, would embrace me and call me freely and boldly, "My Odysseus! My darling boy! The apple of my eye, Odysseus!" And when over our couch, which had never been sullied by either side, the bright angels of God would fly unseen, blessing us (thus it was my mother had prophesied, trying to convince me to preserve my virtue)! Surely that was not such a revolting, tedious picture as Blagov had painted?

Oh, no! Oh, no! He was a complete stranger to me! And I do not know what I can learn from him except, perhaps, how to keep my hands very clean, to speak fluently and cleverly at social gatherings, and that my European suit should be cut in the latest fashion by the best tailor on the shores of the Bosporus or the Neva.

All this of course pleases me very much! But would this please the Father? That is the question. The Father himself dresses very plainly and not at all in fashion, although quite neatly. But did he not tell me so many times:

"It is not by his expensive and 'soft' garments that one can tell already in his youthful years a good master and a good businessman, but by his enterprises and his turnover. A hard-working and clever merchant has no time to gaze at himself in a mirror and to impose fragrant ointments upon his head. If you have money, then even in old clothes you will be sought after by all. . . ."

And observing what was happening around me, I could see how much truth there was in this. *Kavass* Manoli and dear Kolio excelled in their shining cleanliness. Manoli, like a European, even cleaned his nails with a brush, and, at the same time, in the princely luxury of his Oriental garments he looked far more resplendent than Blagov himself; but both of them, Kolio and Manoli, had to stand by the door or serve jam and tobacco pipes, while the wealthy Kusko Bey, whose filthy and shiny old frock coat had at first unpleasantly surprised me when I was still inexperienced—Kusko Bey would sit negligently on the divan beside Blagov and chat with him in whispers about the play of forces in Oriental politics.

What should I imitate then, O Lord? And from whom should I learn?

How angry I was then with Blagov, and how severely and hastily did I begin to judge him. As for you, my friend, I would ask of you only one thing: hasten not to punish him, do not take my former interests too much to heart. . . . Blagov was in many ways better than I. And in many things, in very many things, he was absolutely wrong!

MIRACLE IN SALONIKA

IN REPLY to your request asking me to explain to you what obliged me to give up my diplomatic career, which was proceeding so well (and even *very* well towards the *end*, judging by the comments of Prince Gorchakov and the promises of [Count] Ignatiev), and to think of becoming a monk, I shall refer you to the following aphorism: "Partial frankness and incomplete information often do more harm to a genuine understanding of another person's life than to say nothing at all." But I cannot enlarge on this with entire frankness in a letter. If God wills us to meet (I don't despair of it!), then verbally it will be another matter! I shall attempt, however, to explain a few things. There were many reasons all at once—reasons of the *heart* and of the *mind*—and, finally, those *external* and *evidently* (merely) *accidental* ones, in which not infrequently the higher teleology is more clearly revealed than in those inner regenerations which are comprehensible

From a letter to V. V. *Rozanov, August 14, 1891. First published in* RUSSKY VESTNIK (THE RUSSIAN MESSENGER), *June, 1903, pp. 421–423.*

to man. I think nonetheless that at the bottom of it all lay the following causes, which go back as far as 1870–1871: a philosophical hatred of long standing (from 1861–1862) for the forms and spirit of the *newest European* life (Petersburg, literary vulgarity, railways, jackets, top hats, rationalism, and so on and so forth); and, on the other hand, an *aesthetic* and rather childlike attachment to the *outward forms* of Orthodoxy; add to this the strong and unexpected shock of the most profound upsets having to do with the heart (you have heard of the French proverb *"Cherchez la femme!"* that is, "Search out the woman" in every serious circumstance of life); and the external *accident of a most dangerous and unexpected illness* (in 1871) and the terror of *dying at the moment when I had just planned* but had not yet written my *triune hypothesis* and my novel *Odysseus Polychroniades* (in the opinion of many my best artistic work); and, finally, I had not yet given expression in my essay "The Yugoslavs" to all those accusations I had brought against Europeanism and the lack of faith, which I myself recognize as my decisive historical contribution (Katkov himself did not understand this danger or did not wish to point to it in accord with his opportunism and cunning). In a word: all my most important work was done after 1872–1873, that is, after my trip to Mount Athos and after my passionate conversion to personal Orthodoxy. . . . *For some reason,* at the age of forty, *personal faith* completed my political and artistic education. This event still continues to astonish me and remains mysterious and incomprehensible. But in the summer of 1871 when as Consul in Salonika I lay on a divan in fear of my *unexpected* death (from a strong bout of cholera), I was gazing at the image of the Holy Virgin (just recently brought me by a monk from Mount Athos), I could foresee nothing of all that, and all my literary plans were still rather vague. At that moment I was not even thinking of the *salvation* of my soul (for belief in a *personal* God came to me far more easily than the belief in *my own personal immortality*); I, who was normally not timorous, was horrified merely at the thought of my *corporeal* death and, having been already prepared for it (as I have already said) as a result of a whole series of other psychological transformations, affections, and revulsions, I suddenly and instantaneously began to believe so palpably and firmly that it was as though I saw before me a *living, familiar,* actual woman, one that was most kind and powerful, and I exclaimed, "Mother of God! It is too soon! It is too soon for me to die! I have done nothing yet worthy of my abilities, and I have led a life that was in the highest degree debauched and sinful to the point of refinement! Raise me from the corruption of death. I shall go to Mount Athos, bow to the elders, so that they may convert me into a *simple* and *real* Orthodox Christian, who believes in Wednesday and Friday and in miracles, and I shall even take monastic vows. . . ."

Within a couple of hours I had recovered; all the symptoms had vanished before the doctor arrived; within three days I was already in Mount Athos. The elders dissuaded me from taking the monastic vows immediately, but under their guidance I quickly became an Orthodox Christian. To my *Russian* and aesthetic *love* of the church must also be added that which was lacking for confession even on "Wednesdays and Fridays," namely, the *fear* of sin, the fear of punishment, the fear of God, spiritual fear. To attain to this *spiritual* fear it was only necessary for my pride to experience no more than two hours of *physical* (and hurtful) terror. After this I became *humble* and understood at once that higher *teleology* of chance to which I have already referred. My physical fear disappeared, but my *spiritual fear remained.* And since then I am *unable* to reject faith or the *fear of the Lord even if I wished* to do so. Religion is not always a consolation; in many cases it is a heavy yoke, but he that verily believes will be loath to part with this yoke! Every doubt, every philosophizing that is unprofitable to religion he will easily spurn with hatred and contempt, just as one might wave away an insufferable fly. It is impossible to relate *here* what happened after the conversion, after 1871–1872. The last twenty years of my life, from the age of forty to sixty, I have lived in quite a different way from my first twenty years of maturity (from the age of twenty to forty). I do not say better, less sinfully, but *differently*, on a completely different foundation, more profoundly and more fully. It is in these last twenty years (after Mount Athos) that I have written my best and most original works.

ON MOUNT ATHOS

I HAD learned long ago not to allow circumstances to press too heavily on my mind and imagination, and even in 1871, when I left Salonika in despair *to die* on Mount Athos, at the station stops on the way I pondered clearly for the first time my hypothesis of the triune process * and the secondary simplification. Stopping in Zographie, I did not leave my room for two weeks, writing on the subject day and night; and even when half reclining in bed, I only alternated this occupation with the most bitter, the most sincere, and almost uninterrupted prayers following monastic injunctions and according to the books. I opened in turn Proudhon, St. Paul, John Climacus,† Buckle; ‡ St. Paul and Climacus I read

* See "The Triune Process of Development."

† John Climacus (*d.* 605), ascetic writer, author of *Scola parodisi* (*The Ladder of Paradise*).

‡ Henry Thomas Buckle, English historian.

From REMINISCENCES, *written in 1874–1875. Published in* LITERATURNOYE NASLEDSTVO (THE LITERARY HERITAGE), *nos. 22–24, 1935, pp. 465–466.*

for *my own good, for my soul,* in order to submit to them, to love them, to imitate them; the other two bourgeois writers I read for the sake of *my mind,* for the sake of the work I was writing, which I had already regarded as *posthumous,* in order to hate them, to fight against their influence, to reject them as much as possible, as much as my philosophical conviction would allow.

On Mount Athos the state of my mind was terrible; it was much worse than it had been in Moscow. I had no wish to die, but I did not believe that I would go on living. I thought that everyone had forgotten me, and I only sought to forget everyone; and it was only while I gritted my teeth rather than felt genuine humility that I could reconcile myself to the thought of oblivion and death. I was not reconciled to it; I gave more consideration to the salvation of my soul; and only my reading of the spiritual books and my talks with Hieronymus and Makarius * could raise me to those difficult, thorny heights of Christianity upon which man has the strength, if only for a moment, to say to himself, "The worse it is here, the better; God so wills; and God's will be done!"

Yes! the inner state of my soul on Mount Athos was more terrible than any I had previously experienced. However, there my immediate future was provided for materially; I had no need to think of tomorrow except from the spiritual point of view. There was poetry all around me. All the outward surroundings of life and the whole inner structure of it—nature, customs, the language, the rules, the points of view, the ideals, the clothes, and the buildings, the very absence of straight roads—all this was non-European, all this transported me into an Oriental Byzantine world; almost never did anything there remind me of this bourgeois, prosaic, vulgar, vile Europe (I am not referring to the Europe of Byron and Goethe, Louis XIV, and even Napoleon I, but to Europe at its *latest* stage, the present-day Europe of railways, banks, representative chambers, in a word, the caricature of a Europe of progressive self-delusion and prosaic dreams of universal happiness).

This was what was so good on Mount Athos. There one had

* Russian monks on Mount Athos, of whom more later.

something on which to feast one's soul and eyes; it had almost the same effect on me as Gubastov's * Persian carpets, only on a vaster scale. By contrast, after my long absence from them, Russia and Moscow struck me, first of all, by those of their aspects which I found so repugnant and hideous—by the conceited peasants, who, of their former character, had only preserved their cunning and propensity to drunkenness but had lost that trait of humility and submissiveness which had so adorned and softened them; by the ruined or deserted estates, those estates from which had emerged Pushkin, Zhukovsky, Lermontov, and Fet, in which even the wholesale dealer Koltzov had found for himself esteem and good will; by those iron railroads, which made everything more intolerably expensive and on which one sees in front of one nothing but self-satisfied, two-dimensional figures; by the lawyers, new demagogue-judges, the trial of the unfortunate Mitrofania, whose abuses (I confess without blushing) disgust me far less than a liberal speech by Bright or that blackguard Virkhov, who became so frightened when Bismarck challenged him to a duel. Moscow and Russia looked to me like Katkov's dusty and stuffy editorial office, filled with unbearably colorless and ugly operators and insolent corridor lackeys, who (as I learned from Georgi) were amazed and laughed at the fact that I fasted on Wednesdays and Fridays. To such an extent, indeed, had they become enlightened in this past decade of *beneficent progress!*

(Let Khitrov, the progressivist, ask his *conscience* in *silence*—let him not say a word, for in such cases he will not speak the truth —"Would it not be a good thing to have them *flogged in the stables* in the old patriarchal manner, having first stripped them of their European dress coat?")

Thus the *spectacle* I saw in Russia and Moscow was worse than on Mount Athos. But my health was now improved, the state of my spirit at one and the same time more cheerful, more daring when facing people and circumstances, more humble and more prepared for any eventuality in the sight of God. Here too, as ev-

* A friend of Leontiev's.

erywhere else, God's truth was to be seen. God had first instructed me on Mount Athos, then He had cheered and fortified me in the embassy and in Khalki, and only afterwards had He sent me into the pernicious Russo-European environment, so that there I might overcome obstacles and even enemies whom I did not suspect of having, enemies who nevertheless turned out to be present. The Lord evidently does not expect us to engage in battles that overtax our strength.

I began to write with enjoyment in grayly European Russia and in the midst of external reverses, just as I had written with enjoyment amid the poetry of Mount Athos, though my heart was afflicted with ghastly sores that exuded the terror of an imminent death!

THE ELDERS OF MOUNT ATHOS

In the Russian monastery (Russiko),* there was another remarkable man besides Father Hieronymus †—the archimandrite Makarius, a descendant of a wealthy family of Tula merchants, the Sushkins.‡ At one time he had been a handsome, vivacious, and at the same time lyrically inclined young man. He had arrived to pay homage to the monks of Mount Athos, had fallen ill there, and, expecting to die, had taken monastic vows. When Leontiey found him in Russiko, he was a forty-eight-year-old ascetic, a man of ceaseless activity and full of love and benevolence towards all.

* The Russian monastery of St. Panteleimon on Mount Athos, otherwise known as Russiko.

† A Father confessor in Russiko.

‡ The former Mikhail Sushkin (1821?–1884).

Leontiev, *"Reminiscences about the Archimandrite Makarius,"* with introductory remarks by A. Konoplyantzev, from Yury Kartzov, IN MEMORY OF K. N. LEONTIEV, *1911, pp.* 80–83.

"Reminiscences About the Archmandrite Makarius" was published earlier in GRAZHDANIN (*The Citizen*), no. 246, 1889.

103

According to K. N.'s * description of the archimandrite Makarius, "He was a great and true ascetic in body and mind, worthy of the ancient days of monasticism and, at the same time, a completely contemporary man—keen, attractive, and, I would even say, in certain cases almost a worldly man in the best sense of the word, that is, elegant in appearance, affable, vivacious and sociable." It was under his guidance that K. N. began his new life. To illustrate graphically in what manner Leontiev was educated on Mount Athos, what made him so inclined to the monastic life, and in what way Father Hieronymus and Father Makarius attracted him, we shall cite the following incident as related by Leontiev himself:

ON A special occasion one day the archimandrite Makarius had to celebrate mass (I do not recall what holiday it was) in the Vatopedi tower outside the boundaries of Mount Athos. This tower, which had once served as a fortress for the defense of the monastic shores, was now no more than a plain homestead and sort of conventual chapel belonging to the wealthy Greek monastery of Vatoped.

Inside the tower was a very small, impoverished chapel. In it Father Makarius performed the liturgy, assisted by a young Greek parish priest from the nearby village of Ierissos. The inhabitants of this village, according to ancient tradition, hated the monks of Mount Athos, because, once upon a time, one of the Byzantine emperors had confiscated some of their land and had given it to the holy mountain men. Judging by the fact that the Serbian monastery of Hilandare was, of all the monasteries within the bounds of Mount Athos, the nearest from the side of the isthmus, it is probable (if the tradition be correct) that the land had been donated to it. Not long before my arrival at the holy mountain a considerable part of the beautiful, deciduous forest belonging to that already impoverished monastery burned, and everyone suspected that it was the villagers of Ierissos who had deliberately set it on fire. I do not know whether any litigation over this had ever

* K. N. Leontiev.

resulted; but I do remember that Father Makarius himself told me about the hostile attitude of the neighboring villagers. Nevertheless, he not only treated with the greatest consideration the young priest, who had been invited to share in the celebration of the mass but, by way of a farewell present, also gave him for his parish church a very beautiful and entirely new pallium of white glazed brocade with variegated embroidery. (Father Makarius had brought it with him, knowing full well how needy was the chapel in that neglected tower.)

When, after the mass, we mounted—he on his mule, I on my horse—and rode back to Russiko, Father Makarius himself confessed to his good deed, a small one of course from the standpoint of material value but very significant in the ethical sense (for it was a gift from a holy mountain man to a representative of a village hostile to the holy men).

Father Makarius told me with the kindly expression on his face that I loved so much and with that gay and bright wit, "I felt like wishing to console the poor man" (that is, the young priest). "Let him also go home in brighter spirits. . . ." Father Makarius said "him also" because he was aware that certain circumstances of that day had given me pleasure and consolation.

He was also aware how greatly, because of my nature, I loved kindness and generosity, and how greatly during that time I had become attached to monasticism. He might not have found it necessary to mention this to another person; but he guessed it would give me great pleasure to hear this. Deeply felt kindness is very often far more effective when displayed in the trifles of everyday life, in the pure impulses of the heart, than on more important occasions.

Thus it would seem that in this unimportant matter, which had nothing to do with me—in the matter of the beautiful but inexpensive pallium presented to one who was almost an enemy, and in the smile and the words of Father Makarius addressed to me when we started on our return journey—my heart, which was already so favorably disposed towards him, read so much vital and delicate love that I had the immediate impulse to kiss his noble hand! And had we been alone without attendants, I would surely have done this even though I was mounted on horseback. Yes, I was enraptured by this touching movement of his heart: but our great and strict mentor had a different view of the matter.

When, on returning to Russiko, I entered the cell of Father Hieronymus, he said to me in the presence of the archimandrite:

"Did you see what Father Makarius did? He made a gift of the pallium to the priest! What's the sense of giving away so generously monastery property—and to whom? To an enemy of the Athos monastery!"

Father Makarius was silent at first, smiling; and then he said something I do not remember, but which had no bearing on the matter, and went out.

Alone with me, Father Hieronymus sighed deeply and said:

"I am afraid that once I'm gone, he will give everything away. He is so generous that if you let him have his way, he will squash all his paternal inheritance to the size of a nut!"

Needless to say, I began to defend Father Makarius. I felt rather piqued with the elder because, instead of properly examining our small spiritual joy, he was now throwing cold water on it with his critical reservations.

To my protests Father Hieronymus replied gently and gravely with one of those radiant, celestial smiles which very rarely lit up his powerful and austere face and which had the effect of irresistible charm. He said this to me:

"Have no fear, you child of God! We shall not spoil his heart; he is too charitable and good. But the abbot is one hundred years old; I am also approaching my end. Father Makarius will soon have to become the prior, he will have to shepherd all this flock. . . . And where? Here, in a foreign land! In itself it is a good thing he made a present of that pallium, and as you can see by the life our monks lead, they themselves need nothing. But the monastery must have means. And we should ceaselessly try to restrain Father Makarius and teach him to be strict. He is an 'impressive' man!"

Thus spoke the elder.

At the sight of that unexpected and unimaginable smile on his handsome, majestic face, on hearing his even less expected speech, in which he had addressed me familiarly as "thou" and had called me, a forty-year-old and very sinful man, paternally "God's child," I did not feel like kissing his hand, but rather like falling at his feet and kissing his old felt slipper. Even the mistake he made when he said "impressive" instead of "impressionable" *—this small "want of education," combined with such great spiritual powers, delighted me greatly.

* *Uvlekátelni*—"attractive"; *uvlekáyuschisia*—"enthusiastic." Father Makarius had confused the two words, here translated as "impressive" and "impressionable," to preserve a root similarity.

ON THE ELDERS OF THE OPTINA MONASTERY

One

One

❧ "THE PATH of an elder's education in all aspects of Christianity is recognized by all the great eremites, the Fathers and the teachers of the church, as the most reliable and convenient of all known to the church of Christ. Eldership flourished in the ancient Egyptian and Palestinian cenobite communities, then was planted on Mount Athos, and afterwards was transplanted to Russia from the East. But, in the last centuries, as a result of a general decline in faith and asceticism, it gradually fell into oblivion, and many began to repudiate it. Already in the times of Nil Sorgsky an elder's way of life became an object of repugnance to many, and, at the end of the last century, it had become almost completely unknown. The famous, great elder, Paucius Velikovsky, the archimandrite of the Moldavian monasteries, had contributed a great

Leontiev's article "Father Kliment Sederholm," RUSSKY VESTNIK, *November–December, 1879, pp. 38–41, 535–538. Part 1 opens with a quotation from "A Biographical Sketch of the Elder Father Leonid," written by Father Kliment Sederholm.*

deal to the establishment of this ideal of monastic life founded on the teaching of the Holy Fathers. With great difficulty he collected on Mount Athos, and then translated from the Greek into Slavonic, the works of the ascetic writers, in which is contained the teaching of monastic life, in general, and of the spiritual attitude to elders, in particular. The ascetic monk Fyodorov, one of the disciples of the archimandrite Paucius, who had lived in Moldavia for almost twenty years, passed on these rules of monastic life to the ascetic monk, Father Leonid, who, with his disciple, the elder ascetic monk Makarius, planted them in the Optina desert.

"Father Moisey, the then prior of Optina, and his brother Antony, the head of the hermitage, both of whom had laid the foundations of their monastic life in the forests of Bryansk in the spirit of the great eremites, had long wished to introduce the way of the elders in the Optina desert, but were unable themselves to fulfill this task, because they were preoccupied with many burdensome and complex tasks, having to do with the construction and management of the convent, and also because the conjunction in one and the same person of these two obligations—that of a prior and that of an elder, although in former times this was feasible owing to the simplicity of manners—was inconvenient and even impossible in our times. When Father Leonid settled in the Optina desert, Father Moisey profited by this and, knowing his experience in the spiritual life, entrusted to his leadership all the brothers living in the Optina desert and all who came to stay at the monastery.

"Since that time, the whole internal structure of monastic life has changed in the Optina desert. Without the advice and blessing of the elder nothing important was done in the cloister. Every day, particularly in the evening hours, the brethren would gather in his cell and unburden themselves of their spiritual troubles; in front of the elder each one of them would hasten to confess in what way he had sinned that day, whether in deed, word, or thought; they asked for his counsel and solution of the perplexities they had encountered, consolation in any afflictions that had befallen them, help and support in their inner struggle with their passions and with the unseen enemies of our salvation. The elder received all of them with paternal love and spoke words of experience, edification, and consolation. This is how an eyewitness, the ascetic Antony, describes Father Leonid's cell:

" 'The elder's cell, which was filled from early morning till late at night with people who came to him seeking spiritual assistance, represented a picture worthy of an artist's brush. The elder, all in white, in a short mantle, could be seen in the center of a circle of his disciples who knelt before him, and their animated faces reflected a variety of emotions. One would repent of a sin he would never have thought of unless he was passing through his novitiate; another, with tears in his eyes, would admit having unintentionally insulted a brother. One man's face burned with shame because he could not control the thoughts from which he would have liked to escape to the other end of the world. Another's face reflected a cold-blooded smile of disbelief in everything visible: he had come here together with the others just to call on the elder and to depart unhealed; but he likewise, fearing the elder's piercing glance and accusatory words, lowered his eyes and modulated his voice, as if desiring to mollify his judge with pretended humility. Here also one could see true submission, a readiness to kiss the elder's feet; a feeble, sickly youth, rejected by all the world, would not leave the knees of Father Leonid, like a calf keeping close to its mother cow.' "

His wise instructions began to have a favorable effect on the Optina brotherhood, which began little by little to perfect itself in the ethical sense. The elder's wisdom, to which the love and respect paid him by the prior and the brethren bore witness, soon made Father Leonid famous even outside the cloister. A variety of people—nobles, merchants, city dwellers, and simple folk—began to flock to the door of his cell in search of spiritual guidance. The elder received them all with heartfelt, paternal good will, and not one of the callers left his cell without having been spiritually comforted by him. With each year the number of people flocking to

Optina desert increased significantly, an obvious sign that it was flourishing. . . .

In the 1840s, the authorities started to persecute Father Leonid and the Optina desert monastery for this apparent innovation. Through envy and ignorance, they came to regard their conduct as schism or heresy. His Eminence Nikolai of Kaluga had the weakness to yield to these instigations, and in several instances he prohibited Father Leonid from receiving ordinary civilians, who were rushing in crowds to his doors. Father Leonid and the archimandrite Moisey, the prior of the Optina desert, submitted obediently to the will of the archbishop and ceased to admit the common folk; but the people who had become accustomed to chatting with the elder and listening to his words of instruction—the landowners, merchants, army men, the plain folk of the towns and villages, a multitude of women, nuns from many of the convents—demanded to hear their spiritual mentor and suffered unbearably when deprived of his counsel. One day the following happened. Concerned about his spiritual flock, Father Leonid decided at last, contrary to the archbishop's veto, to allow the disappointed laymen into his presence. (It must be understood what terrible despair a man can feel who has lost faith in himself, in his reason, in people close to him, and in the power of human help in general, and who can see nothing around him or in himself except sorrow and sin, if he is deprived of the sole support of his calm and impartial spiritual guide. This is terrible!) Soon after this His Eminence Nikolai of Kaluga arrived in Optina. The archbishop was walking to the church through the monastery courtyard filled with people. Suddenly Father Leonid came out of his cell on his way to the church. In an instant the crowd pulled back from the archbishop and rushed towards the elder, surrounded him, and, thronging around him, asked for his blessing.

Father Leonid, on his part, tried to push his way through the crowd towards the archbishop in order to render him homage.

When he had approached close to him, the archbishop upbraided him: "And you're still involved with people?"

"To God I sing that I am still here!" Father Leonid replied firmly and calmly.

This answer pleased the archbishop so much that from that time on he ceased to trouble Father Leonid, and since then the way of the elders has taken root in Optina and has flourished there until our day.

Father Leonid was succeeded by Father Makarius (a descendant of Kaluga gentry), the famous confessor and a friend of his, afterwards by Father Ilarion, and then by the present chief confessor Father Ambrosy. Fathers Ilarion and Ambrosy had formerly been the cell mates of Father Makarius.

Two

I shall not here enlarge upon the profit I myself have derived in many respects from my talks with my highly educated friend and true believer.* This ideal profit is the acquisition of my inner world, about which it would be out of place for me to speak in print. The matter does not concern me alone; I must touch upon myself only where it seems essential for a better explanation of Father Kliment's character.

For example, consider the question of Catholicism. Here, in order to point to the catechismic propensities of the deceased and to give a living example of his jealousy, I am obliged to confess that I have a certain partiality for Catholicism—not in the dogmatic sense, of course, not in a purely religious sense, but, so to speak, in a cultural-political one. These tastes of mine disturbed Father Kliment very much; on this subject he and I had very many heated arguments; he himself would open the subject; he admonished me, shamed me, and hounded me for this by word of mouth and even in his letters; in the winter—in his cell or mine, or when walking in the forest—this argument was frequently renewed; in Moscow, in Petersburg, everywhere I received letters from him

* Father Kliment Sederholm.

from time to time in which he touched upon this subject, which in his opinion was a very delicate one but in my view was a very simple and clear one. At first I imagined that he did not understand me, that he was confusing in me two absolutely independent feelings and concepts; but later I became convinced that it was I who had failed to understand him. Finally, he resolved to have it out with me to the finish. And then I understood him; and although I stuck to my view nevertheless, I perceived that there was a great difference between us. I can never forget that gigantic cultural conflict between a clear and perfect older system and a vague and undefined new one, a conflict which is now being waged all over the world; he refused even for a minute to put aside entirely his preoccupation with the salvation of souls—not only his own soul but also that of his neighbor. While defending certain aspects of the papacy, I was thinking of the destiny of Europe; while refuting me anxiously and persistently, he thought only of the salvation of my soul. He was afraid of even a spark of sympathy for the papacy. He was apprehensive lest my political sympathy, which I clearly distinguished from my personal religious beliefs, would imperceptibly pass into something else. While listening one day to my apology for Catholicism, he repeated several times, shaking his head reproachfully:

"Look out! Be careful!"

"What's that?" I asked, laughing. "Don't be alarmed, I shan't become a Catholic. But I only regret that the majority of our clergy lack that sense of jealousy which the Catholic hierarchy possesses, and on top of this we are, unfortunately, so deeply bound to the West that every pernicious trend there is reflected sooner or later here with us. Our church has not yet suffered those open persecutions which the Papacy has been suffering from the Western liberals for almost a century now, and yet, in the meanwhile, our church has also been, if not shaken up, at least undermined on many sides.

"Listen," Sederholm exclaimed heatedly. "For a long time you have not been a true Christian; you were converted late. I can understand that it is useful at the start to respect every religion, to love every faith, even Buddhism, and to prefer every confession to the void of so-called progress. Yes, at the start of a conversion. . . . But you cannot remain in that position. You have to go further and feel a spiritual revulsion to everything that is not Orthodoxy."

"Why should I feel this revulsion?" I questioned him. "No! I would find that impossible. I read the Koran with pleasure. . . ."

"The Koran is a revolting thing!" Kliment said, turning away.

"What's to be done? For me it is a beautiful lyrical poem. I shall never agree with your point of view on this. I do not understand this one-sided approach, and it is foolish of you to have fears about me. As you can see for yourself, I fully submit to the Orthodox faith. I accept not only what convinces my reason and heart, but also that which I dislike. . . . *Credo quia absurdum*."

"There can be nothing absurd about the teaching of the church," Kliment objected heatedly.

"You're taking exception to words. Let me express myself in a different way: I also believe even in what seems to me absurd because of human infirmity in general and of the infirmity of my reason in particular, because of the old and indelible habits of a liberal, European education. It is not an absurdity in itself, let us assume, but only seems so to me. Nevertheless I do believe and obey. I shall permit myself to boast and even to fall into spiritual pride for a moment by telling you that this may very well be the best kind of faith. Any astute peasant, for example, can give us the kind of counsel that we may consider reasonable. A strange thought has astonished our mind by its truth. What's so surprising in our accepting it? One involuntarily accepts it, and one is only surprised that this thought had not previously occurred to one. But believing in a spiritual authority, submitting to it contrary to one's reason and tastes, which have been trained for long years in another kind of life, submitting arbitrarily and obligatorily despite a whole storm of inner protests—this seems to me, indeed, to be true faith. Of course I realize that what I am saying is not very humble. It is the pride of humility. I know, I know all this, but, forgive me, I should like you to understand what is going on within me. So please rest assured. I shall not turn to the Jesuits, even though a Jesuit may please me more than an indifferent Orthodox priest who does not care whether the grass is growing and who will not cross himself until he hears the thunder peal."

"That's a national frailty," Father Kliment asserted. "It has no bearing on the teaching of the church; it is due to historical conditions. . . . However, we also had zealots. I am now collecting material for a book about those Russian zealots of the last few centuries."

As this point, I recall, we were interrupted; but Kliment was far from reassured, and the following day he renewed the conversation.

I spoke to him thus:

"As you see, I submit to everything. But I cannot simplify my mind. I grant it the liberty to enjoy ideas; that may take time, of course, but it will not cause me to waver in the foundations of my faith. Let me give you an example. At home I have a copy of Voltaire's *Philosophical Lexicon*. One day I read in it an article about the Prophet David. Voltaire tries to demonstrate that in the eighteenth century, David would have been adjudged only fit for the galleys and no more, and things of that kind. . . . I laughed a great deal. . . . I love the power of the mind; but I do not believe in the infallibility of reason. Thus the one need not interfere with the other. Half an hour after reading that article by Voltaire, I could still pray as sincerely as before, according to the psalm book of David. There is much that all of us do not understand. Better I should submit to everything you like according to the faith than to submit to Voltaire in reason. My own reason is more precious and more dear to me than any other. I cross myself and go to church and try to fulfill my religious duties like any of those old women who come from Kozelsk and gather outside the gates of your hermitage. For this reason, permit me to be apprehensive for all of Christianity and for the whole world when I see how deeply shaken is Catholicism, the mightiest, the most expressive of the buttresses supporting the social structure. Give me the liberty of entertaining some feeling for all these diverse monks with their cowls and broad-brimmed hats, the splendid ecclesiastical processions, the red-robed cardinals. The highest poetry and the highest politics have a deeper connection than people usually think. When poetry declines, the power of the state declines likewise, and so does profound thought."

YOUNG FRIENDS

1. From a Letter to Olga Kartzov, March 18, 1878 (p. 259)

MY OWN position and that of several suffering persons dependent upon me is so critical that I should only sit still, sleep, write, and pray. Yet I allow myself to travel to Petersburg not only to keep an appointment with Ignatiev, for which a single day would suffice, but I stay on there for three or four days. As if I were a man like any other rather than a creature torn asunder by myself and circumstances. Once in the Crimea I saw a dog of very good pedigree which had its back broken by a cart. Its eyes gleamed with intelligence and seemed full of life. From where it lay it strained

From Leontiev's correspondence with Yury Kartzov and his sister Olga. Leontiev had met them and their mother Katerina in Petersburg at the end of the 1870s. Jokingly he had called the young Kartzovs "little tigers." Afterwards, Yury Kartzov entered the diplomatic service. Later he wrote his reminiscences of Leontiev, IN MEMORY OF K. N. LEONTIEV, *1911. These samples of Leontiev's side of the correspondence are from that work.*

towards passersby with an expression of affection, suffering, and love. We fed it, stroked it, and went our way. I must confess I pitied that dog more than I pitied many people. Passersby fed it, and the dog lived on for a long time. When I departed for Russia, it was still there by a wall in Simferopol.

Would it not have been better to kill that dog? It would have killed itself if it had been able to understand that this could be done. But to a man who believes in life beyond the grave such a thing is impossible. On the contrary, he must pray in order to continue to live and have time to expiate what is necessary. He has to live and strive on the spot with a broken back! We used to come on purpose to feed that dog, but here friends (sincere friends) find it impossible even to call in order to offer a morsel of *spiritual food*. I blame life, myself, my legs broken before their time, legs which nobody can now mend, rather than my friends or people in general. People cannot do anything; that is the worst thing of all.

2. *From a Letter to Yury Kartzov, April 8, 1878* (*pp. 267–268*)

And having asked you, you in particular, to come and stay with me for a single day in the whole of your life and mine, I leave the rest to destiny and the laws of deplorable human nature. "Why? Why?" you will ask. This is why: I shall try not to come to Petersburg again unless I am forced to do so, but you I must see at leisure without any interruptions on a literary matter I consider very important. You, and you alone, are essential for me to consult, only you out of all the people I know in Russia. In you alone, my young and cunning tiger-poet, do I find a combination of those qualities and those faults which I consider necessary for my goal. I shall believe in you alone, and I shall follow only your advice in this undertaking. Although one must approach you cautiously, in order not to prick and cut to blood one's hands, it is from you that one can squeeze that precious, rosy juice which it would be impossible to press out of anybody else with all the machines in the world. True, I have not considered, nor do I consider, myself obliged to argue with you to the finish when I have a sore throat or when I wish to talk with K. S.* or with O. S.† more than I do with you. Since I have been living in the world, you were the first I heard say that it was impossible to finish an argument when one wished. But what especially pleases me is that, in your unjustified anger, you are capable of imparting the appearance of logic and legality even to your unjustified anger.

* Katerina Sergeyevna Kartzov.
† Olga Sergeyevna Kartzov.

LEONTIEV'S SERVANTS

I WAS very touched by your having inquired with such inter-est about my favorites, Nikolai and Varya. Their story over the past two years is very complex and might serve as the subject for a very fine novella, far more refreshing and original than anything being written here with us or abroad. There would be no need for me even to poetize their story, but only to understand it.

Last spring they quarreled violently, and feeling that this was very unpleasant for me, they began to avoid me, became very ner-vous, and, indeed, insupportable. After praying to God and dip-ping into the New Testament, I let Varya go away without any intention of letting her depart for good. She stayed for over a year with Masha * in the Orlovsky monastery;† and not long ago, learn-ing that I was in difficulties, she expressed the wish to serve me.

* Martha Leontiev, K. L.'s niece.
† She worked there in a monastery school for children.

From a letter to K. A. Gubastov, January 1, 1883. Published in RUSSKY VESTNIK, March, 1896, pp. 394–399.

120

She is a very noble and reliable girl, clever and kind, but very proud and unpractical, especially as regards herself. After spending a year in the monastery, she began to regard our relationship more seriously, and now I have really come to find her very useful.

As for Nikolai, it is even painful for me to talk about him. He's actually fit to be the hero of a novel, but first and foremost he is his own worst enemy. From being the giddy weathercock you used to know, he—under what influence I do not know, whether that of a brain disease which doctors have claimed to discover in him or that of an unfortunate love affair—anyhow he has turned into a sullen, frequently angry, and even dangerous man.

This came about in this way. Last winter I was angered by some of his escapades and drove him out of the house and decided to have nothing more to do with him. For a long time he traveled about somewhere and was then employed as a caretaker in one of the Moscow monasteries. He was forbidden to see me; but he happened to meet N. Ya. Soloviev * in the street and begged him to intervene on his behalf and ask me not to deprive him at least of my advice. I was very ill at the time and had received Holy Communion; my confessor advised me to take him back. After I did so, he actually behaved in an exemplary fashion, but at the same time he gradually fell in love with another Kudinovo girl, Fenya, whom you may know by name. She was pretty, very like a doll, and her character reminds one of S. P. Kh., only Fenya is quieter and more languid, cold and slyly coquettish. Having encountered obstacles and coldness for the first time in his life, Nikolai tried his hardest, like Don Juan (not Byron's, but Pushkin's), and attained his goal, and was then obliged to marry because Fenya had become pregnant. I was very satisfied with her as a housekeeper, but was utterly against this involvement for Nikolai and tried to prevent it in every way, even perhaps too much so, until I learned (very late) that they were having a liaison and that it was already too late to cast her off. What was left for me as a Christian and an honest man but to help them to get married? Although my financial situ-

* A dramatist.

ation is easier this year than last, I had no money to provide a dowry for her; but on the advice of Nikodem, Archbishop Favorsky at the local Jerusalem conventual church, who counseled me not to be ashamed to do so, I started a collection for their benefit. Two bishops, the Countess Tolstoy (the widow of the chief public prosecutor), Ionin, and a few others contributed a sum to the amount of two hundred and twenty-five rubles. For this sum they were very well decked out, and I myself spent some thirty rubles on the wedding and the entertainment; and that is all.

I could do nothing more for them. The wedding turned out to be a very gay one; they had guests, and so did I. Even Khitrovo, who had just arrived in Moscow (this was in October), heard about the wedding and paid me a surprise visit; he drank to the health of the young couple and reproached me, saying, "Here you are marrying off your favorites and not inviting your old friends." In the quarters of the young people an accordion played, and there was dancing; Varya had come from her monastery, and Nikolai had a dress sewn for her at his expense for the wedding. In my quarters, Khitrovo and Professor Astafiev, a new friend and a very capable man, argued about the soul and God until three o'clock in the morning. Not only did I not argue with them, but I did not hear half of what they said. With the help of Varya I was preoccupied with domestic aesthetics, seeing to it that everything was on time, handsomely and tastily served—and I think the guests remained satisfied. Astafiev and Professor St——ev (a Bulgarian) had plenty to drink. And actually it was a strange combination— the ragged wallpaper and the calico curtains of my reception rooms contrasted with the elegance and the smartness of the young pair and of their small room near the drawing room, which I had furnished for them inexpensively, of course, but in the Russian style. The bride was wonderfully nice, absolutely like a porcelain doll, although she was dressed in the "German" style, but in good taste and not inexpensively on the money that had been collected; while the bridegroom wore a red silk shirt—him you already know. In church the people whispered that the village lad was marrying a young lady, and Nikolai was very pleased at this. But nothing good came of it!

You will understand—all the plastic, picturesque, and sensual elements were beautiful, but alas! the spiritual element turned out badly, so that I can only rejoice that my conscience in this respect was clean and that all this had happened contrary to my tastes. I would never have selected such a cold and cunning girl for Nikolai. She did not love him; she had merely yielded to a moment of weakness, and she showed no appreciation at all of his physical attractiveness, was even annoyed by his caresses, and altogether failed to understand what we found exceptional about him. But the best proof of Nikolai being an exceptional young man was that people singled him out despite his reserved and cautious manner. . . . Now he began to fly into rages, was jealous of her for days on end, did not believe anything she said; and as we observed them, our very depressing impression of them was only mitigated by the fact that they were both young and handsome. Otherwise it would have been an utterly horrible experience. Then, as chance would have it, a truly unfortunate chance, he began to suffer this summer from fainting fits and paroxysms, which, under the influence of all those spiritual shocks, increased terribly in frequency after the marriage. The fainting fits grew more frequent, alternating with mad rages, and he became really dangerous—he began to threaten us with knives. . . .

The worst of it was that he began to get exasperated at those he loved best—myself and my wife—and for me he became an impossible moral problem; for the last month I have not had one day of peace. Fits of rage and fainting, paroxysms, repentance and tears. Doctors advised me to remove him, especially from our presence; but in all the hospitals of Moscow typhus and other plagues were raging, and it was impossible to send him there. Thus, providing them with necessities, I sent them off to their homeland—him to the hospital at Optina and her to his mother in Kozelsk—and I shall help them financially while I can. Sickness is one thing, but it seems to me that, besides this, his character was terribly vitiated in consequence of his unsuccessful marriage. I assume that my education of him is now at an end and that he will now have to be educated by God Himself and circumstances. What of it? We should also be grateful for the past: I had received from him much that was useful and pleasant. That is all about Nikolai. As you see, my friend, one thing is worse, another better.

THE ELDER AMBROSIUS [*]

PERMIT me also to postpone a detailed account of Father Ambrosius. I shall only say the following: *saintliness*, which is recognized by the church, may be acquired, by God's grace, by people of the most disparate characters and the most heterogeneous minds. By the turn of his character and mind, Father Ambrosius was more practical than contemplative. He was "practical," be it understood, in no petty sense, but in the highest and broadest one. In the sense, for example, in which the teaching of the Gospel may be called *practical* in the highest degree. Love, threats, and the highest ideals of renunciation and condescension towards repentant sinners. I shall add, moreover, he is more cheerful and jocular than morose and serious, extremely *firm* and strict at times, but extraordinarily charitable, merciful, and benevolent.

[*] Born Grekov, Leontiev's spiritual mentor and confessor in the Optina monastery.

From Leontiev's letter to V. *Rozanov of August 14, 1891.* RUSSKY VESTNIK, *June, 1903, p. 423.*

He has no knowledge of my *theories* and, in general, of "our ideas," as you call them, and in general he has had for a long time neither the time nor the strength to read. But he has an excellent understanding of the age we live in and of people, and his psychological experience is astonishing. At times, however, he commands that certain short articles which have been recommended be read to him. Thus he commanded that my article in *Grazhdanin*,* which treated of the connection between the class reforms of Tolstoy and Pazukhin and the delay in the coming of the Antichrist, be read to him aloud two times, and he very much approved of the article. *Like all spiritual people*, he does *not love* "equality and freedom." *Sapienti sat!*

* *The Citizen.*

THE DEATH OF FATHER AMBROSIUS

Troitzky Possad *

IF I HAD known, Vasily Vasilievich, that my long silence would alarm you, I would have written you long ago, even if it had been only five or ten lines. But the point is that I am always eager to write five thousand lines rather than five or ten. And that is the reason I sometimes delay. Besides, I admit that, to my shame, I have been lazy, and I am simply afraid to undertake any work that seems serious (and I regard our correspondence as such).

You ask whether I am angry with you or ill. Neither the one, nor the other; that is, I am ill as always, but not especially so; but over and above that indolence and those delays and vacillations of my will which I have just mentioned, I was very preoccupied and

* Now known as Zagorsk, near Moscow.

From a letter to V. *Rozanov, October 18, 1891. Published in* RUSSKY VESTNIK, *June, 1903, pp. 428–429.*

involved in the first days of October with accounts and with business and domestic correspondence. In my life there has now been an abrupt change or, to be more exact, several interdependent changes. The main thing is that I am now breaking up my household, family, order, such as had been firmly established over the past eleven years; and in expectation of the possibility of retiring somewhere behind an *enclosure*, I am meanwhile settling down here alone in a certain kind of "speechlessness." In monastic terms, "speechlessness" does not connote "silence"; it connotes more or less a carefree, irresponsible *isolation*, accompanied naturally by fasting and prayer. The Fathers of old also distinguished between two principal sorts of monastic life—that of *obedience* (in a community) and that of *speechlessness* (in isolation).

Incidentally, I have transferred myself from number 24 to a special quite *spacious* but quiet, and in appearance very monastic apartment *with vaults* (*medieval*), on the ground floor of the same hostel, and I am *very* pleased with it. *There is room here for a visiting friend.* Previously, in the vicinity of Optina I had set up a whole small household on a special, small estate; there I had my furniture (the Kudinovo furniture, my mother's, even that dating from 1811, which was part of her dowry) and so on. A large, good library. It was necessary to correspond about all this, since I had to decide what to sell, what to give away or to leave behind. Of course, all this had been decided in good time and approved by the deceased elder (you must know by now that he died on October 9). However that may be, you will understand that there was a great deal to do in the beginning. (I do not recall whether I wrote you that my w—— * is now weak of mind.) It was necessary for me to place her with kind and trusty people, and so on.

Now that I have accounted for all this, it will be clear to you that I need not have been angry or especially ill, but that I should have written you all the same.

The end of my elder, Father Ambrosius, did not catch me un-

* Leontiev's wife, presumably. The Lisa of the "Army Doctor" episode, whom he later married and who became mentally ill in later life.

awares; he was already so weak that I am astonished how he managed to survive to the age of seventy-nine. From day to day, for many years, I had been expecting him to die, and therefore I was in no wise astonished by his demise. I understand, of course, that there will be many occasions when, if I live any length of time, I shall ask, "Where is Father Ambrosius?" But what is to be done? It's God's will! The Lord, *if necessary*, will send us another man!

Before receiving the news of his death, I prayed every day for his good health, and afterwards I began to pray for the repose of his soul. And that is all. . . . But for many others, less well prepared or boundlessly devoted to him in their hearts (not purely spiritually), this is a difficult moment. I even know those whose personal feeling for him exceeded their very faith in the church. My own feeling for him was more spiritual; I followed his advice, avoided doing anything important without his blessing, and experienced every kind of generosity from him (even the *material* kind in *former days of need*); but I was not as passionately attached to him as many others. I am convinced that there are people (especially the older nuns) who will not survive him for long; indeed, there are young men for whose faith and future I am somewhat apprehensive; for them Father Ambrosius was *everything*.

 PHILOSOPHY

A CONVERSATION WITH A NIHILIST
ABOUT AESTHETICS

THERE WERE no witnesses to this conversation between us, and my interlocutor died very soon after. He was Piotrovsky,* a young man of twenty-two or twenty-three, a Lithuanian, it seems. He was the pupil and an enthusiastic admirer of Chernyshevsky and Dobrolyubov. He used to write for *Sovremennik,* and if I am not mistaken, in one of his articles he had expressed himself very impudently about the Saviour's words, "You are the salt of the earth," and so on. I vaguely recall that after his death, *Iskra* † or another one of our revolutionary journals entered into a polemic with Askochensky, because he had affirmed that God had pun-

---

* I. A. Piotrovsky (1841–1862), a contributor to the radical review *Sovremennik* (*The Contemporary*).

† *The Spark.*

From Leontiev's description of a conversation with I. A. Piotrovsky, as written down by Leontiev's young friend Anatoly Alexandrov, whose commentary follows. First published in RUSSKY VESTNIK, April 1892, pp. 266–268.*

133

ished Piotrovsky for that article. I have not read either Askochen-sky's notes or Piotrovsky's articles; I only recall the disputes they caused and that *Iskra* or *Sovremennoye Slovo* * rebuked Asko-chensky, as was the current practice, saying, "What kind of Chris-tianity is that? You are rejoicing that God punished him."

I met Piotrovsky accidentally, and I liked him very much. Not having the possibility at the time of publishing anywhere what I should have liked, I consoled myself a little with oral expositions of my views. While living in the provinces (till 1861), I could not understand at all the aims of *Sovremennik* and why it was abusing all and sundry. I came to hate it for this thing alone, without grasping as yet its revolutionary designs. In Petersburg, this was ex-plained to me: "We cannot here openly preach as yet a bloody so-cialist revolution, and we must therefore censure and debunk absolutely everything. If hatred is directed against the contempo-rary order of life, then a revolution is inevitable." But it was at this time precisely that I began to understand for the first time that I did not like popular revolts because of their aims, but rather be-cause of their dramatic effects, and remembered and sensed that in history and in novels I had always felt relieved when revolts were suppressed. Let revolts take place, but let them also be crushed! Democratic aims displeased me terribly, and my reading of Herzen (not of his "Kolokol," † but of some of his other articles) had previously prepared me for this switch to conservatism and reac-tion. From the standpoint of his revulsion against bourgeois prog-ress, Herzen proved very useful—indeed, simply indispensable.

Piotrovsky had imagination, I felt; his eyes were so expressive and thoughtful. We often argued. Thus we were walking one day along the Nevsky and were approaching the Anichkin bridge. I asked him the following question, trying to phrase it as concretely as possible:

"Would you like to have a world in which all people every-

* *The Contemporary Word.*

† "The Bell."

where live in identical small, clean, and comfortable little houses —the way people of middle income live in our Novorossiisky towns?"

"Of course. What could be better than that?" Piotrovsky replied.

"Well, then I *am no longer your man*," I retorted. "If democratic movements must lead to such terrible prose, I shall lose the last vestige of my feeling for democracy. Henceforth I shall be its enemy! Until now I was not clear as to what the progressives and the revolutionaries wanted. . . ."

By this time we were already on or near the Anichkin bridge. On our left was the Belosersky mansion; it was of a rosy hue (with some kind of grayish or pale olive ornamentation, I remember), with large windows and huge caryatids; beyond it, along the Fontanka quay, could be seen the buildings of the Troitzky conventual church, painted dark brown and with a gold cupola on the church, while to the right on the Fontanka were a number of fishponds with their yellow huts and fishermen in red shirts. I pointed out these fishponds, the Belosersky mansion, and the church to Piotrovsky and said to him:

"There's a living illustration for you. The church buildings are in Byzantine style—that's the church, religion; the Belosersky mansion is in a kind of rococo—that's the aristocracy; the yellow fishponds and red shirts—that's the picturesque life of the common people. How beautiful and intelligent all this is! But according to you, it is necessary to destroy and level all this in order to have everywhere nothing but small, identical houses or those many-storied, bourgeois barracks of which there are so many already on the Nevsky prospect!"

"How you love pictures!" Piotrovsky exclaimed.

"Pictures in real life," I protested, "are not there for the pleasure of the spectator; they are the essential expression of some kind of inner, higher law of life—one that is as indestructible as all the other laws of nature."

Such was our conversation.

About the same time * *Leontiev apparently began to understand that he must also pay attention to* institutions (*to which until 1861–1862 he had practically given no thought*) *and* politics, *internal and external, in general. He also grasped that it was impossible to remain* personally *in a state of impartial contemplation and that it was necessary to choose* one side or the other. *Once he had divined that there was much more beauty on the side of the church, the monarchy, the army, the nobility, inequality, and so on, than on the side of modern, middle-class leveling, he stopped wavering and decided to become a "conservative." From this point, it was but a smaller step for him to enter, willingly and even joyfully, the service of the state—not as a doctor, but as a Consul in Turkey. He had not previously given any thought to these consular positions in Turkey; a chance meeting had sowed the seed of this idea and decided the destiny, not only of his practical life, but also of all his future literary works.*

In this way, in 1863, he began to form certain fairly firm convictions about the problems of the state, *as well as those of practical politics. Disputes, reading, and encounters with people in Petersburg very quickly developed this side of him. Nine months of work in the Asiatic Department, the perusal of archives in the Ministry of Foreign Affairs and of consular reports, opened his eyes for the first time to Eastern-Orthodox affairs and began also gradually, barely perceptibly, to prepare a revolution in his* religious *convictions, a revolution which came to a head only on Mount Athos in 1871. It was after this that he "finally found," as the author himself excellently puts it, "an outlet to the noble strivings of his spirit in the glitter and splendor of Christian and Byzantine traditions."*

* Now begins the commentary by A. Alexandrov.

THE RAPACIOUS AESTHETE

MILKEYEV's eyes began to glitter, and his cheeks flushed; Rudnev had never before seen such an expression on his face. The chief wished to make some remark, but Milkeyev was already excited and, throwing back his curls, continued to become more and more heated:

"Why be afraid of conflict and evil? A great nation is great in both good and evil. Give evil and good the chance of freely spreading their wings; give them plenty of room. Please understand that it is not a question of taking paternal care to prevent the possibility of every kind of evil. Rather, it's a question of strengthening the creative powers of good. Fling open the gates: there you are—create, freely and boldly! If some one gets trampled at the gates, that's where the road leads! If it's me, then let it be me; if it's you, then let it be you. That's what is necessary, what should happen in all the great epochs. To be frightened of evil! O Lord! Evil at lib-

From the article "Russians, Greeks, and Yugoslavs," 1878. WORKS, *vol. I., pp. 305–306, 413–415. Here Milkeyev, a student, expresses Leontiev's thoughts.*

erty gives birth to good. It is not necessary that nobody should be wounded; it is necessary that there should be a hospital bed, a doctor, and a nurse for the wounded man. It is not a question of nobody being deceived, but that the person deceived should have a defender and a judge; let the deceiver have the right to exist too, but let him be a bold fellow, and let him be punished in the bold way befitting him. If a Lady Macbeth is essential for the existence of a Cordelia at the other end, then let us have a Lady Macbeth, but let us be rid of impotence, drowsiness, indifference, meanness, and a shopkeeper's prudence.

"But what about blood?" Katerina Nikolayevna asked.

"Blood?" Milkeyev questioned with heat, and his eyes glittered again with strength and inspiration rather than anger. "Blood?" he queried again. "Blood does not hinder the benevolence of heaven. You have all read that treacly Fredrika Bremer*— too much! Joan of Arc spilled blood, but was she not as kind as an angel? What is the point of tearful, one-sided humaneness? What is our mere physiological existence? It's not worth a cent! A simple one-century-old, majestic tree is worth more than two dozen faceless people; and I shall not cut it down to purchase medicine for peasants suffering from cholera."

"I cannot now understand," Milkeyev continued, "how I can reconcile from any angle my ideal with what I see around me! To love the peaceful and universal democratic ideal implies loving vulgar equality—not only political equality but also social, almost psychological equality. Developing under uniform impressions in the midst of those pitiful inclinations, with only one division of useful labor, incapable of giving, men's characters must become similar. A mere difference of temperament is insufficient. Suffering and a wide area of conflict are essential! What need have they of great military leaders, of deep-thinking diplomats? The poet will have nothing to write about; the sculptor will then only decorate railway stations or mold columns for gas lamps. I myself am prepared to suffer; I have suffered, and I shall suffer. I am not obliged

* Fredrika Bremer (1801–1865), a Swedish author.

to pity others with my reason. If my heart feels pity, it is an organic matter rather than one of rules! The ideal of universal equality, labor and rest? The Lord preserve us! True aristocracy is a fine thing in this respect, in that it has *many other* implications. If we destroy the artistocracy, we are only left with two principles: a middle class in dress coats and the people. When we destroy, in its turn, the middle class, which does not allow the people near it, we destroy in essence, not the bourgeoisie, but the people itself; because the worker, as things are, is already crazy about donning a frock coat, dirty and smelly though it be, but a frock coat nevertheless! As they say, "It all depends how it ends." Why are we all afraid of talking about the finite goals in the exact sciences, which are simpler than life, and not afraid of solving the final goal of life, which has been boundless until now? "Man's will is as nothing when confronted with general statistics," say the exact sciences. "*L'homme s'agite, mais Dieu le mène*," the theologian affirms. The final end is unknown to us. You may understand it thus; I interpret it in a different way. But nature, which adores diversity, the splendor of forms, gives us certain directions; according to her example, life should be complex and rich. The personality is the principal element in diversity; nature is higher than its works. The multifaceted strength of the personality or of one-sided prowess— this is the clear goal of history, clearer than any other; true men will appear again, also their works! Which is better—the bloody but spiritually splendid epoch age of the Renaissance or some kind of present-day Denmark, Holland, Switzerland, peaceful, prosperous, and moderate? Beauty is the goal of life, and good ethics and self-denial are valuable only as one of the manifestations of beauty as the free creation of good. The more man develops, the more he believes in beauty, the less he believes in mere utility. A man who is little developed sees utility everywhere; but the more consciously we approach life, the more difficult it becomes to decide what is truly useful to others, to the *family*. Preserving you, I may restrain or even destroy a dozen people; destroying them, I may be saving indirectly a hundred others. Last week, as a doctor, you cured a cruel old man who will return to his village and start beating his bride again. The bride will die earlier, and her husband will then marry a young girl. The first wife bore only girls; from the forty-year-old widower, the young wife will bear boys, workers, and the family will prosper. The beautiful never perishes; it dies here, revives there. Arming ourselves with the beautiful, we can understand and love history; armed only with utility, honesty, and love of peace, we perceive in the life of nations only tears, blood, and cheated hopes. I am not afraid of democratic uprisings; I love them; they help development, even though it is imagined they are preparing the way for peace. On the soil of these strivings, thunderous, virile faces spring up; their extremes provoke reaction, forgotten forces drowsing in stupid affluence, and severe guardians shine in rebutting of them; and afterwards, in the tranquil years, from the accumulated riches and contradictions emerge deep, rounded men, who have reconciled in themselves, as far as possible, the past and the future. In the Middle Ages there was the poetry of religious disputes and wars; now there is the poetry of national movements. I do not even wish to maintain that the latter are better than the former, but only to state that they are right here, under our nose. On the other hand, let me state this: 'Let us, perhaps, restrain the social class which kills off the freedom of others, but do not deprive the world of plentiful leisure and luxury.' It is only under these conditions that we can have figures like Byron, Goethe, George Sand, Caesar, Potemkin, the Count d'Orsay. For all his genius, Shakespeare would not be Shakespeare if a variety of scenes had not been sown in his mind by the colorful environment and the compressed forms of life in England. It is not a question of having no violations of the laws, of having no suffering, but that suffering should be of the highest order. The violations of the law should not be the consequence of mere flabbiness or filthy corruption, but rather of the passionate demands made by the personality! In Sophocles, Creon is in the right, like the law that bids him kill Antigone; and Antigone, who buries her brother because she loves him, is also in the right!"

AESTHETICS I

☙ IT IS not at all a question of eternal agreement and constant friendship; it is a question of the *electrolizing contact of the diverse psychic elements of the Orthodox East, of two nations bound by unbroken ecclesiastical ties—nations which from the national standpoint have been almost hostile at certain moments of their historical life.*

Harmony—or what is beautiful and lofty in life—is not the fruit of an eternal peaceful solidarity, but merely the *image* or the *reflection* of the complex and poetic process of life, in which there is room for everything—for both antagonism and solidarity. It is necessary that the component principles of an integral historical manifestation should be elegant and powerful—only then can be achieved what is called the highest harmony. What is valuable is not eternal peace on earth, but a sincere reconciliation after a passionate struggle and deep repose in the virile expectation of fresh obstacles and fresh perils which temper our spirit!

From the article "Russians, Greeks, and Yugoslavs," 1878. WORKS, *vol. V, pp. 318–319.*

AESTHETICS II

THERE was a time when I disliked military men—I was then very young—but fortunately that did not last long!

Brought up on the liberal-aesthetic literature of the 1840s (especially on George Sand, Belinsky, and Turgenev), I was in my early youth simultaneously a romantic and almost a nihilist. *War* appealed to the romantic; *military men* disgusted the nihilist.

I am now astonished how the most irreconcilable tastes and opinions could have combined at that time in my inexperienced mind! I am astonished at myself; on the other hand, I sometimes almost understand very well the confused and misled young men of today.

And is it only the young men? Are there so few old fools among us?

Only now has a great deal of what agitated, consoled, and irritated us (we were very few in those days) thirty years ago

---

From the article "Two Counts: Alexey Vronsky and Leo Tolstoy." WORKS, *vol. VII, pp. 265–268.*

reached those people. *Progress*, for example. *What kind* of progress? How could I, from the age of twenty to twenty-five, understand, *what kind* of progress it was? *Progress, education, science,
equality, freedom!* All these ideas seemed very clear then; apparently even I thought then that they were one and the same thing.
I *even* like the idea of *revolution;* but recalling now my feelings
at the time, I can see that what appealed to me then was merely
the romantic, aesthetic aspect of those revolutions—the perils, the
armed struggle, the conflicts and the barricades, and so on. In my
youthful years I reflected far less on the *harm* or *utility* of revolutions, on their consequences. I almost did not think about this at
all.

Unconsciously, what I liked best about civil strife was its military, fighting aspect, and not at all its civil aim. The martial side
of the democratic movements appealed to my strong imagination
and forced me to forget for a fairly long time about the prosaic
fruits of those dangerous movements. At the bottom of my soul I
turned out to be far more warlike in spirit than might be expected
at a time when I disliked military men. I have said that "for a
fairly long time" the martial aspects of the revolution forced me
to forget their egalitarian and *vulgar* aims. I said "long time" because I was annoyed at the then confusion of my thoughts. But
by comparison with many other people, who have spent their whole
lives, perhaps, striving for a universal, peaceful, and wooden
prosperity, I corrected myself rather quickly. This fortunate break
for me came during the troubled epoch of the Polish rebellion,
the period also of the dominion of the hateful Dobrolyubov, and
the time of the *notes* from European powers and Prince Gorchakov's brilliant replies to them. Personal, accidental, and emotional influences, besides civil and mental ones, also played their
part in this. Yes, I recovered quickly, although the conflict of
ideas in my mind was so violent in 1862 that I lost weight and not
infrequently spent whole winter nights in Petersburg without any
sleep, with my head and arms resting on a table in a state of exhaustion as a consequence of my martyrlike reflections. I never

joked with *ideas,* and it was not easy for me to "burn that" which our own writers and Western authors had taught me to revere—our own writers by means of artful and subtle negation or false, one-sided enlightenment of life (Gogol, for example—"How bad everything is with us in Russia!") and the Western authors openly and directly (George Sand, for example—"How beautiful is democratic progress!"). But I *wished* to burn and burn what I disliked! The last rag of Gogol's worn-out clothes was burned; consumed to ashes was the last branch of that false, artificial olive tree with which the enchanting but sly Aurore Dudevant* had served me so pleasantly and for so long. I began to find that Gogol was a monster of a genius, who himself had grasped too late all the harm he was doing with his mighty comic talent. I began to suspect very angrily that Dudevant (whose slipper or the hem of whose skirt I had formerly thirsted to kiss—I had seriously dreamed of journeying to France, to Berry, to *Nohant* itself, for this purpose)—I began to suspect that she was, in turn, now *herself,* now not herself; now sincere, now dissembling. In *Lucrezia,* she is sincere; in *Tévérino* and her charming pastorals, sincere; in *The Sin of M. Antoine* and in her other socialist novels, false; for she was too clever not to understand that the wholesale destruction of the monarchy, of the nobilty, of the mystical, positive religions, of wars and inequality, would lead to such a ghastly prosaic existence that it would be terrible even to imagine it!

The aesthetic of *life* (not of art! the devil take art without life!) and the poetry of *actuality* are impossible without that diversity of situations and feelings which can only be developed thanks to inequality and conflict.

Aesthetics have preserved in me the sense of citizenship. Once I had understood that, for the *poetry of life* I so idolized, it was essential to have almost all of those general forms and aspects of

* Aurore Baronne Dudevant, née Dupin, alias George Sand (1804–1876). George Sand's, *Lucrezia Floriani, Tévérino,* and *The Sin of M. Antoine* are novels.

human development, to which I had been indifferent and sometimes even hostile during the ten years of my early adult life, and that it was necessary to resist their utilitarian destruction, it became clear to me which side I should take: the side of a many-faceted development or that of a pseudo-useful destruction.

The state, the monarchy, "the warrior class"—these I understood earlier and assessed them more quickly. The church, Orthodoxy, the "priests," so to speak, I came to appreciate and love only later. But all the same, I did come to *appreciate* them; and they, these benefactors of mine, revealed to me a simple and great thing, namely, that everyone *can believe*, if he will sincerely, humbly and ardently, thirst for faith and beg God to vouchsafe it to him. And I prayed, and I came to believe. I came to believe feebly, unworthily, but from my heart.

Since then I think, I believe, that *that* state is blessed where these "priests and warriors" (bishops, spiritual elders, and the generals of the sword) predominate, and woe to the state in which "the sophist and the rhetorician" (the professor and the lawyer) take precedence. The former impose a form upon life; they assist in its preservation; they do not allow the social *material* to be squandered on every side; the latter, by the *nature of their calling*, are inclined to assist in this destruction, in this deplorable wastage.

Since then I have been prepared to esteem and love so-called science *only when* it *freely* and *willingly* serves not only itself and democracy but also religion, as a dedicated and honest maid will serve a queen; as, for example, in our day this science was nobly enslaved by faith in Bishop Nikanor's * book *Positive Philosophy* or in Vladimir Solovyev's *The Criticism of Abstract Principles*, just as it also served Khomyakov's somewhat willful but nevertheless fundamentally deep Orthodox feeling. I respect science when, as a consequence of a certain *self-negation*, as a conse-

* Bishop Nikanor, or Brovkovich, (1827–1890), a Russian theologian and author of *The Positive Theology and the Supersensitive Existence* (1875–1888).

quence of frequent doubts as to one's own usefulness and useful strength, it prepares man's enlightened mind for the acceptance of *positive* beliefs; that is, of such beliefs, in the presence of which the spiritual, mysterious (mystical) principles cannot be expressed in some one abstract and tedious morality, but seek to incarnate themselves even in the *material* manifestations of outward devotion.

THE TRIUNE PROCESS OF DEVELOPMENT

What is the process of development?

NOW I must put aside for a time both the Slavs and our Russian Byzantinism and stray very far from my main subject.

I shall try, however, to be as brief as possible.

First of all, I shall ask myself the meaning of the word "development" in general. It is not by chance that this term is in constant use in our days. In this respect, the human mind is probably on the right path; it is applying, very correctly perhaps, to psychic life, to the historical life of individual people and societies, an idea worked out by the real natural sciences.

People are constantly saying "the development of the mind," "a developing people," "a developed man," "the development of literacy," "the laws of historical development," "the further development of our institutions," and so on.

From the article "Byzantinism and Slavdom." WORKS, *vol.* VI, *pp.* 187–209.

147

All this is fine. However, there are some mistakes here. When we examine the matter carefully, we see that the word "development" is sometimes used to denote quite diverse processes or states. Thus, for example, the term "a *developed* man" is often used in the sense of a *learned, well-read* or *educated* man. But this is not one and the same thing. An educated, formed, diversely trained man and a learned man are two different concepts. In Faust we have a really *developed* man; however, Goethe's Wagner is a scholar, *but not at all a developed man.*

Another example. "Development of literacy" among people does not seem to be a very appropriate expression.

The *spread,* the *diffusion* of literacy is another matter. The *spread* of literacy, the spread of drunkenness, the *spread* of cholera, the spread of good principles, sobriety, thrift, the spread of railways, and so on. All these phenomena represent the diffusion of something *homogeneous, general, simple.*

In those real, exact sciences from which it has been transposed into the historical sphere, the *idea of development* actually corresponds to a certain complex process; and this process is, let us note, not infrequently quite contrary to the process of *spreading and diffusion,* which is apparently hostile to the former.

Scrutinizing more closely the phenomena of organic life, from the observation of which this idea of development was taken, we can see that the process of development in organic life connotes the following:

A *gradual ascent from the simplest to the most complex, the* gradual individualization, *insulation, on the one hand, from the surrounding world and, on the other, from analogous and related phenomena.*

A *gradual transition from colorlessness, from simplicity, towards originality and complexity.*

A gradual complication of the component elements, *an increase in inner* riches and, at the same time, a gradual consolidation of unity.

Thus the *highest point of development,* not only in organic bodies but in organic phenomena in general, *is the* highest degree of complexity, *held together by a certain inner despotic unity.*

The very growth of grass, of a tree, of an animal, and so on, is already a complication; if we merely refer to growth, we have in view preeminently the quantitative rather than the qualitative aspect, a change in dimensions rather than a change in form.

With growth, the content is quantitatively complicated. The grass, let us suppose, has not yet produced either flowers or fruit, but it has risen, has grown, even though we had not noticed in it any inner (microscopic) or outer, visible, morphological change or enrichment; but we have, all the same, the right to state that the grass has become more complex, because the *quantity* of its cells and fibers has increased.

Moreover, close inspection demonstrates that in the process of development there is always present a ceaseless change in form as well as in the parts (for example, in dimension, and in the aspect of the cells and fibers), as well as in general (that is, there appear new traits, heretofore not present in the picture of the organism as a whole).

The same applies to the development of an animal body, to the development of a human organism, and even to the development of the human spirit and character.

I have spoken of not only whole organisms but also all *organic processes* and all the parts of organisms—in a word, all organic phenomena obey the same law.

Let us take, for example, the general picture of a disease.* *Pneumonia,* let us suppose. For the most part, it begins *simply,* so simply that it is impossible to distinguish it strictly at the start from a common cold, from *bronchitis, pleurisy,* and many other dangerous or slight diseases. Indisposition, temperature, pain in

* I fear being reproached here for the length and the details of what others are prepared to consider to be an ordinary simile. Simile is not only an ornament of language; it makes the main subject more accessible and clear, if it is appropriate and *brief.* Long, boring similes can only confuse and distract the mind. But I hasten to admit that I have here pretensions to something far *grander than a simile:* I can claim to be suggesting something in the nature of a hypothesis for social or historical science.

the chest or in the side, cough. If a man were to die at this moment of something else (if he had been shot, for example), we would find very few changes in his lungs, *very few signs to distinguish them from other lungs*. A disease that is still *undeveloped, still uncomplicated*, and, therefore, *not yet individualized* and strong is not yet dangerous, not deadly, still *little influential*. The more complex the picture, the greater the variety of distinctive symptoms, the easier it is to individualize, classify, and separate the disease; yet on the other hand, it becomes stronger and more influential. The previous symptoms still remain: temperature, pain, fever, weakness, cough, difficulty in breathing, and so on. But there are now also new symptoms: the urine, depending on the occasion, can vary in color from brick red to lemon. And auscultation finally shows a specific *rhonchus crepitans*. Then comes the moment when the picture becomes most complex: in one section of the lungs we note a simple *rhonchus crepitans*, peculiar which is also symptomatic of other processes; in another section, a *rhonchus crepitans* (like the gentle crackling of hair that we rub slowly close to the ear); in a third place, the auscultation of the chest gives us a bronchial *souffle tubaire*, which resembles the sound made by blowing into a pipe. This sound denotes the congestion of the lungs, for the air can no longer pass through. Finally, side by side with this, a swelling, a cavity, and then we can hear and see other new phenomena and discover a more complex picture. A dissection will reveal the same thing: (1) *strength*, (2) *complexity*, (3) *individualization*.

Further, if the organism is recovering its health, the picture of the disease will become simplified.

If, however, the disease is triumphing, then, on the contrary, the *picture of the organism* becomes, either suddenly or gradually, simplified.

If recovery is in sight, the complexity and the variety of symptoms composing the general picture of the disease gradually decrease. The urine becomes more normal (less individualized); the hoarseness becomes more normal, similar to the rattle of other coughs; the temperature declines, the congestion is resolved; that is the lungs again become *more homogeneous, more uniform.*

If death is near, *a simplification of the organism* takes place. In the case of all dying people, their last hours are more analogous, simpler than the middle stage of the disease. Death follows, which, as it has been said, makes all equal. The picture of a corpse is less complex than that of a living organism. In a corpse everything gradually merges, interpenetrates, the liquids congeal, the firm tissues grow soft, all the colors of the body merge into one greenish-brown hue. Very soon it becomes difficult to distinguish one corpse from another. Then the simplification and the merging of the component parts, continuing, turn more and more into a process of corruption, decomposition, dissolution, diffusion in the surrounding elements. The soft parts of the corpse, falling apart, decomposing into their chemical, component parts, arrive at the state of extreme inorganic simplicity of carbon, hydrogen, and oxygen, *dissolve* and *spread* in the surrounding world. The bones, owing to the great strength of the inner chain of calcareous lime, which is their foundation, outlast all the rest; but, given favorable conditions, the bones also soon crumble, first into parts and then into wholly inorganic and impersonal dust.

Thus if we take any *developed* thing, whether a disease (a complex and uniform organic process) or a living, flourishing body (a complex, uniform organism), we shall see only one thing, namely, that certain phenomena precede the decomposition and the *death of the second* (organism) and the *destruction of the first* (process): a simplification of the component parts, *a diminution in the number of symptoms, a weakening of the unity,* of the strength, and, at the same time, a displacement.* Every-

* Whether I am right or not, whether I have expressed my thought ill or well, is another question. I should only like to warn you that it is not a matter here of similes, but of a wish to point out that the laws of development and *decline* of states are, in their general outlines, related not only to the laws of the organic world but also in general to the laws of birth, existence, and death (*Enstehen, Dasein* und *Vergehen*) of all existing things. Everyone knows that a state can fall, but *how?* What are the *symptoms?* And are there such symptoms *now?* If so, where? That is my aim! (K. L., 1874.)

thing gradually becomes lowered, intermixed, merged, and only then does it crumble and perish, passing into a more general substance, which exists not in itself and not for itself.

Before the final death, the individualization of the parts, as well as of the whole, become weaker. Whatever perishes becomes both more uniform internally and closer to the surrounding world, as well as more analogous to more closely related phenomena (that is, *freer*).

Thus the eggs of all females are internally less complex and nearer to the mother's organism than the foetuses, and are more analogous to other animal and vegetable primitive cells.

The various animal foetuses are more differentiated than the eggs; they are *already more* microscopically *differentiated* one from another; they are less analogous. The mature fruits of the womb are even more heterogeneous and distinct. This is because they are at once more complex and more unified, that is, more developed.

Infants and children are even more complex and heterogeneous; young and mature men develop further and further until they fall into senility. They are more and more complex (according to their stage and degree of development) and have more inner unity, and therefore they have more distinct characteristics, more separateness, more freedom from their surroundings, more singularity, more independence.

And this, I repeat, has a bearing not only on organisms but also on their parts, on systems (the nervous, the circulatory, and so on), on the apparatuses (the digestive, the breathing, and so on); it has a bearing also on normal and pathological processes and even on those ideal, scientific, collective units which are called appearance, species, class, and so on. The higher, the more developed, are the appearance, the species, and the class, the more diverse are the parts (the parts composing them), while the collective, integral whole remains extremely unified and natural. Thus a domestic dog is a highly developed animal; for this reason, that division of mammals known under the name of domestic dog is a very complete division, having a great variety of representatives. The species of cats (in the broad sense), the species of the four-armed (monkeys), the species of the vertebrates in general—these represent, despite their extraordinary diversity, an extreme unity of general plan. These are all divisions of extremely developed animals, very rich in zoological content, very individualized, rich in distinctive *signs*.

We can observe the same thing in vegetable organisms, in processes, organs, and the vegetable classification into divisions, collective units.

In the beginning anything is simple, then it becomes complex; and then there is a secondary simplification, first equalizing and merging internally and then simplifying itself still further through the loss of its parts and through a general decomposition, prior to passing into an inorganic "Nirvana."

On further reflection, we can see that this triune process applies not only to the world we call organic but also, perhaps, to all things that exist in space and time. Perhaps this process also applies to the heavenly bodies, to the history of the development of their mineral crust, and to the human character. This process can be clearly seen in the development of the arts, schools of painting, and musical and architectural styles, in philosophical systems, in the history of religions, and, finally, in the *life of tribes, state organisms, and entire cultural worlds.*

I cannot here discuss this at length or develop my thought in detail. I shall confine myself to a few brief examples and elucidations. For example, in the case of a heavenly body, we have (1) a period of *primary simplicity:* a molten heavenly body, uniform, liquified; (2) a middle period, which may be termed, in general, a state of flowering complexity: a planet covered with a crust, with water, with continents, vegetation, *inhabited, variegated;* (3) a period of *secondary simplicity,* the result of a catastrophe: a congealed molten body.

We notice the same thing in the history of the arts: (1) a period of primary simplicity: Cyclopic structures, conelike Etruscan graves (which probably served as the original model for cupolas and, in general, for the rounded lines of the more developed Roman architecture), Russian peasant huts, the Doric order, and so on; the epic songs of primitive tribes, early icon painting, popular woodcuts, and so on; (2) a period of flowering complexity: the Parthenon, the temple of Diana at Ephesus (even the columns of which are sculptured), the cathedrals of Strasbourg, Rheims, Milan, St. Peter's, St. Mark's, the great Roman buildings; Sophocles, Dante, Shakespeare, Byron, Raphael, Michelangelo, and so on; (3) a period of displacement or transition to a secondary simplification, of decline, of replacement by something else: all the buildings of transitional periods—the Romanesque style (from the decline of the Roman style to the advent of the Gothic); all of the present-day utilitarian structures—barracks, hospitals, schools, railway stations, and so on. In architecture, unity is what is called style. In the flowering ages, the buildings tend to be diverse within the limits of a particular style; there is no eclecticism, no giftless, senile simplicity. In poetry also: Sophocles, Aeschylus, and Euripides are all of one style; afterwards everything becomes eclectically and coldly mixed, becomes debased, and then declines.

In literature, contemporary realism may serve as an example of the secondary simplification of previous European styles. It has in it something of the eclectic (that is, *mixed*), the *debased*, the quantitatively lower, the *flat* in style. The typical representatives of the grand style in poetry are all extremely dissimilar; they have an extraordinary amount of inner content, many distinctive signs, much individuality. They have a great deal of what belongs to their age (content) and of what belongs to them alone, to their personality, to that unity of personal spirit which they inject into the varied content. Such are Dante, Shakespeare, Corneille, Racine, Byron, Walter Scott, Goethe, Schiller.

At the present time, especially after the year 1848, all things are more mixed and more like each other: a general style is the absence of style, the absence of a subjective spirit, the absence of love, of feeling. Dickens in England and George Sand in France (I am referring to her earlier works), however they might differ, were the last representatives of a complex unity, strength, richness, and warmth. The realism of plain observation is poorer and simpler, because it has no author, no personality, no inspiration behind it, because it is more vulgar, more *democratic, more accessible* to every nontalented person, whether a writer or a reader.

The objective, impersonal, universal realism of the present day represents a secondary *mixed simplification,* which succeeded the warm objectivity of Goethe, Walter Scott, Dickens, and the earlier George Sand. That and no more.

The vulgar, popular odes, madrigals, and epics of the last century represented a similar kind of simplification, a debased version of earlier French classicism, the high classicism of Corneille, Racine, and Molière.

The same is true of the history of philosophy: (1) a primitive simplicity: the simple sayings of the popular wisdom, the simple elementary systems (Thales and others); (2) a flowering complexity: Socrates, Plato, the Stoics, the Epicureans, Pythagoras, Descartes, Spinoza, Leobnitz, Kant, Fichte, Schelling, Hegel; (3) a secondary simplification, mixing, and elimination, a transition into something entirely new: eclectics, an impersonal mixing of all periods (Cousin); then phenomenal realism, repudiating abstract philosophy and metaphysics: the materialists, the deists, the atheists. Realism is *very simple,* for it is not even a system, but only a method, a device: it implies the *death* of the preceding systems. Materialism is indisputably a system, but of course one of the *simplest,* for nothing can be simpler and cruder, less complex, than to maintain that everything is matter and that there is no God, no spirit, no immortality of the soul because we cannot see or touch these things. In our time, this secondary simplification of philosophy is (applicable) not only to educated youths, who, because of their age, are themselves at a stage of primitive simplicity, at the same stage as apples that are not yet ripe or seminarists of Cyclopic build, as Paris workers even, tavern waiters, and so on. Materialism almost always goes hand in hand with realism, although realism in itself does not give one the right to be either an atheist or a materialist. Realism repudiates every system, every metaphysics; realism is despair, self-emasculation, and *that is why it is a simplification!* But it does not give us the right to draw *materialistic conclusions.*

Materialism is the last of the systems of the preceding age; it will reign until realism is able firmly to say its sceptical word about it. Scepticism and realism are, as a rule, succeeded by a renaissance: some people adhere to ideal systems, while others ardently turn to religion. It was so in antiquity; it was so at the beginning of our age, following the realism and materialism of the eighteenth century.

Both metaphysics and religion continue to be real forces, actual and indestructible necessities for mankind.

Political organisms are subject to the same law, and so are the cultures of the world. Very clearly, they also pass through these three stages: (1) that of *primitive simplicity,* (2) that of *flowering complexity,* and (3) that of *secondary fusion and simplification.* I shall refer to them more specifically further on.

The development of a state is constantly accompanied by the elucidation and individualization of the form appropriate to it; the decline of a state is expressed in the disintegration of that form, in a greater *communion with the surrounding environment.*

First of all, let me ask, "What is form?"

Form, in general, is the expression of an idea enclosed in matter (content). It is the negative moment of the phenomenon; matter is the positive one. In what sense? Let us assume that glass is the matter we are given; its form is manifest in a glass, a cylindrical vessel, hollow inside; the air around or the liquid inside the vessel begins where the glass ends, where it no longer is; the matter of the glass cannot, dare not, extend any further if it wishes to remain true to its fundamental idea of a hollow glass, if it does not wish to cease being a glass.

Form is the despotism of an inner idea, which will not allow matter to spread. The phenomenon perishes when it breaks the bond of this natural despotism.

The spherical or the elliptical shape, which liquid assumes under certain conditions, is form—the despotism of the inner idea.

Crystallization is the despotism of an inner idea. Under certain conditions a certain substance must, while remaining itself, crystallize into prisms, another substance into octagonals, and so on.

These substances dare not behave otherwise; if they do, they will perish, disintegrate.

Vegetable and animal morphology is likewise nothing but the science of why an olive tree *dare not* become an oak tree, just as an oak tree dare not become a palm tree, and so on; from the seed, they are foreordained to have these particular leaves, and no other, these particular flowers and fruit, and no other.

A sculptor chiseling a statue of a human being from stone or casting it in bronze (in matter) or making an ivory ball or pasting and sewing an artificial flower from rags imposes his idea upon matter from the outside, upon matter which he has discovered in nature.

Making a machine, he does likewise. The machine in part servilely obeys the idea put into it from the outside by man's thought; in part it obeys its own inner law, its own physicochemical structure, its own basic physicochemical idea. It is impossible, for example, to make as solid a machine from ice as from bronze or iron.

On the other hand, one cannot make as natural a flower from stone as from velvet or muslin.

He who wants to be a true realist where it is necessary must also examine human societies from a similar point of view. But usually this is not done like that. *Freedom, equality, prosperity* (especially this prosperity!) are taken to be dogmas of faith, and people assure us that this is a very rational and scientific thing!

Who said that this was true?

Social science was hardly born when, ignoring the experience of centuries and the examples of *nature they respect* so much, people refused to see that there was no logical relation between the egalitarian-liberal forward movement and the idea of development. One can even add that the *egalitarian-liberal process is the very antithesis of the process of development.* In the case of the latter, the inner idea holds the social material in its organizing, despotic embrace and sets a limit to its centrifugal and disintegrating trend. Progress, which is hostile to every kind of despotism—the despotism of classes, workshops, monasteries, even wealth, and so on—is *nothing but a process of disintegration,* the process of the secondary *simplification of the whole and the mixing of the component parts* of which I have spoken above, a process of composing morphological outlines, a process of destroying those peculiarities which were organically (that is, despotically) appropriate to the social body.

The phenomena of egalitarian-liberal progress are comparable to the phenomena of combustion, decomposition, the melting of ice (water less free, limited by crystallization); they may be likened, for example, to the phenomena of the cholera process, which gradually transforms originally rather diverse people into more uniform corpses (equality), then into almost completely comparable skeletons (equality), and finally into free elements (relatively so, of course), such as nitrogen, hydrogen, oxygen, and so on.

("*On est debordé,*" many people say. This is another matter. With cholera also "*on est debordé.*" But why not call cholera by its proper name? Why call it youth, rebirth, *development, organization?*)

In all these processes of decomposition, combustion, melting, the progressive movement of cholera, one perceives the same phenomena.

(1) The loss of the peculiarities which have till then distinguished the despotically formed whole tree, animal, whole texture, whole crystal, and so on, from everything else *similar* and contiguous.

(2) A greater *resemblance in the component parts*, a greater *inner equality*, a greater uniformity in the structure, and so on.

(3) The loss of former, *strict*, morphological outlines; now everything merges, ever more *freely* and uniformly.

Thus, what has private, historical, real science to do with discomforts, necessities, despotism, sufferings?

What need have we of these unscientific sentimentalities, so banal in our day, so prosaic moreover, so lacking in talent? Why in such a question should I be concerned with human groans?

What scientific right have I to think about the final causes, about goals, about prosperity, for example, before undertaking serious, lengthy, and impartial research?

Where is this research, this undogmatic, impartial, and I may even say—in the progressive sense—perhaps unethical but scientifically honest research? Where is it? Let us assume it exists, though in a still imperfect state, but it is neither for democrats nor for progressives.

Why should I be concerned, in more or less abstract research, with not only other people's but also *my own discomforts, my own groans and sufferings?*

A political state is like a tree, which attains to its full growth, flowering, and fruitfulness by obeying a certain mysterious, autonomous, despotic, governing inner idea lodged within it. A state is also a machine, fabricated half-consciously by people and maintaining people like machine parts, like wheels, levers, screws, atoms; and finally it is like a machine perfecting and forming people. In the state, a man is at one and the same time a mechanic, the wheels or a screw, and the product of a social organism.

Whichever of the states, ancient or modern, we may examine, in all of them we shall find one and the same thing in common: simplicity and uniformity in the beginning, *greater equality* and greater *freedom* (at least *de facto,* if not legal freedom) *than there will be later.* Closing the book on the second or third chapter, we find that all beginnings are fairly similar, though not quite. Glancing at a plant sprouting out of the soil, we do not yet know what it will become. There are too few distinct features. Afterwards we note a greater or lesser *assertion of power,* a more profound or less sharp (depending on its primordial predisposition) division of classes, a greater *variety* of life and *diversity* of character in the regions.

At the same time, the wealth increases, on the one hand, and poverty, on the other; the resources of pleasure become more varied, on the one hand, while, on the other, the variety and refinement (development) of sensations and needs give birth to greater sufferings, greater grief, greater mistakes and greater undertakings, more poetry and more comedy; the exploits of the educated—of Themistocles, Xenophon, Alexander—are on a grander scale and more appealing than the simple and crude exploits of Odysseus and Achilles. Then a Sophocles appears, an Aristophanes appears, the ranting heroes of a Corneille appear, the laughter of a Molière resounds. In other places, a Sophocles and an Aristophanes, a Corneille and a Molière, merge together to produce a Shakespeare or a Goethe.

In general, these complex, flowering ages are dominated by some kind of aristocracy, either a political one with privileges and a position, or one merely representing a way of life, that is, an aristocracy with a social position but without decisive privileges; or again an aristocracy more often standing on the dividing line between politics and a way of life. The eupatridae of Athens, the feudal satraps of Persia, the *optimates* of Rome, the marquises of France, the lords of England, the warriors of Egypt, the Spartans of Laconia, the notable *dvoryane* of Russia, the pans of Poland, the beys of Turkey.

At the same time, because of the inner necessity of centralization, there also exists a tendency towards absolute monarchical power, which, either *de jure* or *de facto*, always asserts itself in an age of flowering complexity. There appear on the scene remarkable dictators, emperors, kings, or, at least, demagogues and tyrants (in an ancient Hellenic sense) of genius, such as Themistocles, Pericles, and so on.

Between a Pericles, the *de facto* dictator, and a lawful hereditary and religiously consecrated sovereign, there is a whole ladder of diverse personal rulers, who are needed everywhere in complex and flowering ages in order to unify all the component parts, all the real social forces, full of life and ferment.

In such times the provinces are always varied in their way of life, their rights and laws. The tree has completely fulfilled its inner morphological idea.

And what about pain? Pain is equally part of the process of growth and development, as well as of the process of disintegration.

Grain aches with pain in the initial stages of germination. The first shoots ache; stalks and stems ache as they grow; so do the developing leaves; and the blooming of luxurious flowers (aristocracy and art) is accompanied by moans and tears. An equal pain is felt during the rapidly developing egalitarian process of corruption and the process of slow drying up and stagnation which not infrequently precedes the egalitarian process. (For example, in Spain, in the Venetian Republic, in the whole of Italy, the *withering* of the seventeenth and eighteenth centuries preceded the decomposition that set in in the nineteenth.) From the standpoint of *the social sciences* this pain is the ultimate, the most elusive *of the symptoms*; it is subjective, and it is impossible to establish the true statistics of sufferings, the exact statistics of feelings, until some kind of graphic equivalent is invented for feelings of joy, indifference, and grief, some kind of graphic symbol, some kind of objective standard, as when it was unexpectedly discovered that spectral analysis can be used to detect the chemical composition of the heavenly bodies so removed in infinite space from us!

Oh, you realist friends, open some medical books! In them you will find to what an extent the musical, subjective standard is regarded as less important than the sum of all other plastic, objective symptoms; the picture of the organism, as it is manifest to the eyes of a doctor-physiologist, is the important thing, rather than the feelings of a suborned patient who does not understand! Terrible neuralgias, which drive patients to despair, do not prevent them from living a long time and from doing important things, while a quiet, almost painless gangrene can send them to their grave within a few days.

Instead of taking up naïvely or dishonestly, with some finite happiness in view, various preconceived positions, communist, democratic, liberal, and so on, it would be more scientific to submit all these points of view to an identical, impartial, ruthless, evaluation; and if the sum total were to favor either a liberal or a conservative, with a class or a classless view, then the fault, so to speak, would not be ours, but that of science.

No statistics exist for the evaluation of the subjective happiness of individuals; no one can tell under what rule people live more pleasantly. Revolts and revolutions have little proof to offer in this connection. Many people enjoy a revolt. The Cretans of our day, for example, lived positively better than the Bulgarians and Greeks in Thrace and incomparably more gaily and pleasantly than the not so rich inhabitants of any of the large towns. A conscientious man, an alert one, not corrupted by politics, not blind, was in the end astonished by the flourishing aspect of the Cretans—their beauty and health, the modest cleanliness of their dwellings, their excellent, honest family life, the pleasant self-assurance and dignity of their gait and their hospitality. They were the first of the Turkish subjects to revolt, imagining themselves to be the unhappiest of mortals, whereas the Bulgarians and the Greeks in Thrace lived far worse and suffered at that time incomparably greater personal injuries and oppressions both from a vicious police and from their own cunning elders; but they did not revolt, and the Bulgarian elders even supplied the Sultan with addresses and offered to support him with arms against the Cretans.

There are no statistics for determining whether it is better for private individuals to live in a republic than in a monarchy, in a limited monarchy than in an absolute one, in an egalitarian state than in a class-structured one, in an affluent state than in a poor one. For this reason, setting aside the standard of affluence as an ideal unattainable as yet to contemporary social sciences (an ideal perhaps forever inexact and of little use), we would be far less in error if we turned to objectivity and inquired whether there do not exist any universal and quite simple laws of the development and the disintegration of human societies.

Since we do not know whether a universal kingdom of happiness is possible, let us try, at least in accordance with the means at our disposal, to attain, by our efforts, what is appropriate for the *good* of *this or that exceptional state*. To find out what is good for the organism, it is necessary first of all to understand clearly the nature of the organism itself. For hygiene and medical training, it is necessary in the first place to base ourselves on physiology.

Form (as I have said above) is an inner idea expressed on the surface of the content. The idea of a circle, for example, is the equidistance of the center from all the points on the circumference. Is this idea not expressed by the circumference of a circle? Does it not impart this form to bones, to a tree, to a drop of water, to a molten heavenly body, and so on? To content and matter, in general?

This is evident in such a simple phenomenon as a sphere, but it is not so evident in such a complex phenomenon as human society.

Nevertheless, the metaphysical foundation is the same in the case of a small sphere or a great state.

Each nation, each society, has *its own* political form of state;

in its main aspects these foundations are immutable to the historical grave; but from the start to the finish, the parts change either more rapidly or more slowly.

To begin with, the formation of the state is neither sudden nor conscious; it is not immediately obvious; it reaches its full expression only in the middle period of maximum complexity and highest unity, a period which is always succeeded sooner or later by the frequent deterioration of this form and its subsequent disintegration and collapse.

Thus the political form of ancient Egypt was a monarchy based on a sharply defined class society, a monarchy in all likelihood profoundly limited by a priestly aristocracy and religious laws in general.

Persia was evidently more feudal in character; but her feudalism was kept in check by a monarch who was absolute in principle and who represented the earthly image of good (Ormuzd).

The history of Greece and Rome was elaborated in greater detail, and therefore presents us with a much clearer picture of all this.

In their period of flowering, the Athenians had elaborated a political form most suited to their idea of the state.

This was a democratic republic, but one based on privileged classes, the eupatridae, on a property qualification for voting, slaves, and, finally, on a tendency towards a *de facto*, unlegalized, instable dictatorship of a Pericles, Themistocles, and so on.

This form, the natural pledge of which was preserved, of course, in the very customs and circumstances, was elaborated during the flowering, complex period of Athens, from the days of Solon to the Peloponnesian War. It was during this war that the damage was done—the egalitarian *progress* had started.

There had been plenty of freedom before this. What the Athenians wanted now was greater equality.

Sparta, from the age of Lycurgus to its humiliation by the Thebans, had also elaborated its own extremely original, coercive, and despotic form of aristocratic, republican communism, with something like two hereditary presidents.

The Spartan form was incomparably more coercive and despotic than the Athenian, and for this reason there was more vitality and creativity in Athens than in Sparta, but Sparta in the end proved stronger and more enduring.

All the remaining states of the Greek world probably wavered between the Doric form of Sparta and the Ionic form of Athens. The necessity for form, coercion, despotism, discipline, resulting from the need for self-preservation, was so great in this loose and centrifugal Hellenic world that in many states of a democratic character (that is, probably there, where class despotism was more weakly expressed) tyranny was established, that is, the discipline of peronal power (Polycrates, Periander, Dionysius of Syracuse, and others).

Feudalism, that of the village or of the landowner and the knight, was apparently almost as insignificant in Hellas as it was in Rome. All the aristocracies of Hellas and Rome had an urban character; they were, all of them, of municipal origin.

The history of Macedonia, poor as it is, provides us with very little evidence concerning the primitive organization of the Macedonian kingdom. But certain historians suppose that in Macedonia feudalism was more strongly entrenched than the municipality (actually, there is hardly any mention of Macedonian cities; one only hears of the kings and their *armed retainers*, and of Alexander's "generals").

The weakened world of Greek city-states, having later become unified with the crude, vague (undeveloped, probably) feudalism of the Macedonians, instantly attained to state unity under Philip and Alexander, and only then became strong enough to expand its civilization as far as India and the interior of Africa. *It would seem again that a great complexity of form—the conjunction of aristocracy and monarchy—is essential in order to produce the maximum greatness and strength.*

The flowering period of Rome must be considered, I suppose, to extend from the times of the Punic wars to the age of the Antonines approximately.

It was at this time that the Romans elaborated their own form of municipal elective dictatorship—that of the Empire, which disciplined Rome for so long and which later proved of service to Byzantium.

We can observe the same thing among the European states.

The Italy that grew upon the ruins of Rome in the age of the Renaissance elaborated earlier than any other European state its own political form of state in the *shape of two extreme antitheses* —on the one hand, a form of the highest centralization as exemplified in the papacy as a political entity, which embraced the whole Catholic world far beyond the borders of Italy, and, on the other, for Italy itself, an extremely decentralized form of city-states and small aristocratic states, which perpetually wavered between oligarchy (Venice and Genoa) and monarchy (Naples, Tuscany, and so on).

The form of the state innate to Spain came to be clarified somewhat later. The Spanish state assumed the form of an autocratic and aristocratic monarchy, but one that was not strongly centralized and was hard on local and partly corporate liberties and privileges, something between that of Italy and France. The age of Charles V and Philip II was an age of flowering.

The form of the state peculiar to France was to a high degree *centralized, extremely class-divided, autocratic monarchy*. This form gradually clarified itself in the days of Louis XI, Francis I, Richelieu, and Louis XIV. It became distorted in 1789.

The form of the state in England was (and partly still is) a limited, initially less class-divided, decentralized monarchy, or, as others define it, an aristocratic republic *with a hereditary president*. This form found its expression almost at the same time as the French form—in the reigns of Henry VIII, Elizabeth, and William of Orange.

The form of the state in Germany, (until the time of Napoleon I and the years 1848 and 1871) was as follows: an alliance of small, separate, class-divided, more or less autocratic states, with an elective suzerain and Emperor (it was of feudal, not municipal origin).

All these clearly elaborated forms began to change gradually in some countries from the eighteenth and in others from the nineteenth century. *In all of these states there began an egalitarian and liberal process.*

One may well believe that this process brings some kind of common benefit to the universe, but not in any way to the continued preservation of those distinct political worlds.

Reaction is not wrong, because it does not see the truth. No, that is not the case. Reaction everywhere has an *empirical sense of truth*; but the separate cells, the fibers, the tissues, and the parts of the organism had become stronger in their egalitarian impulses than in the power of their inner, organizing, despotic idea!

The atoms of a globe no longer wish to be the component parts of that globe! The cells and the fibers of a hewed-down and withering tree burn here, wither there, rot elsewhere, mix everywhere, praising the simplicity of the future, of new organization, without noticing that this mixing process is a terrible moment of transition from organic complexity to inorganic simplicity—to free water, lifeless dust, uncrystallized, melted, or ground salt!

Until the days of Pericles, until the days of Cyrus and Darius, of Caesar, Augustus, St. Constantine, Francis I, Louis XIV, William of Orange, Pitt, Frederick II, and so on, all progressivists were right, all conservatives wrong. At such times the progressivists lead a nation or state to flowering and growth. At such times, the conservatives, not understanding it, erroneously do not believe either in growth or flowering, or they have a dislike for this flowering and growth.

Then, after a flowering and complex age, the process of secondary simplification and the mixing of contours sets in, that is, a larger uniformity in the regions, a mixture of the classes, the mobility and the vacillation of the authorities, the abasement of religion, a similarity in education, and so on. But, as soon as the despotism of the formological process falters, then, *in the sense of "for the good of the state,"* all the progressivists become wrong in theory, although they triumph in practice; for they follow the current and rush down the slope. They triumph; they enjoy a loud success.

On the contrary, *all the conservatives* and the friends of reaction are *right in theory* when the process of the secondary, simplifying in mixing begins; *for it is their desire to improve and strengthen the organism.* It is not their fault that their triumph does not last very long; it is not their fault that the nation is no longer capable of suffering the discipline of the abstract idea of the state hidden within it!

They perform their duty, all the same; and insofar as they can, they delay the process of decomposition and attempt to bring back the nation, sometimes by force, to the cult of the political idea that created it.

Until the day of flowering, it is better to be a sail or a steam engine. After this irrevocable day, it is more worthy to act as an anchor or a brake for the peoples that are rushing steeply downhill, striving as they do often naïvely in good faith, to shouts of triumph and with unfurled banners of hope, until some Sedan, Chironeia, or Arbela, some Alaric or Mohammed II, or some city like Paris, set on fire by petrol and blown up by dynamite, will open their eyes to the real state of affairs.

I foresee another objection: I know I may be told that the process of *mixing* is more apparent than that of *simplification* before the collapse of cultured life and the political fall of a state. This is true of antiquity as well as the present day. But, first of all, this very process of mixing is a kind of simplification of the picture, the simplification of both the legal texture and the ornamental aspect of everyday life. The mixing of all colors produces gray or white. But the fundamental point is this. Let me ask: are they simple—the present-day Copts, the descendants of the Egyptians, or the Arabs of Syria? Were they simple, the *pagani,* the rustic idol worshippers, who persisted in their beliefs in the higher strata of society after the decline and fall of the Helleno-Roman religion as cults and culture? Were they simple, the Greek Christians who lived under the Turkish yoke until the rebellion of the 1820s? Are they simple, the Gebrs, who are the last remnant of the fire worshippers in the cultural Persian-Median world?

Of course all the communities and national remnants just enumerated are *incomparably* simpler than were the people, the communities, and the nations in the age of the flowering of Egypt, the Caliphate, Greco-Roman civilization, than the Persians in the times of Darius or the Byzantines in the days of John the Goldenmouthed. People are simpler personally in their thoughts and tastes, in the uncomplicated character of their consciousness and needs; communities and entire national or religious residues are simpler in character because the people of their milieu are *all very alike* and *equal* among themselves. Thus, first comes the process of mixing and a *certain degree of secondary abasement* (that is, of a *quantitative simplification*); then comes the *death of an original culture in the higher strata of society* or the *fall of the state* and, finally, the *secondary simplicity* of the national and religious remnants, which are still experiencing their original political form. Now (in the nineteenth century) people tend to think of the *disease* that precedes death as the ideal *hygiene* of the future! The ideal of a Proudhon and a Cabet is a state of the most complete uniformity for people as regards their position, their education, and so on. What can be simpler according to this ideal?

THE AVERAGE EUROPEAN

OH, HATEFUL equality! Oh, base uniformity! Oh, thrice-accursed progress!

Oh, the massive, blood-soaked, but picturesque mountain of universal history! Since the end of the last century you have been laboring in torments of new births. And out of your suffering depths merely a mouse crawls out! A self-satisfied caricature of the people of former days is born, the *average rational European,* in his comic clothes that even the ideal mirror of art cannot reflect, with a small and self-deluded mind, with his creepy, practical good will!

No! never yet in the history of our times has anybody seen such a monstrous combination of mental pride before God and ethical submission before the ideal of a homogeneous, gray, laboring, and godlessly passionless all-mankind!

Is it possible to love such a mankind?

From the article "The Average European as the Ideal and Instrument of Universal Destruction." WORKS, *vol.* VI, *pp.* 268–269.

Should one not, with all the strength of even a Christian soul, hate—not the people who are stupid and have lost their way—but a *future* of theirs such as this?

Yes, one should! One should! Thrice, one should! For it hath been said, "Love thy neighbor, and hate his sins!"

PROUDHON AND HERZEN

AFTER Proudhon, who, like Bazarov,* desired that all people should resemble each other "like trees in a forest," I shall cite the opinion of Herzen, his contemporary and, a thinker of almost the same views as Proudhon until he was *horrified by the prosaic perspective of reducing all men to the mire of the European bourgeois and the honest laborer that Proudhon so admired.*

Herzen, as an aesthete of genius of the 1840s, was sickened first of all by the image of this average European figure in a top hat and frock coat, a figure which, though worthy in a small way, persistent, hard-working, self-satisfied, stoical perhaps in his own fashion, and undoubtedly honest in many respects, bore in his heart no ideal except that of transforming all and sundry into a

---

* Bazarov—the "nihilist" hero of Turgenev's novel *Fathers and Sons* (1862). His views on the subject may be found on p. 88 of the Signet edition of this novel. He and his friend Arcady represent the revolt of the younger generation of the 1860's against the "idealists" of the 1840's. Tr.

WORKS, *vol.* VI, *pp. 28–29.*

semblance of himself and was in *appearance* incredibly prosaic, a figure out of the stone age.

Herzen was so audacious and noble that he did not attempt to conceal his aristocratic squeamishness. And for this let him be honored and famed. He was a specialist, so to speak, in the sphere of the real aesthetics of life, an expert in the elegance and expressiveness of life itself. (Thus, for example, what he liked about Byron was *his life*—his eternal wanderings in the then savage lands of southern Europe, in Spain, Italy, Greece, and Turkey; his bravado, his yearning, his physical endurance in athletic exercises; his capricious demagogy for its own sake rather than for immediate political purposes; his original detestation of his own country, of which he was, however, the natural product from head to foot.) Initially Herzen and Proudhon walked hand in hand, but very soon their paths diverged radically.

Herzen represents the best antithesis to Proudhon. Proudhon has no concern with the aesthetics of life; for Herzen this aesthetic is everything!

As soon as Herzen perceived that the French worker, whom he pitied so much at the beginning and on whom he set so much hope (to stimulate new aesthetic trends in history), desired nothing more than to become himself a *petty bourgeois*, that there was nothing in the least enigmatic about this worker's soul, and that there was nothing original or actually *new* in his notions, Herzen cooled off towards the worker and turned away from him as he did also from Europe as a whole; and after this he began to believe more in Russia and in her original, non-European, and nonbourgeois future.

Herzen wished to see *poetry* and strength in the human character. John Stuart Mill wished that, too. Proudhon's ideal of a universal *bourgeois assimilation* horrified him. But he suggested an impossible antidote, that of bold and original thinkers, of peculiar and diverse thought on a social soil, in the midst of a public life which was ceasing more and more to provide *varied and distinctive impressions*.

THRACE

THRACE and Southern Macedonia, the two provinces of European Turkey closest to the Bosporus and Tsargrad, are of vital importance to us. They are important not only because of this proximity but also because both these countries have a mixed population; they are neither purely Bulgarian, like Danubian Bulgaria and Northern Macedonia, nor purely Greek, like Crete or the Epirotic-Thessalian districts. These two nations, the Greek and the Bulgarian, are, each in its own way, of extreme importance to us. For many reasons, historical as well as geographical, the Bulgarians and the Greeks are of greater importance to us than the Serbian tribe. I shall here enumerate certain of these reasons.

The Bulgarians, until lately, were the most backward, orphaned, so to speak, tribe of all the Christian peoples subject to Turkey. They were, *all of them,* under the sovereignty of the

---

From "My Recollections about Thrace," 1879. WORKS, *vol.* V, *pp.* 323–335.

Sultan—beginning with the borders of Serbia, from the suburbs of Solun and the holy Mount Atros, from the lower Danube to the last Bulgarian villages at the gates of Tsargrad itself. At that time no free center of national political attraction had as yet established itself in the milieu of the Bulgarian people, as Athens had done as head of free Hellas in the midst of four or five million Greeks, as Serbia had done with Belgrade as its center, and as Montenegro had detached itself out from the Serbian provinces subject to Turkey. For the Bulgarians this circumstance was, it would seem, unfavorable; but for Slav politics in the Orient, for the general interests of the Slavs as a whole, whose natural leader Russia would become sooner or later, there was a certain advantage in this circumstance. These independent, Europeanized centers such as Athens and Belgrade were much more easily subject to all *Western tendencies*, and not infrequently (as we have observed in the latest events) they avoided committing themselves to an agreement and alliance with Russia so natural for the Serbs and the Hellenes. During the three-year struggle on the island of Crete, when almost all Greek parties were pro-Russian and when Russia was able *freely* to reveal her sympathy within the confines of a pure Greek sentiment for the Greeks on this beautiful island where there was no admixture of Slav elements—at this time of ardent Greco-Russian cordiality, the Serbs deceived both the Greeks and the Russians. While promising an alliance with Greece and threatening Turkey with war in alliance with dread Montenegro, the Serbian government was, at the same time, conducting underhand negotiations for the evacuation of the fortresses then still in the possession of the Turks on the territory of the Serbian principality. Naturally, England, France, and Austria were all united in supporting Serbia in the arena of this double diplomatic game. The Turks gave up the fortresses, and the heroic population of Crete laid down their arms on their native soil that was soaked with their own blood!

It is well known to all what the Athenian government was doing in its turn—how it restrained for a long time the natural aspirations of the Greek population of Crete, Thessaly, Epirus, and Macedonia, how it intrigued against the Slavs and Russia.

We must, however, remember one thing: that not only the Greeks but the Yugoslavs also are "sycophantic to this day"; this should be remembered not in order to repudiate them, God forfend!—this would be impossible anyhow—but in the perspective of a rather dark future, perhaps, in order to be aware of the truth, in order to have a good knowledge of those conditions, in which we must constantly and inevitably act in that milieu when we are obliged to exercise our influence.

Thus, as I have already said, the political helplessness of the Bulgarians, their entire dependence on the Turks, their backwardness in almost all respects, their proximity to us on the Black Sea and the lower Danube, the lack of their own independent or even vassal capital, the absence of their own higher schools and the comparative scarcity of public schools—all this made the Bulgarian people (surpassing in numbers not only the Serbs but all the Greeks) highly important and, at the same time, under certain circumstances a highly accessible element to us. The Bulgarians were closer to us than any other Orthodox race in the Orient, because they were politically less defined at that time, because the forces hostile to us had nothing to seize on, so to speak, where they were concerned. They had no government, not even a vassal one. . . .

Russian policy in Bulgaria could have taken a direct step from the distribution of prayer books and church vestments, from the education of young Bulgarians in Russian schools, from grants given to public schools, from efforts to form an independent Bulgarian church, to some kind of very real connection with a legally established Bulgarian principality or kingdom. To make of it a vassal, for example, to place it in a certain position of dependence on our crown for our mutual benefit, or to invent some other form of union, which would have served as a cornerstone and a model for the future of the Eastern-Orthodox alliance, an alliance which no efforts by our Western enemies could prevent as long as we ourselves would not undermine by some ill-judged "honesty" of policy our own Pan-Slavist and Pan-Christian future! Neither a Pan-Slavic alliance with Russia at its head, in which only Slavs exclusively would participate, nor a more natural and stronger grand Eastern alliance, of which *volens-nolens* the Rumanians, the Greeks, and the Armenians would form a part in consequence of the racial and political multiplicity of the Orient—*neither the former nor the latter form of confederation is imaginable without having an allied capital in Tsargrad*. Every Russian is obliged to understand this; the statesmen of the West are aware of it, and because of this they use their veto to oppose, as far as they can, every natural move we make towards the southeast. "Peter the Great's testament may be a forgery," a certain European once said to me, "but the man who composed it is a great prophet." "If that is so," I replied, "then the West will do nothing, and the Slavs will bide their time." "The West must fulfill its duty and its vocation to the end," my interlocutor objected.

But if that is so, if, despite the most sincere rejection by Russian statesmen of this or that period of the idea of possessing the Bosporus, the destiny of Russia, her fated growth, to which it is impossible to set a limit until she fulfills her destination, her religious tradition, her commercial interests—if both her most ideal and her crudest motives draw this northern nation towards the *inevitable possession* of the Bosporus, then who *if not the Bulgarians* have been until now the most natural allies of Russia in this historically preordained trend?

The Bulgarians are of the same faith as us (I do not say of the same race, for the Poles, too, are of the same race as us). The Bulgarians are not legally independent as are the Greeks, the Rumanians, and the Serbs of the principality. The Bulgarians, who spread from *our frontiers* (that is, from the lower Danube) *to the very gates of Tsargrad*, have not yet been spoiled by constitutions and absurd ministerial crises. These Bulgarians, though they may be backward, have an awakened consciousness as regards their national and civil rights, and they have been placed by history itself in the position of being the vanguard of the Slavs on the testamentary road of their development!

Such then is the enormous significance of the Bulgarians for Russia and all of the Slavs. Even at the time when I first arrived in Thrace, the Bulgarians seemed to be the most convenient soil for our operations in Turkey; they were our most handy allies in the matter of our vocation.

But if that is so, if all the conditions, political, religious, and geographical (especially geographical), have joined together to make the Bulgarians most closely related and accessible to us, then the Greeks, who are settled in considerable numbers in the towns of Thrace nearest to the sea and to Tsargrad itself, as well as in the southern villages of this province—the Greeks, proud of their past, have themselves aspired since ancient days to annex the Bosporus and actually have greater claim to this than other non-Slavs or the Western nations; these Greeks should be our most dangerous rivals, the most obvious and implacable enemies of ours.

Yes, it is partly so—and partly not at all so. The history of Greco-Russian relations has developed quite differently, and for a long time the Orthodox Greeks (preeminently Orthodox, so to speak) were the most ardent, the most useful allies of ours in our policy in the Orient.

I admit that I find it boring and burdensome to speak in these notes in such detail of such a historical ABC. I should like to pass on as soon as possible to my real task, to the description of the period when I arrived in Thrace;* but, to my amazement, from conversations and newspaper articles I have observed in the most educated section of our public such a superficial and careless understanding of Eastern affairs that I find it impossible not to stop here and say about the Greeks at least as much as I have said about the Bulgarians. Out of respect for my readers (and partly, perhaps, out of indulgence in my own laziness), I shall try to be

* In 1864.

brief insofar as I may not harm the clarity of the exposition of this complex problem.

The *principle* in the name of which we have always intervened in Eastern affairs is one of *religious faith* rather than of race.

Orthodoxy, the belief we hold in common with the Christian population of Turkey, since long ago has given our actions in this country a firm foothold such as no other power of the heterodox West possesses. All other powers in the Orient act almost exclusively by exercising an external, mechanical pressure, by the use of their military and commercial strength, which differs in degrees depending on the nation that personifies it; only Russia alone, owing to its religious principle, finds herself acting under very different conditions. Her *traditions* and the *faith* of her people bind her closely with the religious substance of those small Christian peoples that for a century have formed part of the disorganized and disintegrating Ottoman Empire. Only for Russian policy in the Orient was it possible to have a fortunate combination of traditions and aspirations, of religious conservatism and an advanced movement, of nationality and faith, of the holy relics of antiquity and the exciting trends of contemporary mobility. After the reverses of the Crimean War, in many respects and in many of the Turkish provinces the Russian consuls became *stronger than before* (this will become evident further from my stories). Where this did not occur, the fault may be attributed to certain *individuals*, their lack of talent, their indifference, their stupidity very simply, rather than to the mood of populations and those ethical forces a Russian official might have at his disposal. After Sedan the French officials, who until then had behaved in a blustering, noisy, and quarrelsome manner, more so than the consuls* of any other country, suddenly became hardly noticeable; as soon as the faith in French might had suddenly diminished, her political significance declined to nought. The Russians (those of them,

---

* See Mr. Breché in my novel *Odysseus Polychroniades*. This is a true picture of a French consul in the time of Napoleon III. (K. L.)

I repeat, whom it was permissible to have in the service of the crown) had remained influential even after the reverses, thanks to the organic ties of a common faith.

Thus if Orthodoxy, far more than race, has always imparted so much vitality to our Eastern policy, then is not that nation the most important of all the Christian nations, more important even than Turkey or her vassal or neighboring lands, in which the colors of Orthodoxy are more solid than in all other countries? Should we not seek above all every kind of support in that people in which there is a deeper accumulation of Orthodox forces, of these real and not at all imaginary forces, which are still so strongly present among us? Should we not seek friendship and close relations above all with that Christian nation in the Orient which expresses most strongly and vividly our own sacred traditions?

If the Bulgarians, as I have stated above, were more important to us than the Rumanians, the Serbs, and the Greeks, then the Greeks, on the other hand, were no less important to us for a completely different reason—for the completely opposite reason that they expressed to the greatest extent all those forces which, with us, are comparatively weak. The Greeks had baptized us. Of course that was very long ago, but we need only to remember a simple thing—we need only remember that the holy places of Jerusalem, where the stones speak, are in the hands of the Greeks; they also have Mount Athos, where, even in our day, one can very quickly and with pleasure forget that one is living in a so-called Europe and in the so-called nineteenth century; we should remember that the austere deserts of Sinai and *four* patriarchal thrones are in Greek hands; we should remember that the best traditions of our monastic hermitages have descended to us chiefly from there; we should remember that our people have learned *only yesterday* that Serbs and Bulgarians exist in the world and that, if some plain folk have gone to fight in Serbia and Bulgaria *for the salvation* of their souls, they did so only because these Serbs and Bulgarians were *Orthodox*, and that in our people's mind the thought of these Orthodox peoples in the distant East, who have been oppressed and beaten by the heterodox Turks, is closely connected with what they have read of and heard about these same *holy places*, about Mount Athos, Jerusalem and Sinai, which are all Greek in spirit and are in Greek hands. Tsargrad itself, this presently Turkish, commercial, half-European Constantinople, is in the eyes of our people Tsargrad the holy, the Tsargrad of the apostolic Emperor Constantine, the city of St. Sophia, the city of ecumenical cathedrals, a holy place, too, only temporarily defiled by the nonbelievers. It is not only a question of the simple people; I shall assert directly that the closer a Russian assimilates the general educational level of our time with the Orthodox faith, the more sincerely he lives both in his heart and in his soul *in* the church and *with* the church, the more alertly, deeply, and inalterably will he become convinced of the following, by no means new, but unfortunately not often enough reiterated precepts:

(1) Nobody until now has seen any long-enduring political states which were not based upon mystical foundations, but on purely economic and legal conditions. When a country like the United States, approaching closely enough the latter ideal, will continue to exist without breaking apart or changing altogether its form of government for at least five centuries, then it can be held up as an example. In the meantime, this republic is only a hundred years old, and therefore cannot be taken as an example.

(2) If some new states of the future should be capable of quite separating the *"profanum"* from the *"sacrum"*,* it does not follow from this that an experiment of this kind would not prove fatal to such ancient states as, for example, the thousand-year-old (or eight-hundred-year-old, if taken from the year of baptism) Russia. At the end of the last century, France executed priests, closed the monasteries and churches, declared a cult of reason, and was then obliged again to turn her eyes to Rome; and France would, perhaps, have found herself in an incomparably worse sit-

* For how long? (K. L.)

uation if her Catholic feelings and her traditionally Catholic policy had been completely forgotten and powerless. Almost everyone attacks clericals, but no one has yet seen France without clericals. *Would it have been possible for France to be without them for even a decade?* Would she not have fallen apart immediately? That is the question; *but for me it is not even a question.*

(3) If Orthodoxy, this mighty, real force in Russian life beneath the banner of which we have gained so many victories and have conquered so many foes, is still a vital force with us, if this Orthodoxy is essential to us, then we should remember that a policy founded on a religious principle is not feasible *without sincerely felt mystical beliefs, which the political mechanism is obliged to employ as a weapon.* We should even remember that the more sincere the mysticism of many, many individuals, the more successful and more convenient is the wisest, the quietest, and even, if you wish, the most cunning policy of the nation as a whole. Without the sincerity of Catholicism, for example, without the sincerity of the majority of seventeenth-century Frenchmen, the grand, most astute policy of Richelieu would have proved impossible. *A certain measure of cunning in politics,* I will note, is *obligatory;* for politics are a mechanical matter. They are nothing more than a natural, mutual ponderation of social-political forces. The old Muscovite princes and boyars were all of them very sincere Orthodox people and at the same time very cunning and astute politicians.

(4) If this mystical, sincere Orthodoxy is, in its sincerity, rather indifferent to politics, but in consequence of this sincerity so essential for the successful conduct of foreign policy in difficult times, if it is so important for Russia, then should we not be apprehensive of everything that violates the peace of the church and that hinders the communion between the various national churches which form part of the Orthodox family? Should we not value inexpressibly and ardently all that which strengthens the influence of the priesthood on the people? The monasteries, for example, exercise more influence on society than the best representa-

tives of the white clergy, who are unable, owing to their family situation and their *too ordinary* though honest manner of life, to distract so much the thoughts of their flock from the trivialities of everyday life as a single good Father confessor in the Optina desert or in Valaam can do, or a single hermit in Mount Athos who has retired to a cave! How many indirect, imperceptible benefits have been brought to the Russian people by some five or six Greek or Bulgarian holy men who are quite unknown to us Russians, even though we are reputed to be well educated, and who live in the grim clefts or desert shacks of Mount Athos? About these Mount Athos eremites (Father Daniel the Greek, Father Vasily the Bulgarian, and others like them) authentic accounts and descriptions reach our monasteries—some in print, some by means of personal letters, and others by word of mouth. These rumors and descriptions help to strengthen the spirit of our monks. The image of these saintly, non-Russian men, whom their Russian admirers envision living in that far-off Turkish East, rouses their enthusiasm and consoles them.

For this reason, when I say Orthodoxy, I mean the priesthood; when I say priesthood, I intend monasteries; when I say monasteries, I remember the holy places; *when I remember the holy places, I can involuntarily see with amazing clarity how important is for us the role of the Greek priesthood, which is predominant in these holy places and, indeed, in possession of them.* I am not referring to Hellenism. In itself Athenian Hellenism does not deserve any special, extraordinary attention. Athenian Hellenism should be of importance to Russians only insofar as it is the bearer of Eastern Orthodoxy. It is impossible to distinguish these two principles not only mentally but in many cases practically; and our diplomacy formerly knew how to carry this out—if not constantly, then successfully and over a long period.

This is what I wished to state here, and I have spoken very cursorily and briefly about the Greeks. This is their importance to us; this is why Thrace, as the chief bone of contention between the Bulgarians and the Greeks, that is, between two Christian peoples in Turkey equally necessary and dear to us, is so very important a province in our eyes. It is almost the most important province, if the question is examined from the standpoint from which I have here examined it and from which (I do not know how it is now!) the ministry had examined it. The ministry had constantly and strictly enjoined upon us moderation and the spirit of pacification.

Of course, when I first arrived there, I could not understand everything as clearly as I understand it now. But in its general outlines, the problem was understood even then by every Russian official who could not have managed to read, as I had while still in Petersburg, a hundred or more consular reports.

I shall later speak of the extreme aspects of both the absurd Hellenic "great idea" and that of Bulgarian racial radicalism.

GREEKS, BULGARIANS, AND RUSSIANS

LET US first of all compare the Greeks and the Bulgarians and then compare them both with the Russians. We shall discuss the Serbians later.

By its temperament, perhaps, but more exactly by its historical position, the Greek nation is more sensational, more prominent, more famous than the Bulgarian one.

Everyone who is even a little involved in politics knows something about the Greek spirit. The Greeks have an independent state, their own capital, university, army, chamber of deputies. The number of newspapers in Athens alone, which has no more than fifty thousand inhabitants, at times reaches almost a hundred, they say. Hellas is diplomatically represented at all the courts.

In Constantinople, the Greeks have an ancient hierarchy recognized by all the world, a hierarchy that serves in many respects

---

From the article "Russians, Greeks, and Yugoslavs," 1878. WORKS, *vol.* V, *pp. 269–286.*

as the political representative of the people; they have newspapers which are now fairly free to write as they please. Conversations in Turkish cafes, retail shops, and pharmacies (where many people are in the habit of meeting) have been since days past fearless and frank.

In addition, in many cases, when one does not get enough information in Turkey, one can learn things from Athens, Trieste, Moldavia-Walachia.

With the Bulgarians, on the contrary, who have no chamber, no army, whose newspapers are unimportant and are read only by themselves, everything takes place under Turkish rule, quietly, imperceptibly, by means of underground activity.*

In consequence of these differing conditions of life, it is easier on the whole to judge the Greeks than the Bulgarians. As I have already stated, in the past half century since the days of their first rebellion, the Greeks have developed a far more historical physiognomy.

They have managed to develop more than the Bulgarians not only mentally and in scholarship but also in the sense of a certain organization, and for this reason they are more diverse in their Hellenic racial unity.

From the beginning they have had no class structure; they have been deprived of this element of heterogeneity and harmony. But geographical and historical conditions have imparted to them far more national color than to the Yugoslavs.

If we only look at the map, we shall understand this. We shall see the austere desert of Sinai, the wild valleys and mountains of Asia Minor, commercial Smyrna, so close to these wild countries, the many islands of the archipelago, of the Mediterranean and Adriatic seas, Athens at the foot of the Acropolis, beautiful Crete, pastoral and bandit-ridden Morea, Epirus, where the natives still wear the *fustanella* and still compose even in our day epic songs amid their barren mountains. A couple of hours away by boat from this half-wild and at the same time (is it not strange?) very literate

* Written in 1873–1874. (K. L.)

Epirus, there lies the almost Italian island of Corfu, still full of monuments and traces of the British protectorate. In Cephalonia the inhabitants are again of a different character. The Corfiotes are gentler and more educated, the Cephalonians more passionate, savage, and clever. In his daily life, the Macedonian Greek almost does not differ at all from his neighbor, the Bulgarian; you cannot distinguish a Thracian Greek from a Thracian Bulgarian—they both wear dark blue turbans and brown *shalvari*.

There is something Italian about the Cretans, but they are quite unlike the Corfiotes. They are more original, handsomer, more poetic, more warlike, more elegant, and so on.

As a consequence of the same historical conditions, the Greek middle class is more diverse than the Bulgarian. The fine, cautious, thoughtful Phanariot * is much more of a gentleman in appearance, more capable of engaging in serious politics, far better educated in the public sense than the enterprising Athenian. What is an educated Athenian? A little bit of an ancient rhetorician, a little bit of a Parisian demagogue, and a bit of swindler; a bit of a Kolomna philanderer and *mauvais genre* when he starts paying attention to ladies. He still believes blindly that the Greek is more astute than anyone else in the world, that the Greek nation is the only phoenix in history and will keep being reborn till the end of the world in order to bestrew mankind with flowers and nourish it on the fruits of his genius.

His progress, however, does not go further than his domestic threshold. In his family life, he insists on being the head (like any Serbian or Bulgarian). Having visited Russia, he cannot hide his astonishment at the carefree attitude and the condescension of Russian husbands, brothers, and fathers.

I am convinced of the following: if at some university three young revolutionaries and political dreamers—a Greek, a Bulgarian, and a Russian—were to become friends and if they started to read together the works of public exterminators, then a Russian might like the anarchistic principles of Proudhon but would dis-

* Greek merchants living in Phanar, a quarter of Constantinople.

like the utilitarianism of his godless family. He would probably begin to praise either the polyandry of the Fourierists or the aluminum palaces of Chernyshevsky.

The Bulgarian and the Greek, without rejecting political anarchy, would willingly combine against the Russian over the family question and would take the side of Proudhon.

The Russian would immediately exclaim, "Don't say that! This Proudhon is a terrible bourgeois!" But he would never succeed, however hard he tried, in making the Greek and the Bulgarian understand his interpretation of a bourgeois.

"A bourgeois is a *politis*, a citizen, an inhabitant of a town, an educated healthy man. What is wrong with that? Now if you had said a countryman, a *khoriatis*, a peasant, a barbarian, that would be another matter. But a city dweller is a bourgeois! That's just an ordinary man, a progressive man, a liberal, a man conscious of his human dignity. What do you mean?" the Greek and the Bulgarian would ask in perplexity. And they would be partly right in not understanding the idea of their Russian comrade.

Very likely this Russian would belong to that numerous class which certain of our conservatives have labeled "the gentry proletariat"; he would be a chip off a disintegrated gentry class and as a result would unite in himself two different kinds of protest, two kinds of dissoluteness, the envious protest of poverty allied to fastidious nerves and the squeamish protest of a certain *comme il faut* and a certain romanticism, tired of the restrictions and the humble duties; he would have united in himself the remnants of his ancestral, aristocratic abandon and the acquired irritability of demagogy.

The nerves of the Bulgarian and the Greek are more stolid; this Bulgarian's elder brother is still pasturing his father's herds in the Balkans; it is true that one of this Greek's uncles is a minister in the government of Hellas, but another of his uncles is selling tobacco in a small, chilly shop in Yanina, while his youngest brother is serving as a dishwasher in some cafe. Both the Greek and the Bulgarian have a more restricted imagination, as well as a colder and more practical mind; neither the one nor the other seeks the absolute or even understands it. Their *comme il faut* and aesthetic demands in general on themselves and others are far more limited; and their fantasies, compared with the play of the Great Russian imagination, are extremely poor and simple. In this connection, perhaps, they are like a Manilov * dreaming of friendship with a Chichikov and the beautiful view over the bridge—but this will only last until their first litigation in a commercial court.

We must picture the Bulgarian nation in the following way. In a considerable, continuous, continental space set between the Black Sea on the east, the Danube in the north, the Serbian tribe in the west, and the Greek tribe in the south, there lives a racially identical people. In certain regions, especially in upper Bulgaria, this people lives unmixed with any other tribe; to the south, in Thrace and Macedonia, it lives mixed with the Greeks. Here the Bulgarians are more numerous in the villages, the Greeks more numerous in the cities.

The majority of the villages, varying in degrees of wealth and poverty, the fruitfulness or the barrenness of the soil, and other conditions, are inhabited by small holders who are hard-working, sober, stubborn, patient, thrifty, not at all disposed to debauchery in the Great Russian manner, and very cautious and fairly cunning despite all their apparent simplicity. There are very insignificant shades of difference in their external physiognomy, in their daily life, in their clothes, in their habits, even in their spirit (the Bulgarian mountaineers are bolder and braver than the Bulgarians of the Thracian countryside); but, though they have all been united long ago on the continuous continental expanse and though all of them have been subject to one Turkish rule, they were unable to develop within themselves such local peculiarities and significant shades of difference as the Greeks were able to develop under the influence of more varied geographical conditions and of a more complex history in later times. Since the invasion of the Turks, the

* A character in Gogol's *Dead Souls*, of which Chichikov is the itinerant hero.

Bulgarians have not experienced those vacillations and political *coups* which the Greeks have undergone so often. They have not changed their rulers as often as the Greek islanders (for example, the Cretans were dominated for a long time by the Venetians, and then, not so long ago, they suffered a Turkish conquest; the Ionians, that is, the Corfiotes and others, have had a whole succession of different masters—the Venetians, the French, the Russians, the English, until finally they united with independent Hellas). All this has influenced their spirit, their customs, even their petty habits, and has built up various shades of difference in the Greek people, shades that are sometimes very distinct and that are blurred only in the all-European type occupying the highest social position. The Bulgarians, by contrast, have suffered only two influences, which have made themselves felt constantly and uniformly through the ages: the Turkish and the Greek.

It is understandable that such a people must be very simple, uncomplicated, uniform: to our day, this people is still in a state of primitive simplicity. Because of this, the Bulgarian people are not very interesting; they are aloof, impoverished in spirit, but extremely stubborn and true to their image of themselves (that is very natural, however; the fewer tastes a man has, the fewer his impressions and ideas, the easier it is to achieve the inner unity of a stubborn self, the less he is divided). To the outside spectator, the Bulgarian people offer only a small variety of impressions. All that the simple Bulgarians possess the Greeks have also. But from the wild shores of Asia to the flowering islands near the Italian littoral and the dreary Thracian fields, the simple Greeks, taken as a whole, possess many heterogeneous qualities and many shades of difference, which cannot be found in the uniform Bulgarian nation and which can both attract and revolt; but, in any case, these Greeks impress the outside observer much more vividly than the somewhat tedious, though extremely respectable, appearance of the Bulgarian common folk.

Since the family customs, the manner of receiving and entertaining guests, the strict and pure family ideals, even the clothes and dances (the authentic Bulgarian folk dancing takes the form of a closed circle, whereas the Greeks dance in an open semicircle; however, there is no greater difference between them than between one European pair dance and another) are in places very much alike in the case of both the Greeks and the Bulagrians, it is possible, in general, to state that the Bulgarian is, in the typical sense, rather like a Greek, but only as a paler, more colorless version; that he is nothing but a Macedonian or a Thracian Greek in his customs, type, and character, but one who speaks only Slavic and whom his leaders have persuaded through propaganda that he has absolutely different political and religious interests from his so similar a neighbor, the Greek.

If we write a purely political article about their interests and aspirations, the Bulgarians and the Greeks will confront each other as extreme antitheses. And had they not been restrained by Turkey, they would, of course, have resorted to arms long ago. If we should write a novella bearing on the reality of the situation or an ethnographic sketch dealing with their customs, types, and personal character, then the Bulgarian and the Greek customs, especially in the intermixed continental provinces, and the Bulgarian and the Greek types would greatly resemble each other. We would see the same strong, honest family, the same hard-working character, almost the same Oriental garb, the same customs, the same caution and secretiveness, the same primitive naïvete, which is so often charming and pleasant.

It is mainly a rural population. The big difference, however, lies in that the mass of the Bulgarians are a trifle more uncouth, primitive, and illiterate than the mass of the Greeks. But the Greeks everywhere have a great deal of simplicity and patriarchalism—on the islands, in Epirus, in Macedonia, in Hellas itself.

What shall we say about the urban population? If we mentally separate from the people the so-called intelligentsia (the bourgeoisie), the merchants, doctors, lawyers, teachers, and so on, then comparing those two nations, the Bulgarian and the Greek, we shall see again the very same thing: on the one hand, a considerable similarity in type, understanding, tastes, character, and, on the other, a difference in that the milieu of the Greek intelligentsia, because of foreign admixtures, historical heterogeneity, and older enlightenment, is incomparably more varied, spiritually richer, and abundant in diversity than the milieu of the Bulgarian middle class.

If we compare the Europeanized Greeks and similar Bulgarians with the Russians, our first impression will be that Eastern Christians are drier and colder than Russians in their private life. They have less idealism of the heart, the family, and religion; everything about them is cruder, less refined; but, instead, they have better health, more common sense, sobriety, and moderation. Fewer chivalrous feelings, less conscious good nature, less generosity, but more self-control, more domestic and inner order, less debauchery and loose behavior, less profligacy.

They have fewer original characters, fewer sharply defined types, than we have, and far less poetry; but, in return, there is not even a whisper among them of girl nihilists, of sisters imploring their brothers to kill them because they find life tedious, of husbands who hang their young wives because things have gone badly, of youths, almost adolescents, killing a coachman in order to train themselves as revolutionaries, and so on. Even the crimes of Eastern Christians (Greeks and Slavs without distinction) have a more comprehensible, calculating character. There is not even a rumor here, among the Greeks, Bulgarians, or Serbians, of those strange murders caused by despondency, disappointment, simple sorrow, or a Herostratian desire to become personally famous without any aim or sense—murders that reveal a profound heartache in Russian society and at the same time a profound moral dissoluteness. A desire to rob, quarrel, revenge, jealousy—in a word, more natural, perhaps more crude, simple, but in general more calculating and dryly reasoned motives are the causes of crime in the Near East.

In the intellectual milieu one does not hear about crime; the intelligentsia is too prudent for this; but there is also far less magnanimity and kindness. Here is one example. I was acquainted with Greeks and Bulgarians who were no longer young, who still remembered Russians who had owned serfs. With amazement they complained to me that it was impossible for them to employ in their homes any servants who had served even six months for Russian officials in the Near East, because they had been spoiled by the condescension and generosity of their masters.

This is all a comparison between Russians and Eastern Christians. But if we compare the Greek intelligentsia with the Bulgarian, then we shall see the following. Insofar as the Greeks seem to be colder than the Russians, and each of them is, or all of them taken together are, more uniform than the Russians, so do the Bulgarians seem colder and more uniform than the Greeks to anyone who has lived with both.

Compared with us Russians, the Greeks and the Bulgarians excel in practicality, cunning, self-control, caution, and the commercial spirit, a somehow diplomatic one, rather than in impulse, feeling, and ideality; nevertheless, among Greeks I have known eccentrics, idealists, people who despise commerce, cunning, and diplomacy in private life, caution, and even those who are indifferent to nationalist policy. I knew, though they are fewer in number than with us, fluent talkers, witty, amusing, sympathetic characters; while, among the so many Bulgarians I have seen, I have met until now only one or two such men, and they were not very remarkable. A member of the Bulgarian intelligentsia is above all a bourgeois—always reserved, always calculating, more or less niggardly and cautious, always a diplomat or always a merchant whether in friendship, in marriage or in politics. . . .

It's the same thing again. He's a secondhand Greek; a rather tedious Greek. A Greek merchant (even though he is not a merchant by trade); a Greek speaking Slavic. . . .

It seems that in this way I have pictured clearly enough the psychology of the Bulgarians.

Now if we examine the Bulgarians in relation to each other,

without going beyond their particular milieu, and analyze their mutual relations within their class structure, we shall see the following:

Bulgarian national affairs are conducted by a comparatively small number of men, who have issued, for the most part, from the same simple rural class of Bulgarians, which constitutes the mass of the people, or from simple city dwellers.

These men—bishops, doctors, merchants, lawyers, wealthy proprietors who were educated in Europe or in Constantinople by the Greeks, or in Russia or in Moldavia-Walachia—have acquired their European veneer only to the extent of being able to represent their people fairly badly, needless to say, in a social, mental, and worldly way, but politically very astutely, on the contrary. They learned to conduct political intrigues very deftly in the contemporary spirit and by contemporary means, and did not educate themselves well enough to lose touch with the common people or vice versa. In Russia a peasant would rather deceive a man of the highest society; in the case of the Bulgarians, their elders lead their people by the nose at will. These elders are like our Russian rural extortioners *en grand*, wearing frock coats that are not too well cut.

Behind a handful of these solidly skillful doctors, the Sultan's *kapud zhi-bashi*, traders holding in their hands a newly created priesthood, comes the stratum of more or less young teachers who are scattered through large and small towns. These teachers, trained rather haphazardly and not infrequently in Catholic and Protestant schools, are all ardent fanatics of their national cause, poor people, who have also all emerged from either peasant or lower-class urban families; but they have not had time to learn much or to get rich and therefore they depend entirely on that narrow circle of important representatives who are received by Turkish ministers and foreign diplomats.

Following this young fanatic of Bulgarianism, who is saturated with cheap, realistic European concepts and who is dressed in a tattered or soiled European frock coat, the intelligentsia comes to an abrupt end. Almost immediately after this young progressive and demagogue comes a plain rural extortionist, a *chorbadzhi*, garbed in a thick brown aba, *shalvari*, and a lambskin cap or a dark blue turban. He is for the most part illiterate, sits at home, has no knowledge of the world, and has a deficient understanding of his religion; he is very distrustful and slow; but the teacher Insarov,* who has come out of almost the same kind of village, has no difficulty in persuading him of anything at all, especially of the fact, for example, that it is only out of greed, in order to collect their dues, that the Greek bishops have no wish to free him, the poor man; or that schism does not exist at all, that the "Gretzky patrik" † keeps speaking the untruth when he maintains that our priests dress in the same way and chant in the same way as the Greeks, and perform their liturgy in the same way, and that there is nothing illegal or sinful in the fact that in Philippopolis, Tulcea, and in Tsargrad, there are two Orthodox bishops—a Bulgarian and a Greek one. How can an illiterate Bulgarian peasant possibly understand these things when even very cultured and even religious Russians ask, "Really, where is there a schism here? And where's the harm? All this seems so easy to reconcile!"

Thus we get the following political picture:

Millions of a very uniform simple Bulgarian people are very artfully and deftly ruled under Turkish sovereignty by an insignificant number of *de facto* rather than *de jure* privileged elders and mentors, who emerged from the same milieu but who differ sharply from them in education and understanding.

Such a national structure, very democratic and extremely simple, may lack future stability and may, after the liberation, be the cause of violent demagogy and strife when questions of internal policy predominate over those of foreign policy (that is, when there are no more Turks or Greeks exercising pressure from the outside); but now, in the presence of these external instruments of

* Presumably the "strong," revolutionary and Bulgarian hero of Turgenev's novel, *On the Eve* (1860). Tr.

† The Greek Patriarch.

unification, in the presence of external pressure, such a state of society is very convenient for the accomplishment of contemporary national affairs and for a skillful transference of a political problem to a pseudo-religious ground. Many of the low and few of the high; the domination by a cautious, fairly concordant, skillful cunning plutocracy.

Unlike the Greeks, the Bulgarians had no independent state of their own, no Hellas, no people already spoiled by a constitution, no succession of internal rebellions, no general franchise, no habit of everyone interfering in everything. The Bulgarians have incomparably fewer of those intermediate types—the brightly literate, smart, ordinary folk—that are so numerous among the Greeks; they have very few men like the Greek devil-may-care sailors, Greek small shopkeepers, craftsmen, and servants who constantly read newspapers, all of them, sailors who discuss politics, and so on.

This more notable development of Europeanism (I cannot say enlightenment, for I am unable to understand why the popularization of European bourgeois ideas should be termed enlightenment) among the Greeks confuses the state of things; everyone interferes in everything, everyone has a right to his opinion. But to compensate for this, every Greek understands more; among the Greeks, it is more difficult for an elder, a bishop, or a teacher to deceive the people in church matters, to present black as white, for example—church canons as not canons, and so on.

That's where the difference lies.

Until recently, historical conditions have made the Greek and the Eastern Christian society, as a whole, more church-minded in its education than the Russian. The church was more fused with the rest of the nation; the people and high society stood nearer to the church.

The religiosity of the Greeks, a consequence of their submission to the Turks, assumed a political character imperceptible even to most of them. Of course, while political, national fanaticism was being added to all the rest, to the strong personal feelings, to a personal mystical mood, religion was attaining the crest of its power among the people. It had been formerly so with the Greeks.

But as soon as circumstances changed, the Greek soil, so much more uniform than the Russian, turned out to be less sincerely religious than ours.

While the Turks were harsher, while their laws were more merciless, while there were more arbitrary persecutions, while it was easy to kill the peasants, there was still personal faith, there was still fear, sufferings, prayers, the strictest fasting; there were voluntary martyrs; the monasteries were filled with ascetics.

But as Turkey grew weaker, the laws were made lighter; greater order was established; there was greater literacy, more learning on a small scale, more freedom. In demagogy, Hellas surpassed many of the countries of Europe; there was a multitude of schools everywhere; the teachers in the villages said what they wished without any control. And then, despite the ecclesiastical nature of its education, this purely commercial, practical, industrial, superficially trained Greek society cooled off far more than Russian society towards religion in its emotional aspects. In general, it is vain to entertain any hope in the common people; it is not the people who adorn the higher strata in the course of time, but it is these higher strata which everywhere have an identical influence on the lower strata.

For a long time I have wondered why it all happened in this way.

It happened, first of all, because the subtle and deep psychological needs of a higher civilization did not bring to this deeply democratic, continuous society of Eastern Christians any inner excitement in exchange for the now blunted Turkish scimitar. Secondly, because the mind in the East is only practical and still unpretentious. Too little thought for thought, too little ideal culture. Both the mind and the heart are still elementary.

If we examine in turn the Russians, the Greeks, the Serbians, and the Bulgarians and compare them all with each other from the

standpoint of religiosity, we shall become convinced without difficulty that the strength and the degree of this quality are appor-
tioned in the four Orthodox nations of the East as follows:

As I have said before, the Russians occupy the first degree.
They are followed by the Greeks, the Serbians, and the Bulgarians.

This will become clear from the details. Let us compare, first of
all, the Greeks and the Russians. The Greeks share many features
peculiar to them also with the Serbians and the Bulgarians. Thus,
when speaking of the Greeks, we shall have in mind the Turkish
Slavs; afterwards, it will be easier to explain why the Yugoslavs
lack even those conditions, which make it possible for the Greeks
to redeem their deficiencies and weakness in relation to Orthodoxy.

In Russia, when we enter a church at Easter or on some other
important holiday, we realize that this is a mystical, emotional
holiday. When we enter a Greek church, all we see is a national
holiday.

This true observation was imparted to me by one of the most
gifted of our consuls in the East. He expressed it briefly and
clearly. But it is clear only to those who have lived a long time in
the East and who have reflected while living there.

But more details are necessary for him who has reflected without living in the East or who has lived in the East without bother-
ing to reflect.

Since the days of Peter the Great, Russian society has been educated far more by the state than by the church.

In the Near East, Christian society, which had long been subject to the Turks, found its natural teacher in the church.

In Russia, society was further removed from the church, from
the clergy; between the priest and the nobleman (until our day almost the only leader of the people and the only representative of
the nation) everywhere stood the petty officials; the frequently
heterodox teacher, French or German; the mother, a society
woman, who read extensively; the father, who abused the monks
and the priests without knowing why he did so; and so on. In the

Near East all laymen stand closer to the clergy: they are all more on the same level, intermixed among themselves and with the priesthood. The position of the priesthood here was absolutely different from what it was with us. It was at the same time humbler and freer. It was humbler in relation to the Turks in the sense that it lacked the external respect which the Russian clergy received; also in the sense that it was poorer than our clergy and that it might have to face the perils of death, exile, and so on, more readily than our clergy. Thus the famous patriarch Grigory was hanged by the Sultan Mahmud, despite the fact that not long before his tragic death, he threatened in a pastoral letter to excommunicate all the rebellious Greeks.

The Eastern clergy was freer because it was ruled over by a heterodox government which had been until recently very harsh. By its early *firmans* (decrees) addressed to the patriarchs, the Turkish government deprived itself of any rights to intervene in the internal affairs of the Christian church. Being heterodox, it had not the means of interfering in all the details of ecclesiastical affairs, as an Orthodox government would have been able to do. To this end, it had no principles that were homogeneous with those of the church; but it did not have any particular desire to do this. The Koran commands that Christians be judged according to the Gospel.

In addition, we should not forget that despite the contempt they felt for the *giaours*, the religious Turks, who knew their laws, always entertained a rather original respect for Christ (the Prophet Issa), the Holy Virgin (the Prophetess Mariam), and certain Christian and Jewish holy places. It is understandable that, side by side with oppression, external insolence, and even cruelty, the Turks often had an inner feeling of respect for Christianity.

All these circumstances had the result that in the Near East, the church ruled, uncontrolled, over all the details, over the people, and served it in the capacity of a national, political representative in all things. In the eyes of the Turkish government, until our day, a bishop was not only a spiritual shepherd but also a political, administrative representative of Christians in many questions.

Since long ago, this had brought together and fused the clergy and the people. The schools did the same; family life and the internal organization of the spiritual estate pursued the same goal.

The Christian schools were for a long time exclusively in the hands of the church: for a long time the priests were the only national instructors. It is understandable that the education of society in the East must be more ecclesiastical than with us.

In Russian schools sacred history and the catechism were merely an obligatory course. An adolescent received his religious impressions far more from the church, which he attended with his family, from the book he read at home (more often a French or a German book; from Chateaubriand or Schiller, *Count Hapsburg*, for example) than from the lessons of a teacher of religion in a silk cassock.

Formerly, the church in the East, received a great deal of help precisely because of its dependent position. The sacred history of Christianity, the dogmas, the cathechism, the priest, the bishop— all these proved to be national, political supports. Nothing divided the nation from the church; there were no other issues, no other banners, no other competing force. For a long time there was not even any other poetry, no other literature.

In Russia, since the times of Catherine, there had been, among the nobility, elegant Voltairians rather like the grandee whom Pushkin celebrated in the line, "To you, courteous descendant of Aristippus," or something like Herzen's father (See his *My Past and Thoughts*), or like the worldly old man in Turgenev's novella, *An Unhappy Girl*.

At the beginning of this century, from the 1820s to 1850s, we observe that in Russia the clergy constituted a special estate, almost a caste, for there was a hereditary principle involved in its organization. The absolutely special, completely ecclesiastical education of the seminaries; the far from ecclesiastical education of the lay schools; the domestic education in the most enlightened gentry households, the reading and the background which disposed one either to indifference or romanticism, to contemplation, to the religion of the heart rather than to a national-ecclesiastical one.

In the Near East we observe the opposite.

There we see not only monks but also a white clergy fused with the people, issuing from it and returning to it. The priest does not come from a clerical family, but from a family of farmers, shopkeepers, lay teachers, from the family of a rural captain; one priest is the son of a *kavass*, another was a watchman in his youth; the son of yet another priest becomes the *kavass* of a European consul, and so on.

In the East, we do not see a sharply individualized, seminarian education. On the other hand, here all were almost more seminarist than with us.

The public schools at that time were managed here almost without any control by the clergy, while with us they were directed by society people. (The Turks for a long time did not interfere with the public schools, and the Christians have fended off very skillfully all their attempts to do so.)

In the wealthiest families in the East, life was very harsh, coarse, heartless in many respects; but this family system of the Christian East is all built on secrecy and not on a free romanticism tinged with Christianity as it has been with us from long past—on the will of the parents and not on love and free choice. The maidens do not dream of love, but of marriage. Like the German women in Tacitus, they love marriage rather than their husband.

To picture the Christian East more graphically in this respect, let us imagine Russian society (that of the early nineteenth century) without a nobility, especially without the highest nobility. Let us imagine something in the nature of the merchants and the officials in Ostrovsky,* but with certain shades of difference, with fewer passions, for example; on the one hand, the older men have less of what we have called *samodurstvo;*† on the other hand, they

* Alexander N. Ostrovsky (1823–1886), famous Russian dramatist.
† A stubborn, wild willfulness.

have fewer kind, generous impulses and incomparably more coldness, reserve, avarice, and indifference of the heart.

On the other hand, we must raise a Moslem storm, hang a Moslem scimitar above this ecclesiastically educated, devout but not in the least romantic, rather stiff, cold Eastern society of the first half of this century.

And then all will be clear. The picture of society in the Near East is, on the one hand, chillier than ours; on the other, it is more tragic. Imagine the intrusion of Janizary violence into a life that is purely domestic and very church-minded in many of its principles, and then it will become even clearer how the Turkish rule, which was often a real yoke, assisted in the unification and fusion of all Christian elements—of the church, the nation, the school, the family, the races even; for the awakening of the Bulgarians and their movement against the Greeks and the Greek church began comparatively recently, during a temporary lightening of the Turkish yoke. Formerly, the Turks had regarded the Bulgarians and the Greeks as simply "Christians," and the Orthodox peoples had also called themselves by this name.

RUSSIA AND THE RUSSIANS

IN THE character of the Russian people there are very pronounced and important traits which remind us far more of the Turks, Tartars, and other Asians (or even of nobody at all) than of the southern and western Slavs. We are more indolent, more fatalistic, far more submissive to the authorities, more depraved, good-natured, desperately brave, unstable, incomparably more inclined to religious mysticism (even to religious creativity, to various heretical contrivances) than the Serbs, Bulgars, Czechs, and Croats.

They have more firmness, patience, far more physical and mental sobriety; their family virtues are far stronger than those of the Russian people; they are little inclined to nihilistic extremes, but their indifference to religion is astonishing; their mechanical, matter-of-fact conservation of *something or other* to which they are accustomed or which they value only in the political sense, without any of the passion or pain of "seeking," is unpleasantly

---

From "The Letters of a Hermit." WORKS, *vol.* V, *pp.* 386–389.

surprising to a Russian on closer acquaintance. They are all more or less predisposed to *moderate liberalism,* which, to our good fortune, is not so deeply ingrained in Russia and which can be *so easily crushed to bits between two extremely nonliberal forces*—between a hysterical nihilistic impulse and a firm, fearless defense of our great historical principles.

In a word, our western and southern brother Slavs in their virtues and vices resemble far more than we do the European bourgeois of the most average style. In this sense, that is, in the sense of their psychic, existential, and mental originality, these Slavs are far less cultured than we. For I have already stated that by the word "culture," I understand, *not any kind of civilization,* literacy, industrial maturity, and so on, but only a civilization that is based on its own sources and is universal by the order of its succession and its influence. By the phrase "original, universal culture" I understand *religious, political, legal, philosophical, existential, artistic, and economic* (it is necessary to add *"when* it is a *question of our own time;"* for it cannot be denied that the economic question has its place *everywhere* today and that the nation or state which will have the fortune to seize in its mighty and *protective* hands this advanced and hitherto unimpeded movement of minds will assume for ages to come its place at the head of mankind and will not only gain unheard-of fame for itself but will also preserve from violent destruction a multitude of objects and principles that are dear to this mankind).

I apply the term "cultural" to this system of abstract ideas, which exists unconsciously in life and is also consciously carried through into our life, and which is then drawn therefrom into the sphere of remotest thought. To understand each other, we must agree on the terminology; and in this sense China is to me more cultured than Belgium; the Hindus are more cultured than the North Americans; a Russian Old Believer or even a Skopetz * is far more cultured than a Russian provincial teacher "according to *Baron Korf's* book."

* A member of the sect of Skoptzi, who practiced castration.

In this sense precisely, I may allow myself to state a strange thing about Russia, namely, that she is, of all the Slavs, both the *least Slavic* and *at the same time the most Slavic nation*. She is the least Slavic nation because, by her history, by her composition (by her blood perhaps), by her psychic and mental structure, she is very distinct from all the other Slavs. On the other hand, Russia is the most Slavic of all not only because she is called upon *to be the head of the Slavs politically* but also because she already has and is engendering that which, affirming itself, can develop further—those many elements which, until the present, were not peculiar to either Europeans or Asians, either to the West or to the East. This is natural enough, for only out of a more Oriental or, so to speak, a more Asiatic—Turanian nation, in the midst of the Slavic nations, can emerge something spiritually independent of Europe. Without these Asiatic elements influencing them through Russia, all the other Slavs would very rapidly become the worst of the continental Europeans, and nothing more. For such a sorry goal it would not have been worth their while to "cast off their yoke" or for Russia to undertake for their sake and benefit self-denying crusades. It is not for this that Russian eagles have flown beyond the Danube and the Balkans, not in order that the Serbs and Bulgars should later, in freedom, hatch the chicken eggs of middle-class Europeanism à la Virkhov, à la Cobden or Jules Favre.

That would be horrible!

Of course we shall liberate the Slavs; that is essential; that is inevitable; circumstances, independent of us, will oblige us to do this, and probably very soon. No coalitions will be able to restrain us; no militant Germany with all her schoolmasters can prevent this. Even if Germany defeats the Slavs on the field of battle, she will be defeated politically, fatalistically annihilated, like Austria, which had to surrender the Venetian provinces after her victory at Custozza. Historical destinies *must be* accomplished, despite human considerations; the liberal destruction of the whole social-political order of Europe, established by ages of past greatness, has not yet attained a "point of saturation." Purely political nationalism, that is, one that is defined, not in terms of the cultural-existential originality of the race, not by the originality of *every-thing* in it, from religion to fashion and taste, but only by its political *independence*, is nothing more than one of the chief manifestations of *one and the same thing*, that is, of that powerful and not always understood movement which some call renewal and progress, others revolution, but which I prefer to call more precisely the *egalitarian-liberal decomposition* of Germano-Roman civilization. This disintegration infects, and will continue to infect, all of mankind until such time as the moment reaches the point of return, or, speaking more plainly, until such time *as what I* am stating here, which many may think *to be merely eccentric, becomes as much of a commonplace as has become a great deal of what, half a century ago, seemed to be mere foolishness!*

People who liberate or help to unify the men of their own race in the nineteenth century aspire to some national ideal, but, achieving their political aim, they *produce* something *merely cosmopolitan,* that is, something that obliterates more and more the nationalism of everyday life or culture and mixes more and more these liberated men, or the freely unified men of their race, in a general type of progressive-European middle class. Cosmopolitan democratism and political nationalism—these are but two shades of one and the same color.

BYZANTIUM AND RUSSIA

RUSSIA began her historical life in Novgorod; but very soon after she transferred her center to Kiev, then to Vladimir and Moscow; then to Petersburg; and now she is evidently breaking away from it to the south again. . . .* Thus the religious culture of Islam and the state power of the Russian race are analogous from the standpoint of this "instability." But on the other hand, the difference between them is enormous. Islam, changing its center, *went no change,* as was to be expected from an original religious also *changed races, changed the state structure, but itself under-* culture. The Russian race and the Russian state structure, having always had very little originality in them, also *changed* something extremely important in their cultural type, in the whole *structure of their life and in the spirit of their world outlook* every time they *changed their center.* Novgorod was the first embryo of the Russian state and racial unity—the invitation to the Varangians; Kiev

* It is interesting to note that Lenin transferred the capital back to Moscow.

From "Letters about Eastern Affairs." WORKS, vol. V, pp. 424–426.

—Orthodoxy and the beginning of the appanage system (a kind of unsuccessful attempt at an original organization); Vladimir (not for long—the same sort of door to Moscow as Novgorod had been to Kiev); Moscow—the fall of the appanage federation; tsardom; the establishment of an Oriental-Byzantine cultural style; a fresh impulse, so to speak, "from the Varangians to the Greeks"; Petersburg— Europe; a backward impulse "from the Greeks to the Varangians," while yet preserving an enormous, firmly acquired, Byzantine reserve. Since 1861, extreme Europeanism is apparently triumphing; the *illusion* of a "prosperous," *eudaemonic democratization* has allured the *Petersburg-minded* intelligentsia of the *whole of Russia*; the decomposition of Petrine Russia has begun in accordance with the latest European models. *A monument to mark the millennium of the Russian state has been erected in Novgorod; but a millennium is a fatal and terrifying figure for any state, for very few state structures have survived for more than a thousand years; the majority have lasted much less!* And probably, if there had not been this salutary Eastern question and this great city of Tsargrad, the memorial to our pride in 1862 * would have become a memorial to our disillusionment and despair—*almost our gravestone!* But in these same fatal years (1861, 1862, 1863) there was a revival with renewed strength of those Yugoslav and Greek movements which gradually broke up Turkey, rendered impossible a *Hellenistic Byzantium,* and prepared the way for us to something new, to something which should be authentically creative, so as not to become merely destructive (and let us note, not destructive in the European sense, but to a far greater extent)!

There can be no third way, and we are no longer in a position to retire in the matter of Eastern-Slavic affairs.

That is why I consider *the sooner, the better.* A Russia in possession of Tsargrad will bring fresh life to Muscovite Russia, for Muscovite Russia originally issued from Tsargrad; it would be more cultured, that is, more authentic than Petrine Russia; it would be less rational and less utilitarian, that is, less revolution-

* 862 A.D. was the year of the foundation of Russia.

ary; it will outlast the *Petersburg* Russia. And the sooner Petersburg becomes something in the nature of a Baltic Sebastopol or a Baltic Odessa, the better it will be, I maintain, not only for us but probably also for so-called humanity, for would it not be horrible and downright injurious to think that Moses ascended Mount Sinai, that the Hellenes built their graceful acropolises, the Romans waged their Punic wars, Alexander, that handsome genius, crossed the Granicus in a plumed helmet and fought at Arbela, that the apostles preached, the martyrs agonized, the poets sang, the artists painted, and knights shown in tournaments—*only in order that the French, German, or Russian bourgeois in his ugly and comic* clothes should thrive "individually and collectively" on the ruins of all this magnificent past?

One would have to be ashamed of mankind if this vulgar ideal of universal utility, mean labor, and disgraceful prose should triumph forever!

FUNDAMENTAL THESES

(1) The state should be diversified, complex, strong, class-structured, and cautiously mobile. In general, strict, sometimes to the point of ferocity.

(2) The church should be more independent than the present one. The church hierarchy should be bolder, more powerful, more concentrated. The church should have a *mitigating* influence on the state, and not vice versa.

(3) Everyday life should be poetic, varied in its *national* unity, and insulated from the West (either one does not dance and only prays to God, or, if one dances, then in *one's own fashion*; to contrive or develop national elements to the point of elegant refinement, and so on).

From a letter to Father I. Fudel. Published in Yury Kartzov, IN MEMORY OF K. N. LEONTIEV, *1911, pp. 111–112*.

(4) The laws and principles of authority should be stricter; people should try to be personally kinder; the one will balance the other.

(5) Science should develop in a spirit of profound contempt towards its own utility.

THE PATHS OF RUSSIA

ONE OF our former writers (K. S. Aksakov, if I am not mistaken) noticed that European history takes a sharp turn in its
course at about the second half of *each century*. Perhaps this did
happen and does happen everywhere, but in European history we
not only notice this more subjectively, because it is more familiar
to us, but actually *an und für sich more objectively and acutely,* for
the Germano-Roman civilization is the most complex, the most
prominent, the most self-aware, the most expressive of all previously existing civilizations. Let us remember what occurred in the
middle *decade* of our century, that is, between 1848 and 1860, or,
if you prefer, between 1851 and 1861. (This small fluctuation in
figures is, of course, of no importance.) The *first socialist revolts* in
the West; the severest conservative reactions of the Emperor
Nicholas I of Russia and his armed suppression of the racial revolt
in Austria-Hungary.* The beginning of the Second Empire in

* I have demonstrated more than once that all the purely racial movements of
our century bring directly or indirectly liberal-egalitarian results. They merely

From "*The Average European.*" WORKS, *vol.* VI, *pp. 46–49.*

France (1851); our Eastern war (1853–1856). The accession of Emperor Alexander II to the throne of Russia and of King Frederick Wilhelm in Prussia (both these monarchs, each in his own way, brought about in Russia and Germany *for the second time a fusion of groups and social and political strata*). The unification of Italy (1859–1860); as a result, the weakening of France and Austria; because of this, the strengthening of the liberal forces in both countries. The preparation in Germany for the Schleswig-Holstein tribal (that is, mixed) war and for liberal-egalitarian reforms in Russia. In 1861,* the beginning of the one and the other. At the same time, the opening of the Civil War in America, which ended in a political fusion of southerners and northerners and social equalization of blacks and whites. *In this* interval of time (1859–60), the Far East, India and China, as if awakening from their thousand-year-old sleep, claimed their right to participate in universal history; India was the *first* to rise; China entered for the first time into a serious struggle with the two most advanced nations of Europe, France and England. India was pacified; China was defeated. But it was not the end! Both were now involved in the noisy and terrible torrent of universal fusion, and we Russians, with our gray-European, drab-bourgeois, imitative ideals, with our drunkenness and lack of character, with our lack of belief and mental fear of taking any nonexemplary step in the contemporary West—we Russians now stood between those two reawakened Asiatic worlds, between the *ferociously state-assertive giant* of China and the profoundly mystical monster of India, on the one hand, and, on the other, the perpetually growing hydra of *communist revolt* in the West, which was now undoubtedly "decomposing," and was all the more contagious as a result and all the more capable of destroying a great deal in its death agony.

Shall we survive as a state and culture? Or shall we be infected by the Chinese state system, so indestructible in its spirit, and by

share the old and the inorganic fusion with some other, not especially new element. For example, Poland and Russia in the 1860s. (K. L.)

* The year serfdom was abolished in Russia.

the mighty, mystical mood of India? Shall we be able to fuse together this Chinese state system with Indian religiosity and, *subjecting European socialism to them,* capable of gradually forming *new, stable, social groupings* and rearranging society in new horizontal strata? That is the gist of the matter! If we cannot accomplish this, then we shall find ourselves in such a central position that, having finally fused all and sundry, we would have to write the ultimate *mani-tekel-farés!* on the building of the universal state.

To end history, having destroyed mankind; by spreading universal equality and by diffusing universal freedom to make human life on the globe altogether impossible! *For, in that case, there would be no more new wild tribes, no more drowsy cultural worlds on earth.*

Groups and strata are essential. They have never been completely destroyed; they have only been reborn, passing from one sufficiently stable form through less stable and more mobile, more mixed forms *into other new, more stable forms.**

The real forces in societies are ultimately inevitable, irreversible, really immortal, so to speak. But in the course of their historical conflicts, they reduce each other alternately to a minimum of power and influence, or allow the highest degree of expansion and the greatest possible usurpation, depending on the time and place.

Whatever revolutions may occur in a society, whatever the reforms a government may introduce, *all the elements remain;* they merely reappear in different combinations of forces and of preponderance; nothing more.

The difference lies in that some combinations are favorable to the stability of the state; some, to cultural productivity; others, to both; others again are not unfavorable to either the one or the other. Thus the form which is the most deeply differentiated and contains the most groups—the form which is at the same time sufficiently concentrated in something general and higher—is the most stable and spiritually productive one; whereas the mixed,

* Guizot, *The Ancient Commune and the Feudal Commune.*

equalized, nonconcentrated form is the most unstable and spiritually barren.*

I have said "*all the elements remain*"; but they combine in a different way. I have cited examples and have said, moreover, that even *slavery* has never been entirely eradicated; it not only will not be eradicated but will probably *very soon assume* new and, probably, *more stable forms*.

Speaking of this, I have, of course, deliberately expanded the meaning of this word "slavery." Sometimes it is very useful to expand or narrow terminology in this way, because, from frequent and habitual use, it ceases to have any impact on the mind. In the presence of such mental extensions, the mind not infrequently discovers altogether unexpected perspectives. Even now slavery exists in capitalist societies; that is, hungry labor is subjected to all-powerful capital. Very many people have maintained this thesis even before I did. This expression is not new. They have also stated more than once that the *feudalism of capital* has replaced the *feudalism of the nobility*.

But insofar as the first statement seems to me to be apt, that is, *that slavery exists even now*, the application of the word "feudalism" to the present-day relationship between capital and labor is much less apt.

Slavery still exists; that is, there exists a strong involuntary dependence of working people on the representatives of mobile capital. *Great is the power of money* that the rich have; that is a fact; but if we compare the former state of affairs, say with us in Russia, with the present one, then we shall see that the same thing is true of any country where there has been a mixing of the classes—there the rich have power; the poor depend upon them. But the power of money is not stable, not legalized by privilege, *too mobile*; and the dependence of labor is also *unstable, too mobile*, fixed neither by law nor by *free right* to make a *very lasting*, eternal contract. The question is, would our Russian law permit a man to give himself a bondage for ten or fifteen years? I do not know. I am no

* Proudhon, *About the United States*.

lawyer. But it would not, it seems to me. Five years is the legal term, if I'm not mistaken.

But I know, and everybody else knows, that the contemporary liberal law does not grant a poor man, a very young one, for example, or one with a weak character, the liberty to give a rich proprietor, with whom he is drawing up a contract, the right to inflict corporal punishment on him. Not only would the courts not approve of such a contract, but very likely they would start prosecuting that proprietor.

FREEZING RUSSIA

IN THE winter it is cold, in the summer hot; many people find the one and the other unpleasant, even harmful. What is to be done? . . . Such change is natural, and the reaction, back and forth, is inevitable; everyone knows that spring follows winter, and hot days succeed spring. But who in the heat of summer will rage against the cold days long past? On the contrary, every living person is glad of everything cool in July. What follows from all this? It follows that the evils of Russia, which have now been destroyed by history, have been transformed by a series of events and the movement of minds into evils that are *too liberal!* It is impossible now to act against privileges which no longer exist; but it is necessary, on the contrary, to act in our day against *equality* and *liberalism*. That is, it is necessary to *freeze* Russia, if only slightly, in order to prevent it from "rotting." . . .

From an editorial in the newspaper WARSAW DIARY, *1880.* WORKS, *vol. VII, pp. 123–124.*

Finally, the West has had its own shades of "bureaucratism" and "barrack rule," while the communist movement is everywhere the *same,* and in the West it is more deeply rooted in the masses than with us. What has the *Russian nobility* to do with this?

THE WARMING UP OF RUSSIA

BUT WHAT shall we do with Russian society, if its historical education has been such, that it is incapable of achieving anything good *without the assistance of the government,* despite all the "constitutional" and like pretensions? Everything great and solid in the life of the Russian people was achieved almost artificially and *more or less arbitrarily.* When (as we have seen lately) the initiative of the government has assumed the character of a certain self-denial or self-limitation for the benefit of this so-called society, then the intervention and the comparative freedom of the latter have contributed nothing except *revolutionary* fruits or, at least, those of the *opposition* (with us in Russia the difference between these two political terms is quantitative rather than qualitative).

The Christianization of Russia was a government matter. The consolidation of Russia also; it was the government which also gradually imposed the *right to possess serfs*—a right so salutary in

From "A Note about the Necessity of a New Large Newspaper in St. Petersburg," 1883. WORKS, *vol.* VII, *pp.* 504–506.

its time and even so essential to *culture* (for the diversity of education, so necessary to culture, was the fruit of that *artificial feudalism*). By creating a privileged *cultural* stratum, that is, the gentry,
the government performed its great historical duty. Peter the
Great's European reforms, which were also artificial and extremely
arbitrary, are too well known, and many of their aspects have already been submitted to the judgment of history, but, evidently,
this special kind of artificiality is natural to Russia. Catherine II
also artificially attempted to impose upon her gentry a more aristocratic character. Nobody had demanded this of her; no *press*, no
mob, no *public corporations* had compelled the Empress to take
this direction. But her own genius demanded it, so to speak, also
the *nature* of Russia where only that becomes established *which, I
repeat, is created somewhat arbitrarily and artificially* by the government. Let us take another example: *officialdom*, or the *bureaucracy*, as they call it. It has many defects, many vices; officialdom is preeminently, so to say, a *governmental institution* which,
in the opinion of the liberals, is in the highest degree unnatural.
We need only turn to the best judge in such questions, to the
common sense of the Russian commoner, to understand that this
is not altogether so. The Russian commoner often suffers from the
mistakes and even the oppressions of our administration; but,
though he may be dissatisfied with the details, he nevertheless regards the bureaucracy as essential and salutary. "Officialdom" and
"Imperial servants" he says with respect, and one way or another
he will always sooner understand a good "Imperial servant" than
some independent "regional" landlord, who *charges* him (*for his
own* benefit; not that of the Sovereign) a great deal for the land.
The peasant is prepared to love even the governor, as long as he is
the Imperial governor, whereas he is ready to suspect the independent landowner and landlord of being a malefactor, and he would
be very glad to deprive him of all *his land*. It was not in vain that
the landowners of former days, when they donned their military
uniforms to face a rioting crowd of peasants and thus reminded
them that they were not only landowners (who were in a natural

conflict of interests with them) but also the servants of the Tsar, were able to pacify their inflamed spirits without having to resort to arms.

I shall even say more: if *socialism*—not as a nihilistic revolt and delirium of self-negation, but rather as a lawful organization of labor and capital, as a new kind of corporate, *coercive* serf-state imposed upon human societies—has any future at all, then nothing but a monarchical government will be able to create this new order, which would not harm either the Church, the family, or higher civilization.

ANTICHRIST IN RUSSIA

OTHERWISE, some half a century later, no more, it * will turn little by little, without noticing it, from being a "God-fearing people" into being a "God-fighting people," and become so more rapidly than any other nation. For actually, it is capable of great extremes in everything. . . . In their day, the Jews were more of a chosen people than us, for then they alone in the whole world believed in the One God. However, it was they who crucified Christ, the Son of God, when He descended on earth to them.

Without strict and well-established limitations, without a new and firm stratification of society, without all possible, persistent, and ceaseless attempts to reconstitute our shaken class structure, our Russian society, already sufficiently egalitarian in its habits, will rush more headlong than any other society along the deadly path of *universal mixing*, and who knows—like the Jews, who did

* The Russian people.

From the article "Over the Grave of Pazukhin." WORKS, *vol. VII, p.* 425.

222

not expect a Teacher of the *New Faith* to emerge from their depths, we likewise will give birth unexpectedly, some one hundred years from now—from the depths of our state, at first classless, then churchless or having only a weak church—to that same Antichrist of whom Bishop Theophanus and other spiritual writers have spoken.

CATHOLICISM

WHETHER Catholicism has been deformed or not is a theological question which I do not wish to touch upon here (since I personally believe in the rightness of Orthodoxy, I would even be obliged to agree with this); but when we wish to pose the question in an objective-scientific way, as Danilevsky * did, we cannot take as our criterion or as the basis of our dispute a purely *subjective belief*. The cultural-organic point of view is not really a Christian one; it may have a close connection with my personal Christianity, but to judge objectively, I must be able to pass outside the limits of my *personal religion*; I may well understand not only through my personal faith, through my fear of God, but in many other respects even through my reason that Orthodoxy is more *sound* than Catholicism in the sense of dogma and salvation. But when one speaks of *development*, of *authenticity*, of *cultural-religious cre-*

* Russian historian. Author of *Russia and Europe*, etc.

From an unpublished article, written in 1890–1891. WORKS, vol. VII, pp. 523–524.

ativity, I cannot help but see that after the schism of the churches Orthodoxy was arrested in Byzantium, while in Russia (and among the Slavs generally) it was adopted from there *without* any change having taken place, that is, without any *creativity* (whether harmful or useful is all the same for the moment). But it was precisely after this schism that European culture began to differentiate itself from the universal Byzantine civilization. Every step in the history of Catholicism is a creative one, the manifestation of an original, independent force.

The religious truth of my faith is one thing; the truth of the historical point of view is another. The Judaic, Old Testament faith is to a large extent obligatory for every Christian; but can we maintain that in the age of Moses and the Prophets it was as *developed* and rich in diverse content as the, to us, false pagan faith of the Egyptians or the Brahmins? It is impossible to do so. The false may also be original and very developed, intense and interesting.

Catholicism is such a mighty and complete religion that it has never before, perhaps, had its equal on earth. Are its foundations not the reason for this? We do not have to love Catholicism, we do not have to believe in it, we must struggle against it; but how can we fail to regard it as the *third in succession* and the *first in significance* as a cultural foundation for the Germano-Roman history?

THE MIND

BEYOND this mysterious line everything will begin to help faith; all things assist the glory of God, even the pride of my mind! What have I to do with all those great minds and great discoveries? I have known all this for a long time! They can no longer astonish me. I see the weak side of all those great minds, I see their contradictions, their insufficiency. Perhaps they made a mental mistake, failing to believe in the church; mathematically they had not thought far enough—they had lost this or that from sight. If everyone must make mistakes, then I had better make my own mental mistakes in my own way, as I would like to do it, rather than in the way they teach me to make mistakes. . . . In my mind I shall make mistakes in my own fashion, make the mistakes that please me, and not as they would have me do, all those European thinkers! And it is more comfortable and pleasurable for me to make mistakes together with the apostles, with John the Goldenmouthed, with the Metropolitan Filaret, with Father Ambrosy,

------

with Father Hieronymus of Mount Athos, and even with that sly and drunken priest (who only yesterday irritated me with one thing or another) than with Leo Tolstoy, Luther, Hartmann, and Proudhon. . . . Our young philosophers, Grote for example, admit the mental, philosophical rights of feeling.

Thus even the pride of my mind can lead me to submission to the church.

I do not believe in the infallibility of my mind; I do not believe in the infallibility of other minds, even the greatest; all the more, I do not believe in the sinlessness of collective mankind; but in order to live, everyone must believe in something. Let me then believe in the Gospel, as explained by the church, and not otherwise.

O Lord, how fine and easy I feel! How clear everything is! And this does not interfere with anything—neither with aesthetics nor patriotism, neither with philosophy nor a science incorrectly understood, nor, again, with the right kind of love for mankind.

THE REJECTION OF AESTHETICS

I SHALL conclude by being so bold as to add several of my crazy aphorisms:

(1) If the visible variety and the sensed intensity of life (that is, aesthetics) are the signs of mankind's inner *capacity* for life, then their diminution must be the sign that *mankind is getting old and is near death (on earth)*.

(2) The more or less successful and ubiquitous preaching of Christianity must inevitably and significantly diminish this diversity (whereas progress, so injurious to Christianity in its fundamentals, has the same external effect, partly counterfeiting it).

(3) Thus both Christian preaching and European progress strive in combination to kill off the *aesthetics of life on earth*, that is, *life itself*.

(4) And the church affirms, *"The end will be near when the Gospel will be preached everywhere."*

From a letter to V. Rozanov, May 27, 1891. WORKS, *pp. 418–419.*

(5) *What's to be done?* We must help Christianity, even at the cost of our beloved aesthetics, because of our transcendental egotism, because of our fear of the Last Judgment, for the salvation of our souls; but we should oppose progress wherever we can, for it is injurious equally to Christianity and to aesthetics.

 LITERARY CRITICISM

A LETTER TO THE POET FET

I SENT you a telegram expressing my pleasure on the occasion of your jubilee. I would have sent it earlier, on the day of the dinner in your honor at the Hermitage, if the papers had indicated in good time the precise date of this festival of Russian poetry. But we received the news here so late, and it was so inexact as regards the day, that I could not help being late. But what is to be done? Better late than never.

You have long been aware of how highly I value your poetry; for you this is no news. Since the age of twenty I have been one of those few whom you mention in your last, so sincere and beautiful a poem:

> *For fifty years I've waited for the friends of these songs,*
> *Have tried to divine who gave them living refuge. . . .*

With few exceptions, already in my youth I could not bear the poems of Nekrasov, and since my earlier years I have thought that

---

On the occasion of Fet's literary jubilee, 1899. WORKS, *vol.* VII, *pp.* 484–487.

he could have written humane and "democratic" articles without obliging us also to read his "wooden doggerel," as Yevgeny Markov has so truly said about him. It is understandable, therefore, that while living in Moscow some years ago, I decided that the time was long ripe to acknowledge in public, even though by means of an ordinary jubilee, your contribution and your significance.

"Even though by means of an ordinary jubilee," I said. What does "even though" mean? Allow me to digress as far as possible. I dislike present-day jubilees. Let us suppose that the idea behind them is good, their intention excellent. But what am I to do if I am terribly displeased by the *forms* taken by present-day festivals? I have not the strength to overcome this feeling, all the more so since my reason and my theory justify this feeling. They are terribly ugly! And may I be allowed to put it more crudely: sheer *boorishness!* Not moral boorishness, no, God forfend! Why should we think so? This would be unjust. Both the ethical sense and the spiritual mood at every festival may be beautiful. *No, it is not the ethical, but the aesthetic aspect of almost all festivals of the nineteenth century that is not good. Not their spiritual sense, but their plastic forms are horrible!*

I assure you that I have long been dreaming of your jubilee disinterestedly and even self-sacrificingly (I shall explain further why I do so disinterestedly and even self-sacrificingly). But when I learned from the papers that those who value your enormous and at the same time fine talent were preparing to celebrate your jubilee, my personally amicable delight and my, so to speak, critical and evaluating delight were clouded over—I will not even say slightly, but very much clouded. With horror I was expecting to read in the account of the ceremony again that murderous line which I had read in the description of A. N. Maikov's jubilee (whom I also value highly but with somewhat less subjective predilection).

What was this murderous line?

Here it is: "There entered the venerable jubilarian in a dress coat and white tie!" Alas! Would it not have been better to have passed over this?

Of course, in a dress coat rather than a dressing gown or even a frock coat. One might have guessed it anyhow! Everyone knows that at the time of the declaration of the "Rights of Man," exactly a hundred years ago, there began a plastic deformation of man's image on the democratized (that is, vulgarized) earth. Everyone knows that, out of all nature, the nineteenth-century European man began to wear mourning clothes at his festivals; and this mourning garb is dock-tailed into the bargain: no black cloak, but a kind of black camisole with two black tails behind.

All of nature adorns itself for its festivities. Spring is green, summer is red, and early autumn is golden—they are all more vivid than the winter. The festival of rebirth; the festival of the encounter with life; the festival of unconscious love and flowering; the festival of farewell before long repose and sleep. ("The later flowers are sweeter than the sumptuous first-born of the fields!") What festivals can plants celebrate except the festival of unconscious love and elemental inclinations? They cannot have either religious or public festivals; theirs is only the summer festival of sex urges. And so these plants put on their multicolored flowers.

For their immediate goal, beautiful flowers are not necessary to them at all. Many grasses and large trees bloom with green, invisible flowers, and this does not prevent them from multiplying—but the majority of plants bloom with flowers of many colors, and some with fragrant flowers. *They do not do this for their own sake.* This is a luxury, a surplus of the energies of beauty; this is poetry. The poetry of *life itself*, not the poetry of reflection in human art. Many animals also have this surplus beauty, so unessential to them; they have flowing manes, tails, elegant horns. A not especially beautiful gray parrot lives and multiplies in exactly the same way as a splendid cockatoo or an ara. And let us suppose that our jackdaw, dispensing with a purple head, azure wings, and a tuft, enjoys life no less than other birds. That is so; but on the other hand, neither do all its superfluous and lovely adornments prevent a bird of paradise from enjoying various pleasant sensations any less than a jackdaw. But to observe a flock of jackdaws is not quite the same as admiring a multitude of birds of paradise.

Why then should we not also apply the same *external* aesthetic criterion to people?

Why should we be afraid to admit that to gaze at a troop of Life Guards riding in Petersburg to be reviewed by the Tsar is a delight for a sound taste, while to watch officials or professors in session is a bore? . . .

ON RUSSIAN REALISM

LAST TIME I wished to state that in my short article "Clubbing Together," I intended to expound briefly my general views on contemporary Russian literature as a whole since the days of Gogol and to say that my *critical taste has long been ahead of my creative urge.* For a long time now I have ceased to appreciate the cold objectivity of all our writers, their false, negative outlook on life, their revolting realistic details. Their very language (I am not referring now to some Avseyenko or Kliushnikov, not to the uncouth works of Leskov or Krestovsky,* but to our best authors, to Leo Tolstoy, Turgenev, Pisemsky)—the very language of these best writers of ours has so often revolted me that I have long been seeking an opportunity to express my opinion on this subject.

I have maintained more than once that if the French are too

---

* V. Avseyenko (1842–1913), a minor novelist. Ivan Kliushnikov (1811–1895), a poet. Vsevolod Krestovsky (1840–95), a minor novelist.

From REMINISCENCES, *written in 1874–1875. Published in* LITERATURNOYE NASLEDSTVO (THE LITERARY HERITAGE), *nos. 22–24, 1935, pp. 463–464.*

fond of *elevating* life (*on high heels and stilts,* as people used to say in the 1840s), then Russian writers are too fond of abasing it in every way. *Life itself* is better than our literature. Everything in our writers is more or less coarse—the comedy, the attitude to characters. Even *War and Peace,* a work I myself have read three times and regard as excellent, is spoiled by a multitude of the most unnecessary coarse elements.

In *Anna Karenina* also—in which novel the author evidently consciously strove, more than in his previous works, to be elegant —in his choice of characters and in form we come across those quite unnecessary and disgusting tricks from which none of our writers since the days of Gogol has been able to rid himself entirely. I suggest that we remember the scene where the barber shaves Oblonsky; the whistling sniffle of Karenina's husband; how Count Vronsky pulled his cap over *his prematurely balding head* and how he *poured water over his healthy, ruddy neck.* But in *Anna Karenina* all these faults have been enumerated; they may be forgiven on account of the wonderful artistry and poetry of the rest. But in order to understand fully what I am saying, it is necessary to read those famous *Sportsman's Sketches* and, by way of contrast, fragments from writers who have not been corrupted by Gogol. Take, for example, Pushkin's *The Captain's Daughter* or, from foreign writers, *Werther, Manon Lescaut,* Chateaubriand's *René,* or the prose rendering of *Childe Harold* by Amadé Pichot. Or, finally, something nearer to us—the first sketches and novellas of Marko Vovchok.* Marko Vovchok is a woman, and she has managed to avoid the general coarse manner of our masculine literature. Her talent was not a rich one, and the nihilists spoiled her too soon by suggesting a *direction* to her; but her small works are above perfection. Another woman writer, Kokhanovskaya,† is not at all like her, but these two women writers have one thing in

* Maria Markovich (1834–1907), pseudonym Marko Vovchok, wrote novels in both Russian and Ukrainian.

† Nadezhda Sckhanskaya (1825–1884), novelist. Her pen name was Kokhanovskaya.

common: they have rid themselves of Gogolian elements more successfully than all our men writers.

Kokhanovskaya's content is in the highest degree *positive, and her expression* is ardent, emotional, and rapturous (Gogol has this in his *Rome* and *Taras Bulba*). Marko Vovchok's *content* is more protestant and more negative, but her *expression* is in the highest degree gentle, elegant, somehow *silky-pale* and fragrant. . . .

I have already written an article about her in the *Otechestvennyie Zapiski* * of 1861, and I am *applying this article* here. My taste was formed so long ago, and for as long I have been sickened by the petty realism and the falsehood of negation which have crushed us all and which, even in the case of those writers who would sooner prefer to be positive rather than negative, find an outlet for themselves in language at least, in certain turns of speech, in constant pretensions to humor and comic effects, in the crude surfeit of certain descriptions, which were simply "turned in" rather than written (see the description of the horse in *Anna Karenina* and *Bezhin Meadow* in *A Sportsman's Sketches*).

My taste, as I have said, was formed long ago, but as a creative writer I could not even approach for a long time the ideal I was aspiring to. Only my *Oriental Tales* satisfy that ideal to a certain extent. While correcting proofs, I recently reread my *Chrizo* three times and found nothing there to disgust me; nothing in this novella reminded me of the contemporary Russian vulgarity. On the other hand, when I reread *Podlipki*, published by me in 1861, together with my review of Vovchok's work and my novel V *Svoyem Kraiu*,† I, blushing, came across on every page those very same traits which sicken me so much in other writers. *Chrizo* was written in 1867; six years of living and a sojourn abroad were necessary for me to make the transition from my critical awareness to my capacity to realize even approximately that which I wished to ask of myself and others. *"La critique est aisée, l'art est difficile."*

* *Notes of the Fatherland.*
† In My Land.

DOSTOYEVSKY

IN ORDER to be Orthodox, *it is essential to read the Gospel through the glass of the teachings of the Holy Fathers;* otherwise, it is possible to derive sectarianism from the Holy Writ itself, as do the Scoptzi, the Lutherans, and the Molokans, or other pseudo-doctrines, of which there are so many and which, all of them, claim to be based upon the New Testament (or the Bible in general). Let us note another detail: this young woman (Marmeladova) * somehow does not attend mass, does not seek counsel from Father confessors or monks; she does not kiss *miraculous icons* or *relics;* all she does is to have a requiem mass said for her father. In real life, such a woman would not have failed to do these things, if any vital religious feeling had been awakened in her. In Petersburg and its vicinity, all this may be found. And it is

---

* Dostoyevsky, *Crime and Punishment.*

From the article "On Universal Love: The Speech pronounced by Dostoyevsky on the Occasion of the Pushkin Festival in 1880." WORKS, vol. VIII, pp. 196–201.

even more probable that the lives of St. Fyodora, St. Mary the Egyptian, Taisa, and the Reverend Aglaida would have been found in her hands far more often than the Gospel. From this it is evident that Mr. Dostoyevsky, when he wrote *Crime and Punishment*, gave very little thought to real (that is, church) Christianity. In *The Possessed*, things are a little better. In a square, the reader is made to see an *icon*, which is revered by the "people." The author is evidently expressing his indignation against the nihilists, who have ventured to insult this national holy object, and that is all. In the highest or the most cultured circle of Russians in public life, many talk a great deal about God, about Christ (about "Him")—talk fluently, eloquently, ardently, with great sincerity, but nevertheless in a manner that is not quite Orthodox, not in that of the Fathers of the church, not *ecclesiastically*. From the religious standpoint, all these speeches are nothing more than a beautiful, sweet-smelling "sop", in the highest degree useful *in the beginning* to him who has altogether forgotten how to think about God and Christ; but it is only a "beginning of the way," "only a sop." But a man will relish *the solid, authentic food of Orthodox Christianity* only when he begins to read, with *quivering*, vital interest, for the sincere good of his own heart, the writings of John Chrysostomos, Filaret of Moscow,* the lives of the saints, St. Barsonophius the Great,† St. John Climacus, the correspondence between the Optina preceptors, Makarius and Antony, and their spiritual children, laymen and monks.

True, the epigraph chosen for the novel, *The Possessed*, tells about the possessed man, who, when he had been *exorcised, sat at the feet of Christ*, while the devils that had inhabited him now entered into the swine which then drowned themselves in the sea. In Dostoyevsky, the "possessed" personify *Russia*, in this case a Russia that will be exorcised of all her moral maladies, personal and public, only when she becomes a *more Christian nation in*

* Metropolitan Filaret (Drozdov) of Moscow (1783–1867), author of a Greek Orthodox catechism.
† Ascetic monk (*d.* 550?).

spirit (in the person of its cultured representatives, of course). But this also is very vague. *What kind* of a Christianity? Some kind of general evangelic Christianity or a really Orthodox one, with a belief in the Iversky Holy Virgin, the relics of St. Sergius, the sermons of Tikhon Zadonsky * and Filaret, in the perspicacity and the holy life of certain monks, who are still alive?

What particular kind of Christianity will be the salvation of Russia in the future? The first, vaguely evangelic one, which will unfailingly seek out *forms*, or the second one, already possessing determined forms, which are familiar to all (outwardly at least, if not in their inward sense)?

To this, in *The Possessed*, we shall not find even a shadow of an answer!

The Brothers Karamazov is much closer to the gist of the matter. Here it is evident that the author has followed, though somewhat slowly, the right path.

In *The Brothers Karamazov* Orthodox monks play a significant role; the author treats of them with love and deep respect; certain of the characters of the higher class admit their special spiritual authority. To the Elder Zosima † is attributed even the mystical gift of "perspicacity" (in his prophetic obeisance to Dmitry Karamazov, who in the future will be mistakenly accused of patricide), and so on.

It is true that in *The Brothers Karamazov* the monks say things that are not quite so, or, to put it more precisely, say things that good monks would not actually say in Russia or on Mount Athos, whether they be Russian, Greek, or Bulgarian monks. True, little is said here about church liturgy and monastic vows; there is not a single liturgical service, not a single prayer. Ferapont, *the hermit and strict faster*, who has little contact with other *people*, is depicted in an unfavorable and ironic light. For some reason, a nox-

---

* Russian saints: St. Sergius of Radonezh (fourteenth century) and St. Tikhon of Zadonsk (1724–1783).

† His prototype was Leontiev's spiritual guide the Elder Ambrosius.

ious smell exudes from the body of the deceased Elder Zosima, and this embarrasses the monks who regard him as a saint.

That is not the way, let us assume, that one should write about all this, while remaining completely on the "ground of reality." Let us assume that it would have been better to combine a *stronger mystical feeling with greater precision in the description of reality*: that would be both more truthful and more useful, whereas in this novel of Mr. Dostoyevsky's the strictly mystical feelings are weakly described, while the feelings of *humanitarian idealization* are expressed with extreme ardor and at length even in the statements made by the monks.

All that is so. However, comparing *The Brothers Karamazov* with Mr. Dostoyevsky's previous works, one cannot help but rejoice that a Russian man of this kind, so gifted and so sincere, is trying to follow the authentic path of the church; one cannot help but rejoice that he is apparently striving at last to embody in forms which are definite and sacred to us the lyricism of his ardent, but self-willed and not yet very clear, morality.

One step, two steps more, and he may be able to make us a present that is truly and greatly instructive.

And then suddenly that *speech!* Again those "peoples of Europe"! Again that "ultimate word of universal reconciliation"!

That "universal man"!

"*Et tu Brute!*"

Alas, and *you also!*

From this speech at the Pushkin celebration, for me at least (I admit) it quite unexpectedly appeared that Mr. Dostoyevsky, like the great majority of *Europeans* and Russian *universal men, still* believes in a peaceful and humble future, and is glad that we Russians may soon have to drown and dissolve without leaving a trace in the impersonal ocean of cosmopolitanism.

Without a trace—that's it! For what shall we bring to this (in my opinion, boring to the point of disgust) *universal feast* of universal, uniform brotherhood? What trace of *that which is peculiar to us,* unlike anything else, shall we leave in the milieu of the *intermixed people of the future,* "in a crowd," if not always "sullen," then "soon forgotten"?

> *Above the world we'll pass without a trace or sound—*
> *No fruitful thought bequeathing to the ages,*
> *Nor with the genius of a work begun. . . .*

To our nation was entrusted one great treasure—our strict and unbending church Orthodoxy. But our best minds do not wish to "submit" to it, to its *"exclusivism"* and to that *apparent coldness* which is the effect that all things established, correct, and firm always produce on romantically nurtured souls. They prefer to "submit" to the doctrines of antinational eudaemonism, which has nothing new to show even in relation to Europe.

All the expectations of earthly love and earthly peace may be found in the songs of Béranger and, even to a greater extent, in George Sand, as well as in many others.

In this connection, not only God's name but *Christ's* name, too, has been mentioned in the West more than once.

The too rosy hue introduced into Christianity *by this speech* of Mr. Dostoyevsky's constitutes a *novelty* in relation to the church, which does not expect anything particularly beneficent from mankind in the future; but this rosy hue has nothing in it that is either particularly Russian or particularly new in relation to the predominant European thought of the eighteenth and nineteenth centuries.

While Mr. Dostoyevsky in his novels speaks in *images,* it is evident that the author, fully and to a greater extent than many of us, is a *Russian man,* despite a *certain personal admixture* of *lyrical subjectivity* in all these images.

But the *pure thought* underlying this recent speech, when separated and extracted from these Russian images, from the circumstances of that Russian background, turns out to be, like that of all our best writers, almost wholly European in its ideas and even in its origin.

Until now it is *thoughts especially* that we have failed to bequeath to the ages!

And, reflecting upon this sad characteristic of ours, it is easy, of course, to believe that we shall soon be dissolved in *everything* and *in all things* without leaving a trace.

Perhaps that is how it should be; but what is there to rejoice at here? That I cannot, am unable to understand!

TOLSTOY

THE TWO principal works of Count Tolstoy, *Anna Karenina* and *War and Peace*, not only can be but also must be compared, one with the other. Comparing them in detail and giving preference, during this detailed examination, now to one, now to another, it is essential to admit that the sum of their achievements is identical.

In *War and Peace* the task is more elevated and the choice more rewarding; but for this very reason, namely, that in *Anna Karenina* the author was left more to his own devices and that here he received no external assistance from a given, great historical situation, he was obliged amid the variegated background of the flashing phenomena of the contemporary torrent, to select something and "fix" this chosen material in "enduring thought," one is inclined to give the author of *Anna Karenina* preference over the creator of the national epic.

From the article "Analysis, Style, and Trends (On the Novels of Count L. N. Tolstoy)." WORKS, *vol. VIII, pp. 234–239, 248–255, 295–299, 304–311.*

Needless to say, *War and Peace* abounds in many more tensely dramatic scenes. On top of this, the type of tragedy is superior. In an epic men fight for their country (on both sides, for the French were conducting aggressive wars for the predominance of France, for the advantage of their country). In his contemporary novel *Anna Karenina*, the war of the Russian "volunteers" in support of Serbia is referred to only distantly and is undoubtedly condemned by the author. There are two suicides (an unsuccessful and a successful one), and Levin has suicidal thoughts; this is incomparably gloomier and even more vulgar; but it is not Count Tolstoy who is to blame for this, but rather contemporary life. This material came to him from the outside, just as the fire of Moscow and the battle of Borodino were ready-made for *War and Peace*. It is difficult to write a big, truthful, and interesting novel based on present-day Russian reality without there being present in it at least a few thoughts of suicide, so habitual has suicide unfortunately become in real life.

In any case, it is the great merit of *War and Peace* that its tragic elements are sober, sane, not distorted, as they are in so many of our writers. It is not what we find in Dostoyevsky—the tragic aspect of some kind of flophouses, brothels, and almost the Preobrazhensky hospital. The tragic elements in *War and Peace* are useful; they predispose one to military heroism in the cause of one's country; Dostoyevsky's sense of tragedy may only excite a few psychopaths living in badly furnished apartments.

Even in *Anna Karenina* the two suicides, that of Vronsky and that of Anna, are submerged in such an abundance of health, strength, physical beauty, brilliance, peace, and gaiety that they cannot offend too much the emotions and the taste of a normal reader.

In both novels Tolstoy's incredible subtlety of mind could not kill his healthy feelings or, let us say, his "flair."

The historical or, more precisely, the direct political merit of the author in *War and Peace* is enormous. How many of us were thinking of the year 1812 when Tolstoy reminded us of it so indelibly? Very few indeed! And despite the fact that the count censured the war fairly "tendentiously" and *theophilanthropically*, now in person, now by the mouth of the good-natured but eternally absent-minded Pierre, he is nevertheless so veracious an artist that the reader finds it very easy to heed neither the author nor Pierre and to continue to look at war as one of the highest, ideal manifestations of life on earth, despite all the personal misfortunes it causes. (Misfortunes constantly attended for many people, let us state, with joys so special that peace lacks them!)

And this in our century, which is still far from having been cured from its craze for "universal utilitarian prosperity"—a great political service indeed!

I shall explain now why I preferred to use above the word "political" rather than the word "historical" merit. By the author's expression "the *historical* merit of the writer," I mean the quality of precision and faithful description rather than that of a strong and useful influence. That is why.

It is still not easy to decide how faithful is the description of the epoch in *War and Peace*; but it is easy to admit that this description leaves a deep patriotic trace in the reader's soul. Because of our tendency to be suspicious of ourselves, to see something bad and weak in ourselves rather than something good and strong, Count Tolstoy's external devices, now subtle and carping, now almost coarse—I shall not even say more real, but more *realistic* and *naturalistic*—are very useful. If the novel had been written in a slightly more ideal vein, more simply, in a more generalized way, people would not have *believed* it. But when the Russian reader perceives that Count Tolstoy is far more attentive and critical than he himself is, when he perceives, this foster child of the "Gogolian" and the "half-Gogolian period," that in Tolstoy a hero (a *real* hero) "snorted," another "sobbed," a third "squealed;" that one hero "quailed," another "intrigued," a third was simply a scoundrel, but died for his country (for example, young Kuragin) —when this eternally vacillating Russian reader realizes that Count Tolstoy is laughing a little at almost all of his characters (it seems at all of them with the exception of the Emperor Alexander Pavlovich, Andrey Bolkonsky, and the vicious Dolohov—for some reason . . .), then he, the reader, becomes disposed to everything lofty and develops a stronger belief in the ideal.

The Russian reader of our time (especially the reader who occupies a middle position in society) is not satisfied with the realism which maintains that this man is weak but that one is perfidious, that this one is cruel but that one is comic, tactless, pitiful, and so on. This is still, let us suppose, a moderate and truthful realism; we are all weak and sinful; but that is not enough for us, I say. We find it necessary that someone should snort, and so on. There is no need for the reader not to notice so often that people snort, spit in anger, and so on. But prominent people have educated him in such a way that a wart will make him believe more strongly in nobility, a snort will make him feel love more intensely, and so on; and if someone "with a nervous gesture pours out a glass of vodka" and then, instead of smiling, "smirks," his confidence will be complete! In my eyes—I am prepared to repent—all this is an enormous defect common more or less to all Russian novellas or novels, beginning with *Dead Souls* (where it is still appropriate) and extending almost as far as Count Tolstoy's *What Makes People Live* (here, thank God, there is already nothing of the sort). Perhaps it is only the talented women writers—Yevgenia Tur,* M. Vovchok, and Kokhanovskaya—who have rid themselves of this. I remember how much more freely I breathed in 1860 when I heard the pleasant, musical, and fragrant speech (although a liberally tendentious one) of M. Vovchok. About the same thing, but said in a different way!

"Such am I, Felitza, I'm debauched" in *aesthetics*, but I cannot, like Derzhavin,† say further, "but all the world resembles me." On the contrary! Who is at fault, I or the best of our writers and the public, I have no idea! Let me be at fault in my "feminine" tastes in this respect, but I have not repudiated them in the

* The pen name of the Countess E. Salias de Tournemire.
† Gavriil Derzhavin (1743–1816), Russian poet. His ode *Felitza* (1782).

past thirty years; and I, of course, shall not repudiate them now.

But Count Tolstoy is right all the same; I understand this. He is doubly right: he is right because he has felt for a long time the insuperable need to observe in *this way and no other,* to express himself thus and not otherwise. He could not make the transition to the simple and pure style of his latest folk stories without first having satiated himself earlier on all those bumps and pricks of the naturalistic school, not excelling others very much (Turgenev, for example) even on this ground of crude, everyday slang. It may be difficult and maybe even impossible for a writer to enter upon a new path without having served one style to the point of satiety.

Secondly, Count Tolstoy is also right because, whether consciously or unconsciously, he has rendered his readers a patriotic service by all this slight, external *humiliation* of *life*; the readers like this and, through this, acquire a greater belief in what is lofty and are all the more surprised at the elegance they find in him.

When Turgenev (as Mr. P. Boborykin* has borne witness) stated so fundamentally and nobly that his own talent must not be compared with the gift of Tolstoy and that "Levushka Tolstoy is an elephant," I always think that he must have had *War and Peace* in mind at that moment. It is an elephant, indeed! Or, if you would rather have something more monstrous, then an excavated *çivatherium* in the flesh—a *çivatherium,* the huge skulls of which are preserved in India in the temples of the god Çiva. A trunk, the enormous proportions, the tusks, and, above the tusks, horns as well, as if contrary to all zoological conventions.

Or we can also liken *War and Peace* to the Hindu idol with three heads, four faces, and six arms! The dimensions are huge and the substance is precious, and the eyes are of rubies and diamonds, not only *under* the brow but *also on the brow!* And there is the staying power of the general plan and the great weight of the inexhaustible details; four almost equal heroines (in the eyes of the author and the reader), and three heroes (Bezuhov, Bolkonsky, Rostov; Natasha, Maria, Sonya, and Elena). The psychological

* Pyotr Boborykin (1836–1921), a novelist.

analysis in most of the cases is astonishing, particularly as it is applied to the most diverse people: Napoleon, the sick man near Borodino, and the peasant girl at the council in Fili; Natasha and Kutuzov; Princess Maria and the humble Captain Tushin; Nikolenka Bolkonsky and the two brothers Rostov. . . .

And if I turn with similar demands to both of Tolstoy's big novels, then, despite all the great merits of *War and Peace*, I shall find that *Anna Karenina* has its own qualities, particularly from the standpoint of *good*, healthy realism.

If I ask myself, "Is the external work in *War and Peace* as pure as in *Anna Karenina?*" I must reply, "No, it is not as pure."

Is the psychological analysis in the half epic, half chronicle of *War and Peace* as exact and mature as in the contemporary novel, *Anna Karenina,* which is so skillfully split in two directions?

No, not as exact and mature.

Is the general trend of *War and Peace* as true in spirit and style to the life of the year 1812 as the trend of *Anna Karenina* is faithful to the spirit and style of our time?

It seems to me not so true.

And finally:

Can we say about *War and Peace* what was said about *Anna Karenina* by the Russian critic whose words I have previously cited, namely, that in *Anna Karenina* it is possible to study life itself?

I don't think so.

First, about analysis.

In the second novel, when it became essential to bring the proud, firm, calmly confident Vronsky, who was blessed with all the good things in life, to the point of sudden suicide, Count Tolstoy grasped that Vronsky's passion for Anna and the external obstacles were not in themselves strong enough motives for this. It was necessary, first of all, to humiliate him somewhat *in his own eyes*. But how arrive at that? Another man could not succeed in deliberately humiliating him; Vronsky would kill him or would be killed himself in the contest, but our opponent could never humiliate him in his own eyes, as almost all of Turgenev's weak-souled heroes are, as Tolstoy's Levin, an energetic and courageous but tactless and shy man in company, was often upset, if not humiliated. Vronsky was not a man like that. How was he to be dealt with? In what exceptional but, at the same time, natural conditions should he be placed in order that he might lose his "moral balance"? Count Tolstoy found these appropriate conditions. Vronsky was humiliated in the presence of her unattractive, old, prosaic husband by *the woman he loved* at the moment of his expected death. And let us also remember that, shortly before this, Vronsky, as if on purpose, began to doubt himself for the first time in his life; he became displeased with himself in consequence of becoming acquainted with a certain foreign prince. The prince bored him by his fine and profound arrogance; and in the unpleasant traits of this highly placed foreigner Vronsky perceived, as in a magnifying glass, his own traits and exclaimed, "Stupid oaf! Am I really like that?"

When, *after this*, Anna forced him to beg forgiveness from Karenin, he shot himself without any prolonged qualms. "Lowering his head with an expression of mental strain, he stood there, motionless, for about two minutes with a revolver in his hand, thinking. "Of course," he said, and so on.

How true! Until then, Vronsky had not been accustomed to humiliation and self-abasement, and *this* was enough for him.

Everyone is aware that people who are accustomed to bear mortification and sorrow do not make attempts on their life as easily as those who are not accustomed to bear it with patience. Young people, for example (in our times, at least), resort to suicide more often than their elders. The newspapers not infrequently carry news items in which surprise is expressed that "as it is, the suicide was old."

This special kind of psychic preparation by Vronsky for his suicide attempt is so astonishingly authentic, it represents such a genuine *tour de force*, such talent, that behind it one may, indeed, detect a purely scientific quality. I can cite here another equivalent but not at all similar example. This has to do with the *mushroom* which prevented Sergey Ivanovich Koznishev from becoming engaged to Varenka. As soon as he was about to tell her that she pleased him very much, she found a large mushroom and, in doing so, interrupted *not so much his train of thought as his flow of feelings.* Children also ran up inopportunely. It was his feelings that were really interrupted, for the *thoughts* of a man accustomed to public speaking could not be easily interrupted by such nonsense. But this mushroom and these children's shouts sufficed to cool the recent and not so strong, *calculating* enthusiasm of a solid, impractical man who has long ago "settled" into an excellent public position. The drop of warm feeling which was about to pour out of the vessel of his soul, brimming with the poetry of rural life and the impact of this delightful encounter with a young woman who "suited" him, was instantly frozen. It froze, this drop, and forthwith this experienced intellectual said to himself, "*What is this for?* All this is attractive, but . . . is it not better for a bachelor to live out his bachelor life to the end?"

And not a word more.

This trait of psychic analysis is on a par with Vronsky's preparation to shoot himself in the chest! An original trait this, fully individual and exact. But *this mushroom* would not have stopped either Vronsky, who was passionate and resolute despite his outward reserve, or Prince Oblonsky, the carefree and amorous epicurean, or Levin, a vacillating character, it is true, but also a most impetuous one. This mushroom might, indeed, have interrupted Levin's *thoughts* for a whole day, but in no circumstances would it have broken the flow of his *feelings* forever.

To the number of these observations, astonishing in their beauty, refinement, and truthfulness, we can add the passage where Vronsky, taking his place thoughtfully and absent-mindedly in a carriage on his way to the races, fell to admiring for an instant a "*fluid column of midges.*"

Let us remember that he was at the time both happy and excited: Anna had just informed him that she was pregnant by him.

A far more serious, even tragic principle, perhaps, or, at least, a vague fear of something strict and perilous now enters into their love, into their passion which had seemed *only* pleasant until then. Such a serious shade of feeling, such hints of the possibility of some kind of tragedy, do not frighten energetic men, but merely excite them all the more and incline them to greater firmness and resolution when they are driven by passion and not yet exhausted by their vital struggle. But however firm and calm in *appearance* (that is, when meeting and dealing with other people) a man may be, he has to pay for this excitement; at such moments every man is *not quite* what he usually is inwardly when alone. Vronsky is not a contemplative man; he is not at all inclined to ponder for any length of time *about anything* or to be distracted *by anything*. Besides, he is in a hurry to get to the races. Yet, instead of simply taking his seat in the carriage, he stares at "the midges marking time in the sun." I admit that on reading this for the first time, I thought this was one of Tolstoy's descriptive notes which lead nowhere, analysis for the sake of analysis, a note for its own sake. "*It can happen* that somebody will be lost staring at midges." But as I read further, I soon repented and honored the author with the most sincere enthusiasm. I shall not begin to enlarge here upon the splendid description of the officers' steeplechase; I hope that everybody remembers well the *many* motives that had now come together to upset in Vronsky's soul that particular calm which, according to the words of the English trainer, was essential to him that he might triumph over Mahotin. The news of Anna's pregnancy, the presence of the Emperor and the court, the presence of Anna and her husband, the brother's unpleasant remarks, his sporting feelings in themselves, and, at the very bottom of his soul, a certain predisposition to unaccustomed reflection, to a contemplative absent-mindedness, an untimely inclination to *stare at the midges!* Thus, in another moment of absent-mindedness, Vronsky broke the back of his favorite horse by making a wrong, awkward movement!

When I read as far as the place where Frou-Frou fell, I understood the whole meaning of the "midges in the sun." In Vronsky's case, of course, as regards these very midges, I also note another profound trait, another slender but very strong connection: Vronsky is *something of a painter* by nature, and later in Italy he attempts, though unsuccessfully, to occupy himself with serious painting.

In Anna's preparations for suicide, excellently depicted on the whole, there are also two features which are especially significant and which continue to define themselves further in the future. One feature is the opinion loudly expressed in Anna's presence by the unknown lady in the railway carriage (the lady who, let us note, struck Anna as being very unpleasant): "Reason is granted to man so that he may rid himself of what disturbs him." The other feature is that Anna decides on suicide *only when* a railway worker doing something close to the rails *reminds her instantly* of her whole recent past, beginning with the worker who was crushed by the train when she first met Vronsky.

Until the unpleasant lady spoke that sentence, until the moment when she saw the worker, Anna probably did not yet know what she would do to herself.

Anna had heard, of course, more than once previously the saying "Reason will teach you a way out"; but this is a general psychic law to the effect that the truest and oldest or, on the contrary, the cleverest and newest thought acts upon and strongly influences our acts when our feelings are prepared to accept it.

Our feelings are *prepared*; a strange thought surprises us very much; and our will puts this thought into practice.

The accidental but timely banal opinion expressed by the unpleasant lady had a mental, *rationalistic* effect, so to speak, on Anna's decision, which had already been prepared by her feelings. The sight of the railway worker then produced an *instantaneous*, almost mystical effect on her imagination and will.

This is amazing!

In Anna's preliminary reflections there is also a very true and touching note; she saw a sign: "*Tiutkin coiffeur; je me fais coiffer par Tiutkin.* . . . I shall tell him that," and she smiled; but, at the same moment, she remembered that there was nobody with whom she could now share a pleasantry! This was a momentary gleam of comedy, gaiety, and good nature amid all the horrors of spiritual confusion. This is something that happens often enough, especially to people of a lively character; at the cruelest moments of life some amusing, gay nonsense may unexpectedly come into one's mind. But this true and subtle observation has no connection with the future development of the plot. I have deliberately cited it here for the sake of *contrast,* in order all the better to clarify my views on the various kinds of Tolstoy's analyses and on their comparative value.

It is also interesting to compare the two preparations for suicide—that of Vronsky and that of Anna.

Vronsky and Anna are driven to this act by a whole series of internal processes and external jolts. But the difference, nevertheless, is great. Vronsky is stronger of will, firmer. *He knows beforehand what he wants.* Anna is more impressionable, restless, fearful; until the last minute, until her *encounter with the railway worker,* she does not know what she will do. Vronsky's decision depends, first of all, on his own weighty and attentive argument; he ponders over his decision *alone in his room.* There are no external jolts, no other opinions, no decisive, accidental meetings. He thought it over; he said to himself, "Of course!" and he pulled the trigger.

Anna drove from her house without any plan or decision; her decision is come by almost instinctively, under the impact of accidental impressions. "And *suddenly,* remembering the man who had been crushed by the train on the day of her first meeting with Vronsky, *she understood what she must do.*"

I do not know where else we can find such astonishingly true-to-life, personal variations on one and the same psychic theme.

Nowhere else in the world, it seems. . . .

If this connection does indeed exist in *War and Peace,* not only a hidden connection (as in life itself) but one that is *con-*

sciously revealed by the author, the reader is decidedly *unaware* of it—not only at the first reading but also after many consequent ones (as happened to me).

Napoleon's invasion, Austerlitz and the battle of Borodino, the fire of Moscow; the glittering court, the intrigues and the mistakes of the generals, the famous historical personages, brilliant images such as Natasha and Prince Andrey; all those deliriums, dreams, broad fantasies; the author's strategic review, his philosophy, finally—it may not please us (as it does not please me), but it is all absorbing and demanding of *attention*.

Behind all those large and weighty or vivid, outstanding, and brilliant products of the author's creative process, it was perhaps hardly possible to detect that very fine but likewise vivid and extremely strong net of inner psychic ties which, in the less weighty and less burdened second novel, leap so sharply to the eyes.

I do not know whether only *we can perceive this* or whether the author had consciously wished to elaborate this aspect in *Anna Karenina* and had thrown a brighter light on these leading points, because he was less distracted and less burdened with other things.

I shall not venture to decide whether it has to do with *our*, with my, psychology as a reader, as a problem in the dimensions and quantities of perception, or with the psychology of creation as a problem in the possibility and impossibility of a steady, simultaneous ripening of all the aspects of the task involving artistic work.

I leave that to better-informed people and those more accustomed to the abstract work of thought. As for myself, I cannot, without the assistance of others, repudiate the thought that the spiritual analysis in *Anna Karenina* is more exact, maturer, and more astounding.

There is yet another special kind of spiritual analysis, which came into fashion with us already in the 1840s and 1850s. At one time Count Tolstoy also was much preoccupied with it. It may be called the analysis of *suspicion* or of excessive *scrutiny*.

For example, such and such a lady of honor "looks sad when

mentioning the name of the Empress Maria Fyodorovna or when speaking about the Imperial family"; or Kutuzov, when having an eloquent and subtle explanation with an Austrian general, evidently "is listening to himself with great pleasure" (*War and Peace*, Part II, Chapter 3). Or again (Part II, Chapter 1), "It was apparent that the regimental commander's irritation gave him pleasure," and so on.

In its affectation and refinement, this kind of criticism and presupposition can be often enough quite unfounded and contributes nothing special to the development of the characters, even if we say nothing about how boring this habit of our authors has proved.

There is a passage in *War and Peace* where this *analysis of suspicion* appears entirely out of place and unjust; this is where Count Tolstoy suspects *all* mothers of feeling *envy* at the marital happiness of their daughters.

In *War and Peace* (Part III, Chapter 2), there is a description of that evening reception and supper at the house of the Kuragins when the wealthy Pierre Bezuhov was affianced almost unawares to Elena. Anna Mikhailovna Drubetskaya congratulates the mother on this betrothal; but Princess Kuragin keeps *silent*, "so much did her *envy of her daughter's happiness torment her.*"

But let this incident be! The Kuragin family, generally lacking in moral principles and moral feelings, may be abandoned to the author for his lacerating treatment of them; but whom I am prepared to defend fervently on account of similar faultfinding while attacking the author is the kind, child-loving Countess Rostov, whom the author by all the indications loves. She shows her son Nikolai a letter from Andrey Bolkonsky, who is already engaged to Natasha, *"with that hidden feeling of ill will which a mother always entertains against the future marital happiness of her daughter."*

Well, what is the purpose of this strained interpretation? What is applicable to the Princess Kuragin is not at all natural to the kind and honest Countess Rostov! If this comment had been written by a woman, one might have, perhaps, reflected sadly and asked oneself, "Perhaps she does really know about this?" But if we are going to be suspicious and overcritical, then, in that case, I would rather suspect this lady novelist of some personal pique against her mother or against the mothers of some of her girl friends than accuse *always and all* elderly mothers of such a vicious and stupid feeling.

Now, in my turn, I wish to pick a bone with Count Tolstoy over this issue and insist on asking him why he had to indulge in this almost monstrous and unfounded prank. Perhaps this ugly spiritual gesture on the part of the old countess is connected with something in the future? Perhaps this barely perceptible seed of evil will grow later into a big tree? Perhaps the Countess Rostov, by some arguments and acts, will later break up her daughter's marriage with Bolkonsky? No, there is no mention of that. The old countess will conduct herself in this matter irreproachably to the end, and her feelings even towards her guilty daughter will remain kindly. She will even allow, without protest, Prince Andrey to die in her house in the arms of Natasha. Therefore, there is certainly no *connection* with anything that occurs later.

Or perhaps the author found it necessary to invent this unattractive, impure movement of a mother's heart for one reason only, namely, that he did not wish the Countess Rostov to appear too perfect. The author loves and values people who represent an ideal in life, but he has no desire to idealize in art; he wishes all the best characters in his novels to have frailties, defects, even rather vicious though transient feelings.

But even so the Countess Rostov is no perfect being; she is a good wife, a kind woman, a loving, affectionate mother, but she has no special distinction of mind; she is sometimes a trifle capricious, far less kind and greathearted than her husband (for example, in the matter of the carts for the wounded soldiers after Borodino); towards poor Sonya, who is completely dependent on her, she behaves very cruelly and ignobly, calling her to her eyes an *intriguing* woman because of her so natural desire to become the wife of her unalterably beloved Nikolai. Is all this not enough, as the shadowy traits mingle proportionately with lighter ones, to make her character fully rounded?

Of course it is enough. On top of that, this emphasis on, and creation of, an impure feeling does not have a *specific* bearing upon the soul of Countess Rostov, but upon all mothers who give away their daughters in a good and successful marriage. It is necessary to give them away well, but it looks as though it is *impossible not to envy them or to feel a kind of secret resentment against them.* Good Lord! What a strained interpretation and what excessive psychological pretension! Who will demonstrate the elements there are in common and the inevitability of such a senseless movement? Nobody can.

The gist of the matter does not even lie there, but in the fact that Count Tolstoy, when he wrote those lines, had not yet completely freed himself from the bad habits of the Russian school of which I have spoken earlier. Analyses are not alike. Analysis is *simply* a healthy analysis: a man feels *something*; in the mind and the heart a strong impression is left, let us suppose; afterwards, in consequence of this, he does *so and so*. Or is this a tiresome and, in actual life, an entirely false analysis of *faultfinding* and *suspicions*? For some reason, a man may have an unalterable feeling, whether bad, petty, low, vicious, fainthearted, or directed against *nothing in particular.* Is there not a kind of negative exaggeration in this? Or did not all our authors, nourished on the spirit of the forties, have something like a petty feeling, a kind of *lofty shame*, of a certain deeply rooted literary faintheartedness *when confronted with the habits of negation?* I think this was so, and that L. N. Tolstoy himself, for all his strength and originality, paid in his youth a large tribute to this weakness.

And who has not paid this tribute? We have now become accustomed to raise almost wholesale the literature of the 1840s and 1850s with the aim of opposing it to the crude, directly revolutionary, savage, and, on top of that, very coarse and incoherent literature of the 1860s and 1870s. But in this lauded literature of the forties and fifties we must distinguish two aspects, the theoretical and the practical. On the one hand, the aesthetic views, the aesthetic theories, the aesthetic outlook as a whole; the critique of the philosophy of life and the beautiful. On the other, the artistic *execution*, the artistic *practice* of poetry, novellas, novels, dramatic works. In this distinction we can find a very important point of support for judging certain aspects of our letters.

In those days the aesthetic theories were *very* lofty and profound in their ideals, for they were strongly influenced by German idealist criticism and philosophy, higher than which it is hardly possible to rise in this domain.

Artistic practice with us very soon assumed a more or less negative, ironic, venomous, and gloomy character.

This practice fell under the overbearing influence of Gogol. Or, to be more exact, *under the influence of his latest, most mature, but venomous, gloomy, one-sided satirical works*, which depicted nothing but the mean and the vulgar aspects of our life.

It was not the elevated emotional atmosphere of *Taras Bulba, Rome*, or *The Terrible Revenge* or the powerful fantasy of the novella *Viy* or the charming gaiety of *Evenings near Dikanka* that left a strong, profound, and, until now, ineffaceable trace on the succeeding literature; rather it was the satire of *Dead Souls, The Government Inspector*, and other such works, as well as the portrayal of the bitter, wretched, and sickly phenomena of our life, the ugly, tragic aspects of our everyday life (especially urban life) in *The Overcoat, The Nevsky Prospect*, and *The Diary of a Madman*.

I may even allow myself to say straight out that from the spirit of these three last *Petersburg* novellas of Gogol there issued and developed the whole of Dostoyevsky's sickly and one-sided talent, just as almost the whole of Saltykov-Shchedrin came out of *The Government Inspector* and *Dead Souls*.

A closer and more direct connection can be established, of course, between Turgenev and Tolstoy and Pushkin and Lermontov, for in their works we also find many elegant images taken from Russian life, while not a shade of elegance is to be found in either Dostoyevsky or Saltykov-Shchedrin; they simply did not know how to portray it.

However, everybody knows that both Turgenev and Tolstoy very gradually, rather than suddenly, grew accustomed to perceive in the life of cultured Russian society more positive traits, stronger characters, more elegant images. In the course of time, both of them became more and more daring in this connection.

As the years passed, they both became disaccustomed, in various degrees and under different conditions, from perceiving everywhere only poverty and the insignificance of spirit and life. Unfortunately, Turgenev again yielded more than once to outside revolutionary tendencies and in this way deprived his talent of authenticity; but Tolstoy cannot be accused of anything of the kind. Tolstoy was always independent, and if he was wrong, then he was so in his own way. The tendency to see everywhere only poverty of spirit and the insignificance of life gradually weakened in him; and having begun his literary career with *Boyhood* and *Youth*, where there is so much of that faultfinding and petty suspicion of which we are speaking, he finished with *Anna Karenina*, where there is very little of this, and with his folk tales, where there is no mention even, thank God, of all these "tricks" and expedients. . . .

To describe this real Orthodox life, which is also not lacking in either defects or weaknesses, either drama or poetry, one must possess a special kind of *experience* which Count Tolstoy lacked. Count Tolstoy was too much of a realist and too scrupulous in the artistic sense to depict a life he did know and did not clearly understand.

Because of his lyrical and subjective nature, Dostoyevsky could imagine that he was presenting us with a picture of real Orthodoxy and Russian monasticism in *The Brothers Karamazov*. For Dostoyevsky his own dreams about a *heavenly* Jerusalem on *this earth* were dearer to him than either veracity or authentic church customs. But, in the case of Count Tolstoy, his philanthropical tendency could never spoil the poetry and truth of life.

Whatever the author himself may have thought of the life he

portrayed in *Anna Karenina,* we love it, we love this life. And although we may regret that a more ecclesiastical and ascetic ideal (for it would then become still better in many respects) is not bound up with it and raised above it, yet we can be well satisfied, to a certain extent, by its substantiality and completeness. Especially so, when firmly convinced that there will never be a "heavenly Jerusalem" on *this,* our familiar earth.

Now about the coarseness, the slovenliness, and, generally, the *physical* notations and observations. One coarseness is much like another. I am not at all opposed to coarseness unconditionally. I even love it where it is appropriate. I am chiefly opposed to the "inconsistency" of contemporary language, which has been distorted, turned *topsy-turvy* here and there by those "bumps" and "depressions" of naturalism to which I have referred more than once. I am opposed to a cacophony that leads nowhere and to the cacopsychy of our almost generalized style. I am against this beating up of unclean froth as high as the ceiling—a beating up equivalent to the sugary rhetorical froth of the past century; equivalent in *superabundance* but not at all equivalent in *quality;* for a fragrant and even somewhat sugary froth is a hundred times better and more capable of elevating our thoughts, if the rhetorician is sufficiently gifted, than a whole heap of dirt and garbage splashed with slops. When Tolstoy's Ivan Ilyich uses the "bedpan," that is all right. Ivan Ilyich is a sick, dying man. I like it *here.* But when Gogol's Tentetnikov, awakening in the morning, still lies in bed and "rubs his eyes" and his eyes are "small," this is very nasty and unnecessary. One wants immediately to drive over to General Betrishchev and tell the ideal Ulinka,* "Listen—you must not marry Tentetnikov: according to the testimony of N. V. Gogol himself, he is terribly repulsive in the morning!" Why is that necessary? Ivan Ilyich's distinguishing feature is a vital one; *one pities him.* A young man "rubbing his small eyes," a young man with whom the author's highly respected heroine is in love—

* All three characters appear in Gogol's *Dead Souls* (Part II).

this is not a distinguishing trait, but a kind of cudgel, a kind of log of aesthetic prodding. He might very well not have rubbed his eyes every time; his eyes could have been larger too. There is nothing *organic* here; it is merely revolting.

In *War and Peace* and even in *Anna Karenina* (though far less) we shall find examples that resemble the one and the other.

When Andrey Bolkonsky is driving with Kutuzov in a barouche and Kutuzov is saying that a lot of men will have to pay with their lives for the forthcoming battles, Andrey, glancing at the ancient scar on the old army leader's temple, thinks with respect, "Kutuzov has already undergone all the personal dangers of the military profession and therefore he has the right to argue that." That is excellent as a psychological analysis of Andrey's soul and is also *sufficient* as a *physical* observation. Or, rather, it *would have been* sufficient if it had been said simply: a "scar" or a "deep scar"; but precisely what I call the bad habits of *naturalism* obliged Count Tolstoy to add *"the cleanly rinsed folds of the* scar." The physical tidiness of the famous and worldly warrior pleases me very much, but I cannot, on this occasion, praise the famous and likewise worldly literary man for this unnecessary detail of his toilette. In passing, let me comment again on that page where it is a question of the "rinsed scar." A little before that, Kutuzov, when bidding farewell to Bagration before the battle of Schongraben, blesses him with tears in his eyes. This is beautiful in itself. "With his *left* hand he drew Bagration towards him, and with the *right, on which he wore a ring,* he blessed him with what was *evidently an accustomed gesture and offered* him his *chubby cheek. . . ."* Let me ask why I have to know with *which* hand he drew towards him. And what is the purpose of the ring? And we have long known, often heard, and shall hear again, that Kutuzov was stout, that his cheeks were *chubby* and his neck was *chubby*; his hands probably were *chubby* too. That shade *"evidently an accustomed* gesture" is also not a simple, avoidable expression or observation, but one of those expressions that became established with us in the forties, and there is a great deal of this kind of stuff in *War and Peace*.

Let us turn another page back. Prince Bolkonsky has quarreled with the officer in charge of the baggage train and is about to strike him. "The officer made a gesture with his hand and *hurriedly* rode away." Two lines later, "Prince Andrey *hurriedly* rode away from the doctor's wife. . . ." By itself, this word "hurriedly" is neither bad nor good. But everybody was accustomed to use it *mechanically* to such an extent, considering it their duty to imitate notable models, that it was long overdue for the notable models themselves to stop using it. Again, on the same page (Part II, Chapter 13), "Nesvitsky, *chewing* something with his juicy mouth," calls Andrey Bolkonsky to him. Of course he could have called him without having to *chew* anything. This is that same "*superfluity* of observation" of which I spoke at the beginning. (" 'Yes, Masha, I no longer love you,' Yevgeny Merzavetz *squeezed* through his teeth, *cutting a chop and raising his elbows high*.")

Although every man's mouth is juicy while he is in good health, one need not therefore have mentioned Nesvitzky's mouth, but let it be—let his mouth be specially juicy; but this is something we have known since the days when our troops burned the bridge over the river Enns. And the same officer Nesvitsky was present there, and he joked with other officers, "*chewing a small meat pie in his handsome, moist mouth*" (Part II, Chapter 7).

In all the examples quoted here there is nothing indecent, coarse, or untidy. But they are incoherent and unnecessary—that is the trouble. It would be better to be indecent.

Let us take another example, a most striking one. When, at the end of *War and Peace*, the already married Natasha brings out the *childbed linen* to show it in the drawing room, the *green stain* on the linen *has turned yellow*; although this is unattractive and crude, yet it is *appropriate here*; it has great significance. It demonstrates the extent to which Natasha, like so many other Russian women, has grown slovenly since her marriage, and also the extent to which she has forgotten, behind the strength of her maternal feelings, how uninteresting it is for *others*, even for people who are fond of her family, to be involved in such medical inspections. It would be enough even for the closest friend of the family to learn from her that the child was feeling better. Count Tolstoy *personally* praises Natasha for having ceased to bother about her appearance after her marriage, but the reader is not obliged to agree with him in this. The reader is only obliged to admit, this time, to what extent the author's talent has succeeded in making his beloved heroine appear sympathetic and attractive even in this last, negligent phase of her development!

It is for this reason that I consider this bed linen not only admissible in realistic art, but also very essential.

But when Pierre "dandles" (*"dandles,"* indeed! why not simply *"nurses"?*) on the palm of *his large hand* (those hands) that same infant and the infant suddenly *soils* his hands, this is completely unnecessary and proves nothing. This is dirt for dirt's sake, "art for art's sake," naturalism for its own sake. Or when in the same scene Pierre smiles "with his *toothless mouth*"! This is much worse. What is it for? It is ugliness for the sake of ugliness. An infant does not soil its parents every instant, and Pierre Bezukhov's years (even at the end of the book) are not so many that he should have absolutely no teeth. He might have teeth or not. This is no longer a healthy realism; it is a "bad habit," something like the habits of the Russian common folk when they take hold of a white door, not by the lock, but where they should not touch it.

I shall permit myself to repeat once again that I am not referring here to one *strictly coarse* or *strictly slovenly* scrutiny, but, in general, to *excessive physical* scrutiny, just as formerly people spoke of the excessive psychological carping of the Russian novelists. For example, Natasha, without any need, *strikes her head on a door* when, on returning to ruined Moscow, she first meets Pierre and then departs in a state of agitation. It seems to me that if she had struck her head on the door *before* her *declaration of love* for Pierre or, in general, *before* any conversation rather than *after-*

wards, then some very important psychological element might have established a connection with the physical element in exactly the same way as the mushroom of S. I. Koznishev; or that "piece of paper on the plate" which Pierre was handed at the dinner for Bagration and which Dologhov seized *before* he did, and Bezukhov, already irritated, immediately challenged him to a duel. If Natasha had struck her head on the door *before*, she would have sat down and cried; Pierre would have taken her hand, and so on. They both would have been soothed and moved (she by her physical suffering, he by compassion); they would have declared their love for one another. But this *afterwards* and her *leaving* the room into the bargain—that does not lead anywhere! That is not Sergey Ivanovich's *mushroom*, not Dolohov's and Pierre's piece of paper; that is not even the bed linen—it is merely accident for its own sake; it is *affected* realism. If, let us suppose, one of Count Tolstoy's elder relatives had told him that in the year 1813 such and such an aunt of his, who resembled Natasha, in a similar situation had also struck her head on a door or that Count Bezborodko (let us suppose) was already *toothless* at the time when his first children were born, then, since neither the one nor the other had any inner *organic* connection, and each was in itself very ugly, all this should have been omitted.

If, in this connection, we again remember Gogol, then it will become clear that Gogol is both better and worse. He is worse and weaker than Tolstoy in that he is quite incapable in the *same work*, some five to ten pages later, of *rewarding* us, as Tolstoy does, for all those "rinsed scars," bed linen, snorting, and toothlessness, now by such a fine description of a lady's ball gown that every woman author would envy him, now by an elegant portrayal of the Emperor Alexander, now again by other features out of the life of nineteenth-century people, descriptions so poetic that they might have found room in the most fragrant pages of George Sand. We shall, of course, find nothing similar in Gogol's *later* novels and novellas (*from Great Russian middling-gentry life*). Tolstoy's devices are more varied, more complete, and approach nearer to the fullness and diversity of real life. But *precisely for this reason*—that is, because Gogol is more *one-sidedly intense*—it was essential for him to have "the smell of Petrushka," the "umbilical cord" of Nozdrev's puppy, and the "hiccups" (with which *The Litigation* begins).

"Gogol—*c'est un genre*, but as for *your others*—they're neither town, nor country." Thus a very clever Moscow lady, a friend of Khomyakov's,* expressed herself to me in the fifties. She said this in connection with the sketch *A District Doctor* in *A Sportsman's Sketches*, which were not her cup of tea on the whole but which made me, still a youth then, so enthusiastic that I placed them much higher than *Dead Souls*. Later, I understood with astonishment that this lady was in many respects more correct than I was. . . . *Gogol—c'est un genre!* He almost has no middle ground between the poetry and pathos of *Rome*, *Taras Bulba*, and *Viy* and the abomination of desolation of *Dead Souls* and *The Government Inspector*. But I cannot explain why these superfluous elements were necessary to the *extensive* and almost inexhaustible Tolstoy. It should suffice to have the *organic*, Shakespearean rudeness on a large scale, suffice to have the bed sheets, the dirty toes of Pierre's feet when he is a prisoner of war. What purpose do these small rough passages serve either for us or *him?* A bad habit—nothing else.

I am mortally bored with all this all-Russian "nose-picking." I feel that my word "nose-picking" is nasty and coarse, but I cannot find an expression that is either worse or better! And I am, indeed, a pupil of the same school, but I am a protesting pupil rather than an absolutely revering one.

This lack of simplicity in speech is particularly noticeable when reading aloud. These constant repetitions—"hurriedly," "involuntarily," "involuntary," "alien," "alien," "nervously," "pudgy," "pudgy," and so on; "juicy mouth," "toothless mouth"—these frequent psychological scrutinies and unnecessary corporeal observations when we read aloud not only Tolstoy but the majority of

* A. S. Khomyakov (1804–1860), a poet, philosopher, and leading Slavophile.

our best authors—Turgenev, Pisemsky, Dostoyevsky—are sometimes simply intolerable! And in the case of Tolstoy in particular,
these defects, or more exactly excesses, are incomparably more
noticeable, sharper, and more reiterated than in others.

Perhaps it is because Tolstoy had *everything*, all the energies
peculiar to our school, the high and the low—all of them ten times
greater than any others. The light and the shadow are more
sharply contrasted. As I have already said, he is a *çivatherium* in
the category of pachyderms.

IF PUSHKIN HAD WRITTEN *War and Peace*

FOR A greater clarification of my critical thought, I shall permit myself here to imagine something that is impossible as an
event but is quite natural, I think, as a *retrospective dream*. I shall
permit myself to imagine that d'Anthès missed and that Pushkin
in the forties wrote an epic novel about the year 1812.* Would he
have written it *like* Tolstoy? *No, not like that!* Worse, perhaps,
but not in the same way. Pushkin's novel would probably not be so
original, not so subjective, not so overloaded, and even not so
charged with content as *War and Peace*. But on the other hand, it
would not contain any *unnecessary* perched-on faces or any bumps
from prodding in the language; the psychic analysis would not
have been so "worm-eaten," carping in certain cases, not so
splendid in others. The fantasy of all those dreams and half
dreams, daydreams, deaths, and half deaths would not have been

* The Baron d'Anthès killed Pushkin in a duel in 1837.

---

*From "Analysis, Style, and Trends (On the Novels of Count L. N.
Tolstoy)."* WORKS, *vol. VIII, pp. 328–330.*

270

as *individual* as in Tolstoy, perhaps not as subtle or airy, and not as powerful as in Tolstoy; but on the other hand, it would excite fewer doubts. . . . In Pushkin the philosophy of war and life would be different, and it would not be set within the narrative in whole large lumps as in Tolstoy. The patriotic lyricism would be poured out more evenly everywhere, and it would not be ceaselessly cooled off by *theophilanthropical* provisos; and "With God's martial grace our every step" would be "stamped." *

The Year 1812 by Pushkin would have been (judging by the last turn of his mind before his death) a far more Orthodox Christian work than *War and Peace*. Pushkin would have illumined his creation in a way that resembled the illumination in an excellent recent article in the review *Faith and Reason*, treating of the conflict between Napoleon and Alexander and Kutuzov, rather than in the manner of Tolstoy. Tolstoy's God is a kind of blind and cruel *fatum*, from whose hands I am not certain that anyone can escape even by means of a *free choice of love*. In the article in *Faith and Reason* we find a *living and personal* God, whose "paths" are only occasionally "inscrutable." Pushkin would not have (probably) even called the French marshals and generals, who were running away *from themselves* in carriages and fur coats, "wicked and insignificant men who have done a great deal of evil," just as the Russian heroes, who were chasing them from Moscow, *probably* did not call them that in their soul in the year 1812, but chided them in passion rather than according to the precepts of a tediously moral philosophy. Martial attitudes were then in fashion, and educated people were more direct and frank in their chivalrous outlook than people today. At present even those who, for various reasons, thirst for war tell lies until the very moment of the declaration of war, claiming falsely that they do not want it. "War is a misfortune, that is all!" they say. No one dares speak otherwise today. After the declaration of war, the very next day, they bare their "mental" swords and rattle them (*sincerely, at last!*) until peace is concluded. *At that blessed time for the poetry of life*, a

* From Pushkin's poem *Poltava*.

man's ideal was to be a *warrior* rather than a village teacher or an office worker!

Pushkin's religious enlightment would have been closer to the common national one. Although it might have been very *subjective in its sincerity,* it would have been less *individual in manner* and *less cosmopolitan* in spirit than Tolstoy's. And Pushkin's heroes, and he himself in particular, would have spoken where necessary in *almost the same language as was spoken* then, that is, in a simpler, more transparent, lighter language, not one that was *thick, overloaded, too ornamented in one way or another,* now too crudely and darkly, now in a too refined and "worm-eaten" way as in Tolstoy.

As a result of *this* "general trend," the common-psychic music of the time and place would have been more exact and more faithful in Pushkin; his creation would have instilled greater *historical confidence* and, at the same time, would have furnished us with a more complete artistic *illusion* than *War and Peace.* Pushkin would have written his *The Year* 1812 somewhat in the manner in which he wrote his *Dubrovsky, The Captain's Daughter,* and *The Negro of Peter the Great.* . . .

Returning again for an instant to the proposed novel by Pushkin, I should like also to state that, admiring this nonexistent novel, we would probably submit in *equal measure* to the genius of the author and the *spirit* of the age. Reading *War and Peace* with the greatest enjoyment, we still realize very clearly that we are here dominated not so much by the *spirit of the age as by the personal* genius of the author; that we are satisfied, not by the "trend" of the place and the time, but by an authentic, very dissimilar (as a whole), bold creation on the part of a contemporary of ours.

Admiring *War and Peace,* we still have a certain right to shake our head sceptically. The characters in *The Family Chronicle* * and the characters in *Anna Karenina* are not only true to themselves from the beginning to the end, true humanly and psychologically but are also probable—they are true to their place and

* S. T. Aksakov, *The Family Chronicle* (1856).

time. The characters of the Pushkin novel I have imagined would also be as true *to themselves and to their age*, if we are to judge by his *The Negro* and *Dubrovsky*. The characters, the trend, the people portrayed, and the personal music of their creator would have breathed in *a time not our own*.

In *War and Peace*, the characters are completely true and probable only to themselves, psychologically. I shall even add more: exactitude, detail, and the truth of their general psychic fashioning is so profound that Pushkin himself could not, of course, have achieved such perfection—Pushkin, who by the nature of his gift preferred to look at life *à vol d'oiseau* rather than to burrow into the depths, digging up from there precious diamonds as well as nasty worms of naturalistic provenance. As far as the characters of *War and Peace* (especially the two principal heroes, Andrey and Pierre) are concerned, when taken *from the standpoint of their faithfulness to the age*, then it is permissible to have some doubts. In general, I cannot speak of these *characters* as decisively as I have talked about excessive scrutiny, the carping nature of analysis, the inconsistency of the language, a certain triteness in the all-Russian and the all-naturalistic manner. . . .

When I hear for the tenth time "a fleshy hand," "a chubby hand," "a dry hand," I entertain not the slightest doubt that I am right in deploring this.

When I am assured that Kutuzov "admired his own speech," I squeamishly (not physically, but mentally and morally) exclaim, "*Old hat! Old hat!* We have heard this often enough, to the point of satiety, from Turgenev, from Dostoyevsky, and from Count Tolstoy himself in his *Boyhood* and *Youth*. This is not that healthy, almost scientific analysis which everyone must admire in Tolstoy and examples of which I have quoted. . . . This is broken, unnecessary analysis, which makes a mountain out of a molehill!"

A Selected Bibliography

WORKS OF LEONTIEV

in Russian

Sobranie sochinenii (Collected Works). Vols. I–IX (1912–1914).

Moia literaturnaia sud'ba (An Autobiography), with comments by S. Durylin. In *Literaturnoe Nasledstvo*, pp. 22–24 (1935). Reprinted 1965 (The Slavic Series).

Egipetskii Golub' (The Egyptian Dove). A new edition, with an introduction by B. A. Filippov (Chekhov Publishing House, New York, 1954).

Analiz, stil' i veianie . . . (on L. Tolstoy's novels), with an English introduction by Donald Fanger (Brown University Press, Providence, R. I., 1965).

Leontiev's Letters to V. V. Rozanov. Vols. IV–VI (1903). In *Russky Vestnik* (1891).

in English

The Average European as an Ideal and Instrument of Universal Destruction, translated by W. Shafer and G. Kline, with an introduction. In *Russian Philosophy*. Vol. II, edited by J. Edie, J. Scanlan, M.-B. Zedlin, and G. Klein (Quadrangle Books, 1965).

ON LEONTIEV

Pamiati K. Leontieva, a collection of essays, including Leontiev's biography by A. Konopliantsev; V. Rozanov's essay "Neuznannyi Fenomen"; and Leontiev's letters to E., O., Ju Kartsov (1911).

B. Griftsov: *Sud'ba K. Leont'eva* (K. Leontiev's Destiny), *Russkaiia Mysl'*. Vols. I, II, IV (1912).

S. Bulgakov: *Pobeditel'—Pobezhdennyi*, in the collection *Tikhie Dumy* (1918).

N. Berdyaev: *K. Leontiev* (1926). Also in English, *Leontiev*, translated from the Russian by George Reavey (Geoffrey Bles: The Centenary Press, London, 1940).

G. Florovskii: *Die Sackgassen der Romantic* (on Herzen, Leontiev, and Dostoyevsky), *Orient und Occident*. Vol. IV (1930).

E. Gasparini: *Le previsioni di K. Leont'ev* (Milano-Venezia, 1947, 1957).

Prince S. D. Mirsky: *A History of Russian Literature* (1947).

V. Zenkovskii: *Istoriia russkoi filosofii* (A History of Russian Philosophy). Vol. I (1941). Also in English (1953).

Iwan Kologriwof: *Von Hellas zum Moenchtum. Leben und Denken Konstantin Leontjews* (Regensburg, 1948).

George Ivask: "K. Leontiev's Fiction," *Slavic Review* (December 1961); and a book on Leontiev published (in Russian), in the monthly review *Vozrozhdenie* (La Renaissance) (Paris, 1961–1964).

B. A. Filippov: "Strastnoe pis'mo s nevernym adresom," *Mosty* (Muenchen). Vols. IX–X (1962–1963).

R. Hare: *Pioneers of Russian Social Thought*, 2d rev. ed. (Vintage Books, New York, 1964).

S. Lukashevich: *Konstantin Leontiev*. A study in Russian "Heroic Vitalism" (Pageant Press, New York, 1967).

BIBLIOGRAPHY

A. Konopliantsev: *Rusky Biograficheskii Slovar'*. Vol. X (1914). Another one compiled by G. Ivask (unpublished).

Chronology

Feb. 23, 1812: Nikolai Borisovich Leontiev marries Feodosiia Petrovna Karabanova.

Jan. 13, 1831: Their son, Konstantin Nikolaevich Leontiev, is born on their country estate, Kudinovo, in the province of Kaluga.

1841–1849: He studies in various schools in Smolensk, Petersburg, and Kaluga.

1849: He enters the School of Medicine, University of Moscow.

1851: He meets I. S. Turgenev and other writers in Moscow.

1854: First story published, in the paper *Moskovskie Vedomosti*.

1854–1857: Military surgeon in Crimea, then under invasion by the French and British armies.

1858–1860: Household physician on the country estate of Turgenev's friend, Baron von Rosen, in the province of Nizhnii-Novgorod.

All dates according to the Old (Julian) Calendar.

1860–1863: In Petersburg. Friendship with his niece, Maria Vladimirovna Leontieva (b. 1848).

July 19, 1861: Marries Elizaveta Pavlovna Politova, daughter of a merchant of Greek origin, in Feodosia (Crimea).

1861: Longer novel *Podlipki* published in *Otechestvennye Zapiski*.

1863–1864: Secretary to the Russian consul in Canea, Crete; removed because he offended the French diplomatic agent there.

1864: Longer novel *In His Land* published.

1864–1866: Secretary and assistant consul in Adrianople (Edirne).

1867–1868: Vice-consul in Tulcea, Moldavia. Planning and writing a serial of novels *The River of Time* (unfinished, fragments remain). His wife mentally ill.

1869–1871: Consul in Yanina (Epirus).

February 1871: Mother dies in Petersburg.

April 1871: Consul in Salonika.

Summer 1871: Miraculously cured of cholera or dysentery while praying to the Virgin Mary: he promises Her he will take monastic vows.

September 1871–1872: In the Russian monastery on Mount Athos.

1872–1874: In Constantinople and on the island of Chalki.

1875: *Byzantinism and Slavdom* published.

1874–1875: Returns to Russia; for a short time is novice in the Nikolo-Ugresh monastery near Moscow.

1875–1876: The novel *Odysseus Polichroniades* is published in the review *Russkii Vestnik*.

1876: From *The Life of Christians and Turks*, vols. I-III.

1875–1879: In Kudinovo, Moscow, Petersburg; sometimes visiting Optina monastery.

1880: *Father Kliment* (Sederholm), a book dedicated to the memory of his friend, a monk of the Optima Monastery (died in 1878). In

Warsaw, contributes to the paper published there, *The Warsaw Diary*.

1880–1887: In Moscow, working on the Censorship Committee. Young friends; some of them students of Moscow Lyceum. Meetings with the philosopher Vl· Soloviev.

1881–1882: The novel *The Egyptian Dove* published in *Russky Vestnik*.

1885–1886: The book *Orient, Russia, and the Slavs*, vols. I-II published.

1887–1891: Lives in a rented cottage in the Optina Monastery. His spiritual guide is the elder Ambrosius.

1891: Corresponds with his critic and admirer, Vasily Rozanov.

Aug. 23, 1891: Secretly consecrated as a monk, under the name of Kliment, in Optina Monastery.

Aug. 30, 1891: Moves to the Trinity Monastery (Zagorsk).

Nov. 12, 1891: Dies there of pneumonia.

1911: A collection of (unfinished) works published.

1927: His niece and closest friend, sometimes secretary, Maria Vladimirovna Leontieva (b. 1848), dies in Russia.

Index